Child Welfare
An Africentric
Perspective

CHILD WELFARE

An Africentric Perspective

edited by JOYCE E. EVERETT,
SANDRA S. CHIPUNGU,
and BOGART R. LEASHORE

Rutgers
University
Press
New Brunswick,
New Jersey

Library of Congress Cataloging-in-Publication Data

Child welfare: an Africentric perspective / edited by Joyce E.
Everett, Sandra S. Chipungu, and Bogart R. Leashore.
    p.   cm.
Includes bibliographical references and index.
ISBN 0-8135-1712-5 (cloth)   —   ISBN 0-8135-1713-3
(pbk.)
    1. Social work with Afro-American children. 2. Social
work with Afro-Americans. 3. Child welfare—United States.
I. Everett, Joyce. II. Chipungu, Sandra S. (Sandra Stukes),
1950–   . III. Leashore, Bogart R.
HV3181.C48   1991
362.7'9796073—dc20   90-28752
                                                      CIP

British Cataloging-in-Publication information available

To our parents,

Eddie and Hettie Everett,
Floyd and Katie Stukes,
Bogart, Sr., and Vashtie Leashore

Contents

List of Figures and Tables

Figure

Tables

List of Contributors

BARBARA C. BAILEY, D.S.W., is acting coordinator of the Office of Administrative Review, Commission on Social Services, in Washington, D.C., and an adjunct professor at the Catholic University of America. She is also a consultant on child welfare management.

SANDRA S. CHIPUNGU, PH.D., is an assistant professor at the School of Social Service at Catholic University of America in Washington, D.C. Her research interests are African American families; the socioeconomic status of women, children, and minorities; and evaluations of human service organizations.

RICHARD A. ENGLISH, PH.D., is dean of the School of Social Work at Howard University in Washington, D.C. His publications include research reports and theoretical/conceptual works on African American families, cultural diversity and families, human service organizations, social work education, mental health, and displaced populations. He co-edited *Black American Families, 1965–1984: A Classified, Selectively Annotated Bibliography* and *Human Service Organizations*.

JOYCE E. EVERETT, PH.D., is an associate professor at the Smith College School for Social Work in Northampton, Massachusetts. Her published works focus on child-support enforcement, foster care, and African American adolescence. She is a member of the Consortium on Black Adolescence, a group funded by the W. T. Grant Foundation.

PAULA G. GOMES, PH.D., is a licensed clinical psychologist. She is currently employed as the coordinator of Clinical Services at George Washington University in Washington, D.C.

KETAYUN H. GOULD, PH.D., is professor of social work, emeritus, in the School of Social Work at the University of Illinois at Urbana-Champaign. Her major areas of interest include women and minorities, particularly the development of feminist models of education and practice related to these groups. She is also involved in a major research project on the history and demography of the Parsi-Zoroastrians of India. Her recent publications are on feminist perspective, Asian and Pacific Islanders, women and aging, and women in Zoroastrianism.

ROBERT L. HAMPTON, PH.D., is professor of sociology and dean of the college, Connecticut College, New London; research associate in the

Family Development Program, Children's Hospital Center, New London; and lecturer on pediatrics (sociology), Harvard Medical School, Boston. He has published extensively in the area of family violence.

BOGART R. LEASHORE, PH.D., is dean of the School of Social Work at Hunter College in New York City. He has published articles related to foster-care administrative reviews, family reunification, legal guarianship in child welfare, social services and African American men, and fathers. He has also served as the training and technical assistance coordinator of a regional resource center on child abuse and neglect.

C. ALDRENA MABRY, PH.D., is a licensed clinical psychologist and certified school psychologist in New York State. She consults with the Roosevelt Community Mental Health Center in Roosevelt, New York, and maintains a private practice specializing in marital and family therapy, stress management, and minority child development issues in education.

HARVEY L. MCMURRAY, PH.D., is an assistant professor at North Carolina Central University in Raleigh. He was formerly the coordinator of the Volunteers for Children in Need project. He is a specialist in criminal justice.

TOSHIO TATARA, PH.D., is the director of research and demonstration for the American Public Welfare Association and director of the National Aging Resource Center on Elder Abuse in Washington, D.C. He has published a number of articles and monographs and serves as a technical consultant for the federal government, state and local governments, and professional organizations. His recent publications address the legislative history of the Family Support Act of 1988 and the effects of the current drug epidemic on children.

RONALD L. TAYLOR, PH.D., is a professor of sociology at the University of Connecticut in Storrs. He is co-author and editor (with Doris Y. Wilkinson) of *The Black Male in America: Perspectives on His Status in Contemporary Society* and has published widely on youth employment, role models for adolescents, self-esteem, and African American men. He is co-director of the Consortium on Black Adolescence, a group sponsored by the W. T. Grant Foundation.

ROBERTA J. TURNER, PH.D., is an assistant professor at the School of Social Service at Catholic University of America in Washington, D.C. She has conducted research on parenting and on behavioral problems of children and provides consultative services to an array of community-based organizations, including a foster parents association in the District of Columbia.

CAROL C. WILLIAMS, D.S.W., is senior research analyst, Center for the Study of Social Policy, Washington, D.C., and lecturer, University of North Carolina at Chapel Hill. Her publication topics include child welfare and homelessness; families and children's policies; and the adoption of minority children. Her current work focuses on the restructuring of public services to better meet the needs of families.

MELVIN N. WILSON, PH.D., is an associate professor of psychology at the University of Virginia in Charlottesville. He is the principal investigator of a research project entitled "Social Interaction in Two- and Three-Generational Black Families." His publications include articles on parenting and child rearing in African American families.

Child Welfare
An Africentric
Perspective

JOYCE E. EVERETT

Introduction: Children in Crisis

> Spoke I not unto you, saying do not sin against the child, and ye would
> not hear?
> —GENESIS 42:22

Scorned children are scared children. They are children whose protection is in question. They are children in crisis, children removed from one vulnerable situation and subject to another. They are forsaken children whose lives are affected by the ignorance, callousness, indifference, and neglect of those charged with the responsibility to care for them, the duty to guide them, and the obligation to ensure their safety and well-being. A disproportionate number of these children are African American. The circumstances of their vulnerability vary and are often related to poverty. There is a tendency to view and to treat the experiences of children of color in state custody (with the exception of Native American children) just as we view and treat the experiences of nonminority children in state custody. This book examines the special strengths and needs of African American children and families who become entangled in the child welfare system. The phrase *scorned children* depicts the destiny bestowed on these children and suggests that the troubles of African American families and children necessitate special attention and concern.

Children of color, especially African American children, travel a hazardous and arduous journey through conception, gestation, delivery, and each of the subsequent stages of development. Higher proportions of African American children than nonminority children die before birth or during infancy; have learning, emotional, and physical disabilities; lack educational opportunities; become parents at an early age; are incarcerated in youth; or die as a result of accidents and homicides before and during young adulthood. Children supervised by the child welfare system, without the stable supports of family and community, are at even greater risk than most African American children for these and other negative outcomes.

This book presents a body of knowledge about and introduces a different perspective for assessing the effects of traditional child welfare policies and services for families and children of color. Patterns and trends in family structures, child-rearing practices, and child-development issues are described throughout. With the publication of this book, we hope to elevate the importance of race in the field of child welfare. In future discourses on public policy and practice, as creative solutions to "private" troubles are sought, the critical variable, race, must be addressed with a sensitivity to the preservation and protection of difference.

Background to a Tragedy

In the late 1960s professionals in the field of child welfare and society as a whole acknowledged the rapid growth in the numbers of nonwhite children placed in foster care, group homes, institutions, or adoptive homes. Many were even willing to give lip service to the assertion that conventional child welfare services for children of color were inappropriate and ineffective (Billingsley and Giovannoni 1972). In subsequent years, 1972 to 1980, child welfare agencies intensified their efforts to extend services to families and children of color by providing outreach services and modifying conventional adoption and foster-parenting standards, thereby increasing accessibility. At the same time, the slow but steady development of specialized African American adoption services and agencies successfully demonstrated the efficacy of community-based services. These developments helped to invalidate the assumption that finding adoptive African American homes was difficult.

Since the enactment of P.L. 96-272, the Adoption Assistance and Child Welfare Act of 1980, the total number of children in foster care has declined. Despite these decreases, the percentage of children of color in substitute care has steadily increased. Compared with white children four times as many African American children become wards of the state and are supervised by child welfare agencies (Edelman

1987). African American children constitute the largest minority group in most state foster-care systems. African American children of all age groups, especially adolescents, are represented in the child welfare system. During one year alone, 1986, African American children constituted approximately 26 percent of the children entering foster care, 35 percent of those children in care at the end of the year, and 26 percent of those children leaving care during that year (Select Committee on Children, Youth and Families 1989).

Throughout the 1970s and the 1980s the majority of these children were separated from their families because of neglect. Statistics for 1981 from the American Humane Association (1984) indicate that 25 percent of African American families were reported for neglect only, while 19.5 percent were reported for abuse only. The incidence of physical and sexual abuse among African American families has been consistently lower than that among other groups, though a slight increase in physical abuse was observed in the late 1980s. Today, poverty, homelessness, and parental substance addiction have been linked to the growing numbers of African American and Hispanic children in the custody of state agencies.

These African American families are expert witnesses of the myriad effects of implementing the Adoption Assistance and Child Welfare Act of 1980—the catalyst for a change in the philosophy of child welfare services. The act defined government's role in developing child welfare policies, and the federal and state financial responsibility for supporting services. In the wake of its enactment, however, critical evaluation of the effects of these policy changes was delayed. Nevertheless, it is clear that shortages in the availability and accessibility of supplementary and supportive services, along with culture-free policies and practices in child welfare, have severely impaired prevention and reunification efforts aimed at providing permanent homes for African American children.

Throughout this period reports published by the Office of Civil Rights, the Child Welfare League of America, the National Urban League, the Children's Defense Fund, and other organizations provided numerical descriptions of entry and exit rates, offered a chronology of the patterns and trends in service delivery, and foretold the nation's future for children of color. African American and other children of color remain in foster care for longer periods of time, experience multiple placements, and are less likely to be adopted than white children. Labeled "hard to place" and "at risk," primarily because they are members of racial minority groups, these children are faced with many challenges to healthy development. Their membership in specific racial, cultural, and social-class groups constitutes a significant lens for viewing the self, the world, and future opportunities (Gibbs, Huang, and Associates 1989). A culturally based perspective for understanding the special needs of African American children could be a catalyst for creativity in the reformulation of policy and practice to limit some of the damage to these families and children.

The Consequences of Disregarding Racial and Ethnic Difference

The following fictitious case illustrates the negative consequences of the unnecessary placement of a child in foster care and subsequently in an institution that further jeopardized healthy development. The family characteristics portrayed in the case closely resemble those of other families, especially African American families, who fall into the web of child welfare agencies.

Name of Child: Samuel
Child's Date of Birth: 9/78
Race: African American
Parents:
Father: Mr. Jones   Current Age: 31
Mother: Mrs. Jones   Current Age: 29
    The Department of Mental Health referred the case of Samuel to the child guidance center for evaluation and treatment. Samuel had been a victim of neglect and physical abuse in early childhood and had a recent history of oppositional and defiant behavior, relationship problems, and academic difficulties. Samuel, a twelve-year-old African American male, was unusually tall for his age, 5 feet 11 inches. His appearance was often misleading because he looked older than other children his age.
    Samuel was originally committed to the DMH residential facility when he was removed from the Morris foster home. Mrs. Morris became Samuel's legal foster parent and cared for him until she suffered a stroke. During her illness Samuel's behavioral difficulties intensified both at school and in the home. Because of the behavioral problems and his history of unsuccess-

ful foster home placements, a residential mental health placement was recommended.

Since age four Samuel had been placed in a succession of foster homes following an initial report of parental neglect and physical abuse. The protective services unit of the Department of Social Services filed a care-and-protection petition with the court because he allegedly had been left alone in the home for several nights without adult supervision. Neighbors also reported alleged physical abuse and neglect. During one of those nights, because of a citywide power failure, the home lost electrical power, and water was cut off for routine maintenance on another night. The protective services worker visiting the home for an initial investigation in the early afternoon found Mrs. Jones preoccupied with her chores and anxious about the interview. She expressed anger about the alleged charges of neglect and abuse noting that it was not easy to support and care for Samuel alone. She had very little patience for her neighbors and felt they were out of line in reporting abuse and neglect. She stated, "None of them offered to help after my husband left and besides they are just busybodies. It was none of their business how I raised my son." She and Mr. Jones, her husband, separated over a year ago, when he left after an argument about money. Mr. Jones had frequently physically abused his wife and on two occasions had harmed Samuel.

Since separating from her husband, Mrs. Jones had found work to "make ends meet." She worked as a custodian from 6:30 P.M. till 9:30 P.M. and then as a waitress in an all-night restaurant from 10:30 P.M. until 5:30 A.M. She explained that she thought it more important she be at home during the day to make sure Samuel got to school and home safely before she went to work. She also said a cousin usually watched Samuel from 6:00 till 10:00 P.M., when she came home to check on him before going to the next job. The incidents leading to the investigation had occurred during a week when the cousin had been ill with the flu and was unable to babysit. When asked whether anyone watched Samuel after 10:00 P.M., Mrs. Jones became agitated, saying, "I do the best I can by Samuel. He knows how to use the telephone and has managed well for the last four months without anything happening." The worker indicated she could get parent-aide services to care for Samuel while Mrs.

Jones was working. However, Mrs. Jones, refused, saying she didn't trust government help.

The court ordered Samuel's removal from the home shortly thereafter when neglect was substantiated. The maternal grandmother, Mrs. Jackson, agreed to temporarily care for Samuel until Mrs. Jones was able to secure a better job. Samuel remained with Mrs. Jackson without the benefit of foster board payments to assist with his care. Samuel adjusted reasonably well to his new living environment. He seldom mentioned his mother but often spoke of his father, wondering where he might be. Mrs. Jackson said Samuel seemed shy and often afraid of strangers, and experienced enuresis for several months after the move. He continued to attend school and later was enrolled in public school and an after-school program. Mrs. Jones visited frequently during the day, but continued to work the two evening jobs.

During a six-month foster-care review, Mrs. Jones was told Samuel would remain in the care of the maternal grandmother because she, the mother, did not meet all the established goals for reunification. Specifically, she had not looked for better employment and had not kept several prearranged appointments with the social worker. Mrs. Jones said she had no knowledge of these requirements and that there had been at least two different social workers assigned to the case since Samuel was removed from her home. She stated that it was difficult to get to the worker's office because of transportation problems. The social worker was instructed to maintain close contact with Mrs. Jones and to obtain transportation services for her when necessary.

When Mrs. Jackson, the maternal grandmother, became ill, an aunt, Mrs. Williams, agreed to share her home with Mrs. Jones and Samuel to keep the family together. Custody of Samuel was returned to Mrs. Jones shortly after she moved in with Mrs. Williams. Mrs. Jones and Samuel lived in Mrs. Williams's home for two years until Mrs. Jones remarried and moved to another county. She asked Mrs. Williams to keep Samuel until she and her husband could manage to care for him. Over the next years, Mrs. Williams continued to care for Samuel but reported she seldom heard from her niece. Samuel had been suspended from school twice for throwing things and biting the other children. At a parent/teacher conference regarding Samuel's suspension,

Mrs. Williams learned that Mr. Jones, Samuel's father, frequently walked Samuel home after school. Samuel indicated that his father met him once a month at school to walk home with him. He said his father would talk with him about his schoolwork and his behavior. Mrs. Williams contacted Mr. Jones's mother to find out why he did not visit Samuel in her home. Shortly after this conversation, Mrs. Williams said, Mr. Jones started to call regularly, about every other month, and sent gifts and money for special occasions. Meanwhile, Samuel's teacher indicated he seemed to have a learning disability and wanted to place him in a special class with similar children. Mrs. Williams, unable to reach Mrs. Jones for several months and overwhelmed with the financial and emotional responsibilities of caring for the child, voluntarily requested foster-home placement for Samuel. Workers were able to contact Mrs. Jones, who reluctantly agreed to the placement but refused to consider termination of parental rights. She felt she and her husband would soon be able to assume the care of Samuel. Placement with the Morris family followed. Mr. Jones contacted the agency two months later to protest the child's placement and to inquire about his right to visit.

In cases such as Samuel's, assessments of maltreatment, whether of physical or emotional abuse or of neglect, are usually based on one of three theories: psychodynamic, learning, or environmental. Each suggests a particular cause, set of associated factors, and strategies both to treat the family and to prevent the future occurrence of the maltreatment. Within a psychodynamic perspective, the parent's level of functioning is examined in an effort to explain the abusive or neglectful behaviors. Assessment emphasizes such factors as the parent's ability to parent, level of attachment, ego strengths, psychological or personality disorders, and family history, including parent/child relationships. Treatment tends to focus on increasing the parent's understanding of the parental role, building self-esteem, and providing support. From the perspective of learning theorists, assessments tend to stress the parent's level of knowledge of alternative child-rearing practices, techniques for stress management, and anger control. Treatment emphasizes parent education, involvement in support groups, and provision of home-aide services or respite care. From the perspective of environmentalists, assessments emphasize broad structural and cultural factors, including poverty, social isolation, unemployment, racism, and sexism. Advocacy, public education, systemic reforms, community action, and employment programs constitute the thrust of treatment.

Samuel's case illustrates individual pathology as well as environmental or ecological issues that did not receive the necessary or appropriate attention by service providers. For example, allegations of child neglect were made because a minor child was left alone even though provisions were made for his care by the cousin who became ill in the mother's absence. The mother's age, family history of neglect or abuse, relationship with Mr. Jones, relationship with parents and friends, work history, feelings of personal efficacy, and ability to access support networks, although considered in the assessment of the case, are less evident in the treatment plan. The mother's knowledge of child-development milestones and ability to manage stress and demonstrate affection and concern for Samuel's well-being constitute other aspects of the assessment. Neither of these factors is evident in the case plan. An assessment of the family's cultural and social status might have led to permanent and stable living arrangements for the child, such as legal guardianship with relatives, as well as supportive services to the parent and the extended family. Samuel's case illustrates how little regard was given to the sociocultural context of this family and the supportive nature of the extended family, as well as to some of the family's needs for assistance.

Samuel's case required the use of support services, supplemental child-care arrangements, and community resources for employment. None of these services could have been offered directly through the child welfare office; rather, a referral to the appropriate agency or department would have to have been made. Even then, long waiting periods would have been likely before the particular service could be offered. Consequently, the need for skillful case management was critical. The attractiveness of parent-aide services to ensure the child's well-being while the mother worked might have been reiterated in subsequent meetings with the mother. The mother's limited job skills made occupational mobility difficult, but little effort was made to promote economic self-sufficiency and stability or to improve parenting. Moreover, the agency failed to ensure that the mother understood what she had to do to prevent the removal of her child and, upon removal, what she had to do to have her child returned.

In addition, an African American child often has a wide kinship network consisting of numerous family members who at various times provide care. In Samuel's case, the child's father was ignored despite gestures of parental concern. He and his family might have provided a viable permanent home for the child.

In sum, in this case, decisions should have been based on statutory provisions regarding the definition of child abuse and neglect, federal regulations regarding what constitutes reasonable efforts to provide preventive and reunification services, fiscal provisions for foster-care payment, and judicial provisions regarding due process for parents during court disposition and the case-review process. Despite the tireless efforts of legislators, the judiciary, the legal profession, and other human-service professionals, terms like *child abuse* and *child neglect* continue to some degree to be ambiguous. Definitions of abuse and neglect do not always encompass the range of culturally diverse values and child-rearing practices among families. The lack of supervision was the primary factor for placing Samuel in foster care, despite the allegations of physical abuse, though some might argue lack of supervision is a form of abuse rather than neglect. Needless to say, vague legal statutes permit judicial discretion, but the degree to which that discretion is used to keep families together is uncertain.

Issues of accountability also arise in Samuel's case. Referrals to employment and training programs, child-care agencies, and parent-aide programs do not constitute a reasonable effort to maintain a functioning family unit. Skillful case management and provision of advocacy services for both the parents and child, as well as further utilization of extended kin, might have constituted reasonable efforts to prevent the reoccurrence of abuse and neglect. The nonuse of the federal statutes authorizing foster board payments is also apparent; such payments might have alleviated some of the financial hardship associated with informal adoption by extended kin. The case summary indicates no effort on the part of the worker to acquire funds or medical coverage for Samuel during his stay with relatives. Finally, the case demonstrates a failure to provide due process not only to the mother but also to the child.

Integrating knowledge of people of color into daily child welfare practice has been difficult; the demands placed on child welfare workers seldom permit consistent and careful assessments of children of color within the context of their culture. Instead, practitioners tend to note the ethnic origin of the child during intake but ignore it during assessment and treatment. Moreover, the avoidance and nonacknowledgment of the impact of race on child welfare practice are difficult to overcome.

A culturally based perspective is needed to grasp the intricacies and nuances of any racial minority group. Much of the work on integrating knowledge about people of color into practice has been relatively superficial. In educational institutions and training programs three general patterns or trends have emerged: the occasional inclusion of various, but limited, cultural illustrations as teaching tools; assessments of the dissonance between theory and the existing culture; and modifications in theoretical constructs to respond to cultural differences. In our view, any one of these trends is a much needed improvement in education and training. However, each is subject to limitations, such as the exclusion of important information about different cultures, distortions, and a devaluation of cultural factors in the application of knowledge. The limitations lead to incomplete pictures of families of color. These limitations can be minimized by (1) utilizing conceptual frameworks that provide sound foundations for understanding the cultural context of various families and communities; (2) incorporating specific knowledge about the organization, structure, and functioning of culturally and racially different families, including values, beliefs, attitudes, and behaviors, into practice; and (3) designing responsive service-delivery systems based on this knowledge.

Statement of Purpose and Goals

We had several reasons for writing this book. First, there is growing evidence that institutional arrangements for the provision of child welfare services have dismally failed minorities, especially African American children. Second, the evolution of an Africentric perspective of African American family life and child development provides an alternative framework for educating future generations of professionals to serve these families without further stereotyping. Third, there has been a dearth of published materials on African American children and child welfare policy in recent years.

For these reasons, our first goal is to reframe the public discourse on child welfare issues in light of the condition of African American children since the Adoption Assistance and Child Welfare Act of 1980. Despite enormous efforts since the passage of this legislation to ac-

quire permanent homes for the thousands of children in care, the conditions leading to the removal of African American children have
deteriorated. These conditions, including poverty, social and economic isolation, racial bigotry, and misunderstandings about cultural
and racial differences, receive sparse attention in the public arena.
Though public policy is designed to address the needs of aggregate
groups, the reality of African Americans and other people of color as
aggregates seldom enters public debates. Minority children are the
populace on which this nation's future depends. Presently, the developmental journey of children of color, especially African American
children, is bleak. Something more than lip service must be given to
fulfilling the needs of these children, especially those in state custody.
Through open and critical public discourse about the policies and
practices within the child welfare field innovations that account for the
unique qualities of African American families can be generated.

In this book, a culturally based perspective—the Africentric perspective—is used to describe the social context, value base, attitudes,
and behaviors that shape the belief systems, coping strategies, defensive styles, help-seeking behaviors, and treatment responses of African
American families and children (Gibbs, Huang, and Associates 1989).
Admittedly, the Africentric perspective is evolving. However, when
it is juxtaposed with the Eurocentric and American philosophies, the
contrast in the value base, in ways of knowing and doing, reveals the
incongruencies and inconsistencies in current practice and its effects
on ethnically and racially different groups. By using this approach, we
hope to elevate consideration of race in the practice of child welfare
and in the development of policies that enhance and support ethnic
differences.

A perusal of the textbooks on child welfare indicates that most either omit a description of or offer a cursory overview of the lifestyles
and the socioeconomic and cultural circumstances of African American families and their children. Thus, a second goal for writing this
book is to provide a single source for information pertinent to child
welfare issues and African Americans. We review what we already
know about African American family life, child-rearing practices, and
the developmental needs of their children. Each of the authors in this
book struggled to convey the contributions and the implications the
Africentric perspective offers for increasing our understanding of African American families. Contrary to previous works, which examine
African American families from a deficit model, this book highlights

the strengths inherent in the development of these children. Perhaps
more importantly, we describe some of the implications of African
American family life for providing protective services, foster care, reunification and family preservation, and adoption services to African
American children.

Regrettably, this book cannot include every concern about the child
welfare system for African Americans or other people of color. It does
not deal with the role of the judicial system in child welfare, nor does
it address civil rights protections or new developments in the provision of child welfare services such as group homes, orphanages, and
independent living arrangements. Instead we have attempted to provide a broad overview for understanding the complexity of family life
and the practices and policies that affect people of color, especially
African Americans.

Overview of the Book

The eleven chapters in this book are organized into three parts; they
provide a frame of reference for understanding African American
families, a knowledge base about these families, and a critique of the
effects of current child welfare policy and practices on these families.
In the first chapter English offers a taxonomy for understanding the
subtle dimensions of the world view of African Americans, assesses
organizational behavior within a political economy perspective, and
offers strategies for empowering client groups. In the next chapter
Turner describes the Africentric and Eurocentric perspectives and suggests that cultural differences limit the universal application of existing
theories of human behavior. Gould in the third chapter of this part
assesses the implications of a minority perspective—and, more specifically, the Africentric perspective—for practice and education in the
field of child welfare. Interesting enough, the focus for each of these
chapters is mesosystems, or the interactions among the family, other
primary organizations or bureaucratic structures, and the child.

The second part of the book enhances our understanding of the
inner workings, or microsystems, of the family. Wilson places the
African American extended family in historical context by describing
variations in family structure, roles, and functions. He then argues
for modifications in policy and practice to accommodate the unique

features of extended families. Child-rearing practices of African American families are described by Taylor in Chapter 5. His critical assessment of the previous literature on the topic suggests that African American children are socialized to certain styles and motifs rather than to specific rules of behavior. Gomes and Mabry review the stages of child development in Chapter 6, placing considerable emphasis on the role families play in providing a bicultural identity for African American children, in addition to emphasizing the interactions among the family, the school, the community, and the child.

In the third part of the book we turn to the specific child welfare service areas and assess the impact of policies and practices within these areas for African American children and families. Various aspects of child abuse and neglect policy and practice are described by Tatara and Hampton in Chapters 7 and 8. Tatara provides an overview of treatment, protection, and prevention services. His assessment of protective services policies and administrative issues leads to a series of recommendations regarding ameliorative and preventive strategies. Similarly, Hampton describes the incidence of physical and sexual abuse among African American families, considers various models of causation, and suggests the implications for the development of policy. Chapter 9 illustrates an innovative and creative approach for utilizing community resources to foster reunification and preservation among African American families. In this chapter Leashore, McMurray, and Bailey demonstrate the vitality of resources found in an African American community to reunite children who are in foster care with their families. In the next chapter Williams summarizes the opportunities missed in our quest for permanence for African American children. Because legal definitions of family do not reflect social definitions, she argues for the increased use of legal guardianship and of family-preservation measures. Finally, in Chapter 11 Chipungu considers the value base for child welfare policy and proposes a different set of values for policy development.

We feel this book makes an important contribution to the field by focusing attention on the plight of children of color, especially African American children; summarizing in a single text what we already know about African American families; presenting a different set of lenses for understanding the cultural heritage of African American families and children; and making reasonable policy and practice recommendations.

References

American Humane Association. 1984. *Trends in Child Abuse and Neglect: A National Perspective*. Denver.

Billingsley, A., and J. M. Giovannoni. 1972. *Children of the Storm: Black Children and American Child Welfare*. New York: Harcourt Brace Jovanovich.

Edelman, M. W. 1987. *Families in Peril: An Agenda for Social Change*. Cambridge: Harvard University Press.

Gibbs, J. T., L. N. Huang, and Associates. 1989. *Children of Color: Psychological Interventions with Minority Youth*. San Francisco: Jossey-Bass.

Select Committee on Children, Youth and Families. 1989. *U.S. Children and Their Families: Current Conditions and Recent Trends, 1989*. Washington, D.C.: U.S. House of Representatives.

ONE
Cultural
Consciousness

BECAUSE ONE OF THE GOALS for this book is to redirect public discourse about welfare services for African American children, this first part introduces the Africentric perspective to frame the cultural and sociohistorical context of African Americans. Here we describe the values and world views (or cultural adaptations) of African Americans, as well as the basic constructs of the Africentric perspective. These chapters suggest a different perspective, one that is linked to the broader society and its structures. Concomitantly, they view child welfare services in a context that extends beyond the traditional welfare system.

The Africentric perspective (Mbiti 1969; Nobles 1972; White 1984) describes the ethos of Africans and African Americans and the values that guide the way African Americans interact with the world around them. It goes beyond issues of institutional oppression to offer a global view of the peoples of the African diaspora. It counteracts the all-too-conventional application of a deficit model to the behaviors of people of color. It elicits a proactive stance toward the behaviors, beliefs, and attitudes of African Americans by emphasizing strengths. The application of this perspective uncovers incongruencies and inconsistencies in current child welfare policies and practices and reveals the meaning of interpersonal helping from the point of view of African Americans.

It suggests the need for a reexamination of the basic premise supporting existing child welfare services.

Juxtaposed to this perspective is the minority perspective (Lum 1986; Montiel and Wong 1983; Spencer, Brookins, and Allen 1985), which asserts that racism and oppression place minority groups in the United States in subordinate and powerless positions resulting in differential and unequal treatment. This perspective holds that minorities have unequal access to power and are stigmatized for traits perceived by the majority as inferior (Mindel and Habenstein 1981). Its application is limited to Americans and lacks a sociohistorical context. The minority perspective captures some dimensions shared by oppressed groups including ethnic group behavior, minority versus majority dynamics, and social class. When applied to social work practice, the minority perspective has led to demands for culturally sensitive practice models that acknowledge the effects of racial oppression on clients.

The discussion in these chapters is cultural and political. It is cultural in the sense that the Africentric perspective is a reflection of the real experiences and mind-set of African Americans. It is political in the sense that the minority and Africentric perspectives assume a particular stance—one that integrates the individual within the social environment, rather than focusing on intrapsychic phenomena. The intent of our discussion is to open public debate and to suggest different ways of understanding and serving African Americans and other people of color. The imposition of conflicting norms, beliefs, and traditions on children and families of color is the subject of the chapters in Part One.

World view belongs to a class of social science concepts that encompass the various ways in which people perceive their relationship to nature, institutions, other people, and objects. World views constitute psychological orientations to life and in part determine the way we think, behave, make decisions, and define events. Cultural experiences, life events, and value orientations are significant components of an individual's world view, or cultural adaptation (English 1984). In this context, racism is a critical factor affecting the world views of minorities of color.

English (Chapter 1) draws from a diverse literature on racial minorities to delineate a fourfold typology of world views. The typology, expressed in the form of dichotomies, classifies these cultural orientations as bicultural/multicultural, acculturated/assimilated, native-oriented/traditional, and transitional/marginal. Use of this classification of world views allows one to identify professional and client cultural orientations and to assess the effectiveness of treatment interventions. Obviously world views are dynamic. Alterations in world view occur through the interactions among ethnic culture, mainstream culture, and critical life events and experiences (English 1984), which involve power—the capacity to influence or affect one's life. To supplement the discussion of world views, English explores the power of human service organizations. The implications of the political economy perspective of human service organizations are discussed. Furthermore, English offers several strategies for empowerment, collective action, and advocacy that can alter the power/dependency outcomes for people of color.

African and African American philosophical orientations are examined closely in Turner's chapter. Because social constructions of reality are inherently biased, bound by cultural context, historical time, and place, she asserts there are differences in the world views of African Americans and European Americans that challenge the application of psychological paradigms to African Americans. Turner contends that African values, to some extent, remain as vestiges in African American communities. Illustrations of Africanisms retained include a belief in the interconnectedness of all things; a belief in the oneness of mind, body, and spirit; collective identity; consanguineal family structure; and spirituality. Turner considers briefly the implications of these orientations for child welfare.

In the final chapter of Part One Gould scrutinizes the validity and applicability of the minority and Africentric perspectives as theoretical and practice-based frameworks for child welfare work with African American families. The questions posed in her chapter are provocative. She begins by asking whether the minority and Africentric perspectives are interchangeable, separate, or overlapping. Her theoretical analysis leads her to conclude that the minority world view critiques societal and professional ideologies and challenges the tendency to adopt dominant societal definitions automatically. A minority perspective is part of the Africentric perspective, but the two are not identical. An Africentric perspective offers the lens through which policymakers, practitioners, and students can look *with* rather than look *at* the lives of African Americans. Because the formulation of the Africentric perspective is evolving, as the cultural experiences of African Americans are reconstructed and recorded, Gould examines how this perspective can be defined theoretically and put into practice empirically in the child welfare field. In doing so, she demonstrates the applicability of such constructs as family extendedness, communal identity, and self-help to the practice of child welfare. Finally, she considers the implications of the Africentric perspective for social work education, child welfare practice, and feminism.

On one point all three authors agree—namely, that the interaction among individual, family, and organizations is the critical factor affecting the lives of people of color. Economic, cultural, and institutional environments influence both minority values and minority perceptions of and behaviors toward the helping professions and the organizations in which they work. The attitudes and behaviors within organizations also affect the ways in which resources are provided to people of color. Obviously, all parties (the individual, family, community, and organization) need increased awareness of the unique ways each shapes and directs the interaction of the others. The following chapters offer clues and suggestions for improving exchanges between individuals and organizations.

References

English, R. A. 1984. *The Challenge for Mental Health: Minorities and Their World Views*. Austin: Hogg Foundation for Mental Health, University of Texas.

Lum, D. 1986. *Social Work Practice and People of Color: A Process-Stage Approach*. Monterey, Calif.: Brooks/Cole.

Mbiti, J. S. 1969. *African Religions and Philosophies*. New York: Praeger.

Mindel, C. H., and R. W. Habenstein. 1981. "Family Lifestyles of America's Ethnic Minorities: An Introduction." In *Ethnic Families in America: Patterns and Variations,* edited by C. H. Mindel and R. W. Habenstein, 1–13. New York: Elsevier.

Montiel, M., and P. Wong. 1983. "A Theoretical Critique of the Minority Perspective." *Social Casework* 64:112–117.

Nobles, W. W. 1972. "African Philosophy: Foundation for Black Psychology." In *Black Psychology,* edited by R. Jones, 18–32. New York: Harper & Row.

Spencer, M. B., G. K. Brookins, and W. R. Allen, eds. 1985. *Beginnings: The Social and Affective Development of Black Children*. Hillsdale, N.J.: Erlbaum.

White, J. L. 1984. *The Psychology of Blacks: An Afro-American Perspective*. Englewood Cliffs, N.J.: Prentice-Hall.

1

RICHARD A. ENGLISH

Diversity of World Views among African American Families

They that seek and seldom find and yet all ceaselessly do seek some Truer,
Better Thing—some fairer country.
—W.E.B. DU BOIS,
Prayers for Dark People

The delivery of culturally and ethnically sensitive services by public
and private child welfare agencies is burdened by a major paradox.
When given an option, many ethnic minorities of color will avoid
bureaucratic services to resolve their problems. Rather, they are likely
to seek out family, friends, and others nearby for support and help.
This pattern of help seeking seems to be the case independent of income level, geographic location, and family background (Brown and
Gary 1987; English 1985; McAdoo 1978; Martin and Martin 1985;
Mindel and Wright 1982; Shimkin, Shimkin, and Frate 1978; Stack
1974; Taylor 1985).[1] Yet when confronted with the necessity for child
welfare services—such as for adoption, foster care, child protection,
residential treatment, adolescent pregnancy and parenting, family
counseling and preservation—ethnic minorities of color have little
choice. These are services requiring professional expertise and complex organizational resources. All too often, however, the agency
from which help is sought is understaffed, underfunded, and over-
burdened with heavy workloads to resolve some of society's most
pressing problems: child maltreatment, substance abuse, homelessness, and the abandonment of infants and children (Kamerman and
Kahn 1990; Pecora, Briar, and Zlotnik 1989). As clients of the bureau-

19

cratic child welfare service-delivery system, they are at once vulnerable and powerless. The majority of these clients are single mothers with children who are at risk of poverty and emotional stress. An effective, culturally and ethnically sensitive child welfare delivery system must address both these challenges: their clients' vulnerability and their lack of power.

The intent of this chapter is to present a case for enhancing the organization and delivery of child welfare services for African American families and other ethnic minorities of color. Clearly an effective and professionally competent child welfare delivery system will benefit all children and their families. In the undertaking of this task, three topics are addressed: the world views (cultural adaptations) of professional caregivers and ethnic minority clients; a political economy perspective on the bureaucratic organizations in which most child welfare services are located (Hasenfeld 1983; Zald 1970); and advocacy and empowerment strategies for changing power/dependency outcomes for ethnic-minority clients in child welfare agencies.

It is important to point out that the ideas offered in this discussion will not solve the enormously serious and complex problems of the public service-delivery system for children and families. Solutions to many of the pressing problems of the organization and delivery of child welfare services on the one hand and the poverty and social problems of the clientele on the other hand must be addressed in a larger societal context. However, as Schorr (1988:256–283) points out in her review of social interventions for disadvantaged children and families, those programs that worked incorporated in their interventions the unique characteristics and environments of their clients. Furthermore, successful interventions were likely to be carried out in bureaucratic and professional structures that were flexible, intensive, and comprehensive.

World Views of African Americans:
A Mechanism for Assessing
Cultural Adaptations

The social science literature suggests contrasting models of racial and ethnic experiences in U.S. society.[2] One model posits that ethnic and racial groups have values and experiences different from those of the majority culture because of their unique histories. The other model emphasizes racism, discrimination, and lack of economic opportunities as causes (Farley and Allen 1987:365–368). These two models are not necessarily contradictory. In both models predictions are made about social mobility and other important outcomes throughout the life cycle. In the first model, greater responsibility is placed on the individual and his or her cultural background as critical influences on social mobility. In the second model a much greater role in social-mobility outcomes is assigned to racism and blocked opportunities.

Since W.E.B. Du Bois ([1899] 1967:173) we have known about the double environments of African Americans—the white world and the black world. Du Bois recognized the centrality of race and ethnicity in the daily lives of African Americans. He understood the reality and significance of the influence of the double environments on the enactment of both simple daily tasks—what kind of food to eat and clothes to wear—and complex tasks such as naming children and deciding where to live and how to educate children.

Health is an important area in which the double environments of African Americans are uniquely expressed in the range and severity of particular ailments that are caused as much by their life-styles—the neighborhoods in which they live and their eating and drinking habits—as by their genetic predisposition to certain diseases. For some time it has been well known that certain health problems are associated with particular groups, such as sickle cell disease and hypertension among African Americans, diabetes among some Native Americans, and Tay-Sachs disease among descendants of eastern European Jews. But as Leary (1990) points out, some well-known health problems previously considered ethnically neutral may be manifested in ethnic groups in different ways, may vary in incidence, and may require different treatment approaches. Leary gives several examples: Severe kidney failure, long known to be higher in whites, is now revealed to be much worse than previously believed in African Americans; the risk of developing diabetes during pregnancy is much higher for Chinese and Hispanic women than for comparable African Americans or whites; and the rate of infant mortality among Mexican American women, who often live in poverty and receive poor prenatal care, is low compared with the infant death rate among blacks and in some cases among whites. In these examples, the role of genetics is recognized. But the importance and role of environmental and cultural factors are critical as well.

Experiences with environmental factors such as racism and discrimination are likely to have profound consequences for African Americans. These experiences are critical sources of vulnerability and stress. Brown and Gary (1987) reviewed studies indicating that low income and poverty tended to expose African Americans to a greater number of stressful life experiences than whites were exposed to. Vega and Rumbaut (1991) divided these stressors into subjective and objective factors. Subjective factors are the individual's own perceptions of unfair treatment or blocked opportunity based on race and ethnicity. Objective factors are negative experiences such as "unemployment, disrupted marital relationships, fragmented social networks and physical hardships" (Vega and Rumbaut 1991). Both perceptions and real-life experiences can influence major decisions about future events. For example, as these authors point out, the individual's perception of a hostile, prejudiced environment is likely to influence the choice of where to live, of a mate, of child-rearing practices, and of social ties.

The social science literature defines these perceptions of one's relationships to other people, institutions, objects, and nature as world views. Theoretically, world views are related to one's conceptions of the universe, of one's role in society, of the meaning of life and death, and of the determinants of knowledge and of change in society (English 1983:17). World views are overarching belief systems about the universe and one's place in it. Because the world views of African Americans are shaped and developed by unique realities, it is important and useful for child welfare professionals to take them into account in their practice and service-delivery systems. They can be helpful in providing insights into their clients' presenting problems and reactions to them.

World views of African Americans and other ethnic minorities are useful as a source of knowledge for achieving four distinct goals: assessing the client's cultural background and fundamental orientation toward life, diagnosing problems and planning treatment, empowering African American and ethnic-minority families and individuals, and designing innovative child welfare programs and interventions.

The conceptualization of world views of African Americans began with the identification of traditional practices associated with black family and community life in the revisionist literature on black families published during the late 1960s and through the 1970s and early 1980s. Allen, English, and Hall (1986) documented this literature in an annotated bibliography. Billingsley (1968) is credited with establishing the "strengths" school of black family studies and was followed by many others including Hill (1972, 1977); Gutman (1976); Blassingame (1979); Shimkin, Shimkin, and Frate 1978); Stack (1974); and Martin and Martin (1985).

In this literature the following attributes of traditional black family life and community are identified: strong kinship ties and obligations, care of the elderly and absorption of children into households by other relatives and fictive kin, strong religious consciousness, strong community ties, socialization of the young with emphasis on group welfare over individual welfare, strong helping and mutual-aid tradition, and strong achievement orientation. These patterns are rooted in the African American experience. Not all African Americans share an adherence to these values. Variations occur based on a range of complex factors, including social mobility, urban experiences, the impact of racism and discrimination on life experiences, and childhood socialization.

Theoretically, it is assumed that the more African American culture is an essential core of the individual's life-style, the more these traditional kinship and community values are reflected in the individual's family life. The less African American culture is a component of the individual's life, the more likely "assimilated" family values are an essential part. When one has a deeply felt commitment neither to one's own culture nor to mainstream culture, the result is a "marginal" world view. A "bicultural" world view occurs when the individual deals effectively with mainstream culture without sacrificing African American culture.

Starting with the traditional values and experiences of African Americans and drawing on the assimilation/integration sociological literature (Glazer 1954; Gordon 1964; Shibutani and Kwan 1965), I present here a fourfold typology of these world views: traditional, bicultural, assimilated, and marginal. These world views are characterized as dichotomous variables so as to reflect their continuous character (English 1983:19–20):

Native-oriented/traditional world views reflect patterns of native culture rooted in the history of a particular ethnic group and in past familial and communal experiences.

Bicultural/multicultural world views result from experiences in two different ways of life for racial and ethnic minorities—their own traditional culture and that of the mainstream culture—or from experience with diverse cultural traditions found in a pluralistic environment.

Acculturated/assimilated world views result from the acquisition of the beliefs, attitudes, values, and behaviors of a group of which one is not a natural member; assimilation is the end state of such a process.

Transitional/marginal world views are held by individuals suspended between their own ethnic identity and mainstream culture without a strong identification with either group.

World views can be further classified in two dimensions: (1) the value an individual places on his or her own culture and identity, and (2) the value placed on involvement with and participation in the mainstream cultures, as illustrated in Table 1.1. This model can be used in the analysis of African American clients' cultural orientations.

In an empirical test of the world-views paradigm, an exploratory study was conducted in 1984 of African American middle-class husbands and wives ($N = 150$; 75 husbands and 75 wives) living in a middle-size Texas city with a large public university. A nomination strategy was employed to identify a sample of African American families that met the following criteria: (1) couple-headed or widowed; (2) married at least five years; (3) with at least one child under eighteen years of age living in the same household; and (4) middle class, as defined by the person nominating families for the study. The major purpose of the study was to determine how these relatively trouble-free families handled stress and the problems of daily living, and the role of cultural orientations in their coping styles. The mean years of marriage for the sample was 16.8. A large percentage—87.3 percent (both husbands and wives)—had never been previously married. The median family income for the sample was $50,000 ($N = 147$). The mean years of education for the sample was 16.1. Husbands and wives were about the same age, although husbands were slightly older (husbands' mean age was 41.2 and wives' mean age was 39.5).

Table 1.1. A Typology of World Views

	Level of participation in and commitment to own culture and identity	
	High	*Low*
Level of participation in and commitment to mainstream and other culture	*High* Bicultural/multicultural	Acculturated/assimilated
	Low Native-oriented/traditional	Transitional/marginal

Assessment of world views was made by asking respondents to read a set of four statements and to specify which one described their point of view.[3] These statements were as follows:

1. I have a strong commitment and identification to Black culture and the survival of Black institutions. It is far more important for me to identify and promote a separate Black culture than participate in the mainstream culture. Generally, I stick pretty close to the Black community and prefer to spend my leisure time with other Blacks like myself. [Traditional]
2. I have a strong commitment and identification to Black culture and the survival of Black institutions. I am equally committed to identifying and participating in the mainstream culture as well. Generally, I participate in both mainstream activities and those in the Black community in equal fashion. [Bicultural]
3. I have a strong commitment and identification to mainstream culture. Generally, I stick pretty close to the larger community, and prefer to spend my leisure time with persons like myself who may be of another race or ethnic group. [Assimilated]
4. It really doesn't matter whether one is strongly identified with one's own group or the mainstream culture. Generally, I do what I like whether it's with other Blacks or those who may be of another race or ethnic group. [Marginal]

Two-thirds of the total sample expressed a bicultural orientation (66.7 percent) and a very small percentage an assimilated orientation (2.0 percent) (Table 1.2). Traditional and marginal orientations accounted for 12 and 19.3 percent of the sample, respectively.

When husbands' responses were compared with their wives' responses, there were few differences. As Table 1.3 shows, slightly more husbands than wives held traditional world views. Only two husbands and one wife identified themselves as having assimilated orientations.

Table 1.2. World Views of Overall Sample

	N	%
Traditional	18	12.0
Bicultural	100	66.7
Assimilated	3	2.0
Marginal	29	19.3
Total	150	100

Table 1.3. World Views of
Husbands and Wives Separately, in percent

	Husbands	*Wives*
Traditional	14.7	9.3
Bicultural	66.7	66.7
Assimilated	2.7	1.3
Marginal	16.0	22.7
N	75	75

More wives than husbands were self-described as having marginal orientations. An equal number had bicultural orientations. These data indicate the viability of world views as sources for identifying critical aspects of African American values and cultural orientations.

Other analyses from these data suggest that while the majority of the sample sought professional help with severe problems, they tended most often to rely on themselves and their families. Friends were usually not used as sources for coping with stress but rather as a source of companionship. When families did consult professionals for assistance, they were more likely to hold bicultural world views than traditional world views.

Professional Caregivers and World Views

Traditionally in the human service literature much has been made of understanding the psychological and cultural backgrounds of minorities, largely clients. In addition, however, it is as important to understand the cultural backgrounds of professionals, minority and nonminority, who serve these populations. In the complex professional helping process the ways in which caregivers perceive, experience, respond to, and define even insignificant life events may have critical outcomes for clients.

In a self-report by a Latina social service administrator (Rincon and Keys 1982), a vivid description is provided of the process of "transcending the culture," which is believed to be necessary for professional success. This particular social service administrator was the only female director in a network of approximately one hundred social service agencies across the country for Hispanics and minorities. In the process of transcending the culture, she suggests that one must be able to set oneself apart from his or her origins. She suggests that she had to move beyond her origins in order to perform her professional duties effectively. Specifically, she had to remove herself from the influence of her culture, especially sex roles in which Hispanic males (father, brother, husband) may expect women to be passive and submissive.

One of the ways of understanding world views is to use the techniques of ethnomethodology. Ethnomethodology has been useful as a scientific tool in helping us understand how individuals manage "the presentation of self in everyday life" (Goffman 1959). It is a method for uncovering and discovering the common sense thinking that people use in managing, organizing, or coping with the problems of everyday life. It can be useful to professional caregivers in their work with clients. But it may also be useful in understanding their own interactions and decision making with clients (Korte and Rael 1986:25–26; Spradley 1979).

Summarizing the importance of world views, Hartman and Laird (1983:62) observe: "In summary then, human beings, families, and institutions, out of social processes and in interaction with the world and each other, develop epistemologies or world views that become major guides in organizing perceptions and decision making. Patterned and consistent world views may be called paradigms and are expressed in daily life and action." Analysis of these paradigms can assist in assessing the extent to which one has successfully transcended the culture and adopted the professional role.

However, understanding the world views of either professionals, their clients, or both is not sufficient for serving ethnic minorities of color. Such limited understanding runs the risk of inviting cultural imperialism. There is the necessity of considering issues of politics and power in the bureaucracy.

The Political Economy Perspective of Bureaucratic Organizations: The Loss-of-Power Problem

Most human services (health and welfare) are delivered within organizations. These organizations are ubiquitous in modern societies. We spend our entire lives dealing with these organizations, and they have critical effects on our aspirations, status, values, and behavior.

We are born and die in hospitals; are socialized and educated in schools; seek spiritual guidance and solace in religious organizations; seek a multitude of services and assistance from social welfare agencies; and protect ourselves and properties through law-enforcement agencies. These organizations serve the homeless, feed the hungry, and comfort the dying and those with fatal diseases. In 1974 Hasenfeld and English called this set of organizations, whose principal function is to protect, maintain, or enhance the well-being of individuals by defining, shaping, or altering their personal attributes, "human service organizations" (Hasenfeld 1983; Hasenfeld and English 1974).

These organizations are distinguished from other bureaucratic organizations in two important ways. First, their work is directed toward people whose attributes they attempt to shape. People are their raw material. Second, they are mandated to protect and promote the welfare of the people they serve. Through this societal mandate (which is a form of social support), human service organizations are obligated to provide services based on universal criteria and without prejudice.

Yet the power that human service organizations come to possess over those whom they serve can cause them to fall short of the achievement of these twin objectives. The process by which human service organizations come to have power over their clients is rooted in the transaction between organization and client, and in the nature of human service organizations themselves.

When individuals seek out human service organizations and become their clients, students, patients, prisoners, and so on, they invariably become dependent on them, and the organizations acquire power over their lives. Moreover, organizational elites and officials control the resources these client groups need, as well as the policies that govern the services. The individual's loss of power in transactions is a fundamental aspect of human service organizations. In many instances, individuals have little choice in dealing with these organizations (Hasenfeld 1983:4). This reality has serious consequences for many people, especially those who are poor and underserved by these organizations.

A typical response to this set of events is to cast the problem in a human-relations frame of reference. For example, Johnson (1978:215) identified a list of seven problems preventing bureaucratic mental health agencies from providing effective services to African American clients.

1. Frequently the needs of the entire constituent population are not met.
2. Frequently organizations and their resultant institutions are not definitive as to their function(s).
3. Frequently specialized organizations and institutions do not select priorities which will enable service delivery to the constituency.
4. Frequently provider organizations and those in need of service have different opinions and ideas as to the service need.
5. Frequently provider organizations are not in communication with service users as to what their function(s) should be.
6. Frequently provider organizations do not view the user as capable of making a contribution to the service delivery.
7. Frequently there is distrust between the provider organization and users. Thus, there is little congruence between providers and users in their perceptions of need and remedy.

The human-relations approach, which began with the famous Hawthorne studies, assumes that the goals of the organization and its workers are compatible and, therefore, that organizational goals and worker interests are similar (Hasenfeld 1983:24). Human-relations theorists stop at their solution of improving interpersonal relations in the organization as a means of solving this set of complex problems. Basically, these theorists assume that all problems are rooted in poor communications. Thus, if you solve the communications problems, all problems will disappear.

Not so.

Organizations exist in environments that typify prevailing societal conditions. It is, therefore, difficult for them to insulate themselves from patterns, values, and norms of social inequality. Specifically, they have difficulty in buffering themselves from prejudicial and discriminatory attitudes and behaviors toward minorities of color. They must, as Korte and Rael (1986) suggest, for example, contend with the view of the "tangle of pathology" that lurks behind African Americans, the "machismo" viewpoint among Mexican Americans, and the model-minorities view of Asian Americans. (This perspective considers Asian Americans as "model" minorities because of their industriousness, hard work, and intelligence, and because they have not been victimized by discrimination and prejudice. Thus, they are considered problem free.)

In contrast, the political economy perspective, as developed by Zald (1970), addresses itself to the critical issue of relations between organizations and their clients. Zald suggests that the political economy perspective "is the study of the interplay of power, the goals of the powerwielders, and the productive exchange systems" (p. 223). As Hasenfeld (1983:44) suggests:

> *Political* refers to the process through which power and legitimation . . . are acquired by the organization and distributed internally, operative goals are determined, and major tasks of the organization are defined and controlled by the dominant elite. . . . *Economic* refers to the processes by which resources needed for the service technologies of the organization (i.e., clients, . . . money) are acquired and distributed in the organization, divisions of labor are specified and operationalized, and production of the organizational outputs is maintained.

The role of clients can be assessed from this political economy perspective. Fundamentally, this perspective suggests, as Hasenfeld (1983:48) points out, that "the ability of clients to influence the organization and the patterns of relations between them and staff will be a function of the needed resources they control, both political and economic." He further suggests (p. 48) that "when clients possess few resources, the organization's responsiveness to their needs will depend on the relative power of those interest groups championing their cause."

Although the political economy persepective of human service organizations does not solve all the problems of enhancing health and human services for underserved populations, it does point the direction for interventions. In the case of powerlessness, it suggests strategies of advocacy and empowerment.

Empowerment, Collective-Action, and Advocacy Strategies for Changing Power/ Dependency Outcomes for Clients

At the Howard University School of Social Work, a new curriculum with a concentration in social work practice with displaced populations was recently introduced. Displaced populations encompass a wide range of groups, including the homeless, refugees, migrants, immigrants, undocumented minors and workers, and victims of disasters. In teaching and working with community agencies that provide services to these populations, one is reminded of how our organized social services consciously or unconsciously strip individuals of their independence and autonomy. This loss of power is particularly evidenced in programs for the homeless. Much is required of those who need the services, and often little is provided. The homeless person is frequently required to surrender his or her total self and possessions to the service providers. Many women who are in shelters, for example, are required to turn their SSI benefits over to shelter staff or are discouraged from saving their limited income for another day. The invasive approaches of many shelters may be modified by limiting access to the total biography of persons in them. Providing limited services, for example, rather than comprehensive services is an effective strategy for preventing intrusions into privacy and addressing the feelings of suspicion and fear that characterize so many homeless persons.

Client-advocacy organizations, such as the Children's Defense Fund, the Child Welfare League, the National Coalition for the Homeless, and the Community for Creative Non-Violence (homeless), can serve as a front-line defense for client groups, who are able to advance their own goals in the organization. Empowering clients to enhance their advantage in human service organizations will place them in positions to control transactions with the organization and optimize their interests. For example, the effective leaders of Muslim prisoners in a big city jail were able to join forces with influential Muslim groups in the community to induce jail officials to provide prayer rugs and special meals.

Conclusion

This chapter attempts to demonstrate that enhancing the organization and delivery of child welfare services for African American families is not a straightforward matter. In our society we generally believe that receiving help is good. Yet we all can recall times when the help we received was anything but good. Receiving help is therefore not without its perils and can be potentially costly because of the loss of power involved. The ability of organizations to control effectively the lives of individuals who have little power cannot be underestimated. However, help can be beneficial and can extend the individual's freedom of choice.

None of these limitations mean that African American populations should avoid bureaucratic child welfare services, even in the face of viable informal support networks. To the contrary, organizational theory "suggests that when used in some combination or sequential pattern, *the effectiveness* of family, extended kin resources, indigenous community-based care-givers, and bureaucratic health and human services is maximized. Each makes a unique and specialized contribution to the solution of the individual problem. When both the informal system and the bureaucratic help-giving system are coupled with community networking, self-help groups, neighborhood groups and the like, the goal of serving underserved populations has been greatly advanced" (English 1983:14).

Enhancing the power of clients in child welfare agencies will ultimately serve their best interests and give them increased access to the best the organization's service-delivery system provides. Professionals who take the clients' best interest into account are likely to devalue organizational demands to render them powerless.

Notes

1. In a review of the research literature on help-seeking patterns of African Americans, Taylor, Neighbors, and Broman (1989) reviewed two studies in which few respondents reported that they would go to a social service agency for help with a problem. In their report of data from a national survey of Black Americans, they reveal that 64 percent of the Black adults interviewed ($N = 1,322$) indicated having experienced a serious problem in their lives. Of these respondents, 87.2 percent sought help from at least one member of their informal network. Only 48.7 percent sought help from professionals.

They then analyzed the data from the small proportion of respondents ($N = 91$) who sought help from social services. Seventy-eight percent of this sample was female, and a high proportion was poor and had less than a high school education. A preponderance had been referred to social service agencies by relatives and friends.

In my study of Black middle-class families in Texas, the majority of those who had mental-health problems first sought help from family, friends, and ministers. Only when they believed their problems to be serious did they seek out professionals. These professionals tended most often to be psychiatrists.

Studies of social support among African Americans provide an understanding of the roles of informal support networks. Not only are these networks useful in helping with daily problems, but they also help define the nature of the individual's problems, make appropriate professional referrals, and promote adherence to treatment interventions (Taylor, Neighbors, and Broman 1989:209).

2. This discussion of world views and child welfare is adopted from a previous work (English, 1983).

3. Another strategy for assessing world views involved the operationalization of traditional kinship values in a series of eleven items. Respondents were asked to indicate how their families reacted to these events if they had ever occurred or to imagine how their families would have acted if they had occurred. In addition, respondents were asked to indicate whether they strongly agreed, agreed, disagreed, or strongly disagreed with statements such as these: "When a close member of my family moves to another city where other relatives live, they can live with those relatives until they get settled"; "Responsibility for a daughter's or son's out-of-wedlock children will be assumed by the family"; "Blood ties are more important than marriage ties"; "Elderly relatives who can't take care of themselves are better off in nursing homes." These assessments of world views were highly correlated with the written statements.

References

Allen, W. R., R. A. English, and J. A. Hall. 1986. *Black American Families, 1965–1984: A Classified, Selectively Annotated Bibliography.* New York: Greenwood Press.

Billingsley, A. 1968. *Black Families in White America.* Englewood Cliffs, N.J.: Prentice-Hall.

Blassingame, J. W. 1979. *The Slave Community: Plantation Life in the Antebellum South.* New York: Oxford University Press.

Brown, D. R., and L. E. Gary. 1987. "Stressful Life Events, Social Support Networks, and the Physical and Mental Health of Urban Black Adults." *Journal of Human Stress,* Winter, 165–174.

Du Bois, W. E. B. [1899] 1967. *The Philadelphia Negro.* New York: Schocken.

English, R. A. 1983. *The Challenge for Mental Health: Minorities and Their World Views.* Austin: Hogg Foundation for Mental Health, University of Texas.

————. 1985. "Social Supports in Middle-Class Black Families in Two Texas Communities." Unpublished paper, School of Social Work, University of Texas at Austin.

Farley, R., and W. R. Allen. 1987. *The Color Line and the Quality of Life in America.* New York: Russell Sage Foundation.

Glazer, N. 1954. "Ethnic Groups in America." In *Freedom and Control in Modern Society,* edited by B. Morroe, A. Theodore, and P. H. Charles, 158–173. New York: D. Van Nostrand.

Goffman, E. 1959. *The Presentation of Self in Everyday Life.* Garden City, N.Y.: Doubleday, Anchor Books.

Gordon, M. M. 1964. *Assimilation in American Life.* New York: Oxford University Press.

Gutman, H. G. 1976. *The Black Family in Slavery and Freedom, 1750–1925.* New York: Random House, Vintage Books.

Hartman, A., and J. Laird. 1983. *Family-Centered Social Work Practice.* New York: Free Press.

Hasenfeld, Y. 1983. *Human Service Organizations.* Englewood Cliffs, N.J.: Prentice-Hall.

Hasenfeld, Y., and R. A. English, eds. 1974. *Human Service Organizations.* Ann Arbor: University of Michigan Press.

Hill, R. B. 1972. *The Strengths of Black Families.* New York: Emerson Hall.

———. 1977. *Informal Adoption among Black Families.* Washington, D.C.: National Urban League Research Department.

Johnson, A. E. 1978. "The Organization of Mental Health Services Delivery." In *Mental Health: A Challenge to the Black Community,* edited by L. E. Gary, 212–238. Philadelphia: Dorrance.

Kamerman, S. B., and A. J. Kahn. 1990. "The Problems Facing Social Services for Children, Youth and Families in the United States." *Children and Youth Services Review* 1/2:7–20.

Korte, A. O., and R. H. Rael. 1986. *The Multicultural Study of Families: A Critique.* Tempe: Hispanic Research Center, Arizona State University.

Leary, W. E. 1990. "Uneasy Doctors Add Race-Consciousness to Diagnostic Tools." *New York Times,* September 25.

McAdoo, H. P. 1978. "Factors Related to Stability in Upwardly Mobile Black Families." *Journal of Marriage and the Family* 40:761–776.

Martin, J. M., and E. P. Martin. 1985. *The Helping Tradition in the Black Family and Community.* Silver Spring, Md.: National Association of Social Workers.

Mindel, C. H., and R. Wright. 1982. "The Use of Social Services by Black and White Elderly: The Role of Social Support Systems." *Journal of Gerontological Social Work* 4:107–126.

Pecora, P. J., K. H. Briar, and J. L. Zlotnik. 1989. *Addressing the Program and Personnel Crisis in Child Welfare: A Social Work Response.* Silver Spring, Md.: National Association of Social Workers.

Rincon, E. L., and C. B. Keys. 1982. "The Latina Social Service Administrator: Developmental Tasks and Management Concerns." *Administration in Social Work* 6 (Spring):47–57.

Schorr, L. 1988. *Within Our Reach: Breaking the Cycle of Disadvantage.* New York: Doubleday, Anchor Books.

Shibutani, T., and K. K. Kwan. 1965. *Ethnic Stratification: A Comparative Approach.* New York: Macmillan.

Shimkin, D. B., E. M. Shimkin, and D. A. Frate, eds. 1978. *The Extended Family in Black Societies.* The Hague: Mouton.

Spradley, J. P. 1979. *The Ethnographic Interview.* New York: Holt, Rinehart & Winston.

Stack, C. B. 1974. *All Our Kin: Strategies for Survival in a Black Community.* New York: Harper & Row.

Taylor, R. J. 1985. "The Extended Family as a Source of Support to Elderly Blacks." *The Gerontologist* 25 (5):488–489.

Taylor, R. J., H. W. Neighbors, and C. L. Broman. 1989. "Evaluation of Black Americans of the Social Service Encounter during a Serious Personal Problem." *Social Work* 34 (3):205–211.

Vega, W. A., and R. G. Rumbaut. 1991. "Reasons of the Heart: Ethnic Minorities and Mental Health." *Annual Review of Sociology* 17 (August).

Zald, M. N. 1970. "Political Economy: A Framework for Comparative Analysis." In *Power in Organizations,* edited by M. N. Zald, 221–261. Nashville, Tenn.: Vanderbilt University Press.

2

ROBERTA J. TURNER

Affirming Consciousness: The Africentric Perspective

We wear the mask that grins and lies,
It hides our cheeks and shades our eyes,
This debt we pay to human guile;
With torn and bleeding hearts we smile,
And mouth with myriad subtleties.
— PAUL LAURANCE DUNBAR,
We Wear the Mask

All theories, models, and paradigms of human behavior are inherently culturally biased or ethnocentric; they are bound by the culture, historical time, life experience, and knowledge base of their proponents. The construction of models of human behavior from an Africentric perspective attempts to portray African Americans, the people of the African diaspora in the Western hemisphere, in ways that are free of European ethnocentrism and androcentrism. The Africentric perspective implicitly contends that differences in culture, world view, and historical experiences exist between African Americans and European Americans, as there are differences between Asians and Europeans, and between the indigenous populations of the Americas, the Amerindians, and Europeans. The Africentric perspective delineates and explicates some of these differences, many of which have implications for the construction of paradigms of human behavior. In this chapter the constructs of the Africentric perspective are described and illustrated.

The Primacy of Culture

Culture as a concept provides a set of principles for explaining and understanding human behavior (Hatch 1985). One of the most controversial debates in the field of anthropology focuses on how culture is defined. The debate, which has to do with the inclusiveness or exclusiveness of the meanings assigned to the concept, has implications for the presumed influence culture has on human behavior and vice versa. Culture is defined in this chapter as the "way in which any group has constructed solutions to the universal problem of how to live. It includes religion, family structure, dress, language, values, beliefs, technology, and so on" (Hatch 1985:178–179), and is reflected in the patterns of behavior and ways of thinking and feeling that people have developed. Much of culture is below the level of conscious awareness and tends to structure both thought and perception. Culture is also enduring and dynamic. It adapts to changing societal needs and goals.

Cultural context, then, is an important variable affecting human behavior and perceptions of human behavior. Culture is frequently used as an explanatory concept in that it helps to explain why specific institutions occur when and where they do (Hatch 1985). Cultural analyses examine the life experiences, adaptive responses, and creative struggles of groups. The primacy of culture lies in its ability to provide an interpretive explanation that gives an account of behavior by explicating the values, beliefs, symbols, and so forth, that underlay that behavior.

Because all societies possess culture, it seems reasonable to assume that sociocultural factors shape what is perceived to be objective reality. Culture may also alter the ways in which people perceive reality, starting with physical reality. For example, the images that an object forms on the retina do not always correspond to what the brain interprets as the external environment. As one walks around a living room, a table may form a trapezoidal image on the retina, yet one sees the table as remaining rectangular. Shapes and sizes remain constant; otherwise the environment would be visually chaotic. People thus learn how to see the world (Dember 1979).

Research in the psychology of perception has found there are optical illusions that almost all people in the West see. However, people in non-Western cultures may not be as susceptible to the same optical

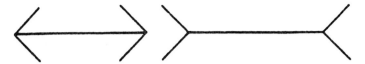

Figure 2.1. The Müller-Lyer illusion. The two horizontal lines are of equal length, but the line on the right appears to be much longer. To make the lines appear subjectively equal, the line on the left must be approximately 25 percent longer than the one on the right.

illusions (Segall 1979; Segall, Campbell, and Herskovitz 1966). One of these is the Muller-Lyer illusion. When people raised in the West are asked to describe the lines depicted in Figure 2.1, most will indicate that the line on the right is longer than the line on the left! However, rural people in East Africa tend to see both lines as the same length. Similar differences are observed with another illusion that involves a trapezoid drawn inside a circle and then rotated. People raised in the West report the rotating trapezoid as a square, presumably because they have a perceptual set for square objects; a trapezoid is a shape not found as often as squares in their everyday environment. In contrast, the Zulu, a South African tribal group, traditionally live in an environment filled with circular objects. For example, houses are circular and are arranged in circles. Consequently, the Zulu do not see the illusion. The rotating trapezoid is seen as a trapezoid and not as a square (Dember 1979). Data demonstrate that optical illusions are culturally bound; the same data illustrate how culture and environment affect perceptions of physical reality.

Language, which some contend is culture, may also have some influence on the perception of material reality. Whorf (1956) and Sapir (1933) postulate that language structures reality. Whorf argues that the language of a culture influences how people view material reality. The Aztecs, for instance, have one word for ice, snow, and sleet, while the Aleutes and Eskimos, who live in a cold, wet, and snowy environment, have dozens of words for different types of snow alone. Each of these words enables them to make fine distinctions about a phenomenon that is very much a part of their environment. Different languages also have distinct ways of describing colors. The Navaho, who work with turquoise, have dozens of words to describe different shades of turquoise, none of which are found in European languages. The boundaries between colors on the spectrum also vary among cultures (Cole and Scribner 1974). For example, English speakers distinguish between shades of blue and green—a continuous gradation of hue. The Zuni, however, use the same word for red and orange. "Different languages make distinctions between colors at different places along a continuum" (Hatch 1985:178). Thus, the languages developed by different groups of people may be seen, assuming the Whorfian hypothesis, as influencing their construction of physical reality.

Different languages also allow different constructions of social reality. The languages in Africa and Micronesia, for example, contain words that distinguish among a wide range of kinship ties. European languages tend to contain one single word, *uncle* to describe a mother's brother and a father's brother. But African languages differentiate these two relatives and also differentiate senior brothers from junior brothers and senior sisters from junior sisters. Similarly, there is no single word in English for an individual who is one's fifth cousin, three times removed. Most people in the United States have difficulty determining who a fifth cousin is. Yet, an African might quickly name individuals who fit into that category, as well as linguistically differentiate relatives who have died and those not yet born. Further, in Twi, a West African language, there are twenty-two different words to describe various types of male/female relationships, most of which are not translated into English by a single word. Some of these words refer to different degrees of concubinage. Thus, family ties and relationships are defined differently and more extensively in many African cultures than they are in Euro-American culture. In effect, how we label a phenomenon is to some extent a function of the implicit assumptions of our culture (Seidman and Rappaport 1986).

Berger and Luckmann's treatise (1967) on the sociology of knowledge analyzes the social construction of human reality and the process by which knowledge comes to be known as reality. These authors postulate that the relationship between human thought and its social and historical context affects what is considered reality. I.Q. scores are an example of a socially constructed reality. Many skills and abilities that can be used to understand, adapt to, and manipulate the environment are not included in measurements of I.Q. Operationally, intelligence is defined by psychologists and others as that which the I.Q. test measures. However, traditional intelligence tests, according to most studies, measure learned behavior—that is, problem-solving styles, language competence, and mathematical skills (White 1984). In addition, they measure a student's exposure to and knowledge of Euro-American culture and thus are not free of cultural biases.

Challenges to the Universal Application of Euro-American Psychological Paradigms

Because cultures are in continual change with increasing Western contact, anthropological studies of the same groups over time are never examining exactly the same cultures. Consequently, the reliability of anthropological findings is questionable. Moreover, anthropological studies are often methodologically flawed, and because they have their own biases, there are caveats about generalizations from Euro-American models. Anthropologists have historically attempted to prove the cross-cultural applicability of Euro-American psychological theory. As early as 1927, for example, anthropologists were trying to apply psychoanalytical constructs cross-culturally.

Sigmund Freud's psychoanalytic paradigm has been a dominant force in clinical practice since its introduction in the United States in 1909. This paradigm emphasizes repression of sexuality as a primary causal factor in the development of psychopathology (Miller 1989). Freud formulated this paradigm during the Victorian era, a period of extreme cultural repression of sexuality, which was rationalized as "Christian." However, the kind of repression of sexuality that occurred in Victorian Europe never occurred in other parts of the world, including the South Pacific and Africa. There are obvious implications about the application of this paradigm in cultures that exhibit less sexual repression and guilt about sexuality. For example, in parts of Africa sexual behavior is governed by social norms, not by religion. In fact, some African American psychologists view repressed aggression among African Americans as more important than repressed sexuality.

Another construct of psychoanalytic theory, the Oedipal conflict, was studied by Malinowski (1927) among the Trobriand Islanders in Micronesia to ascertain whether the conflict was present in cultures with family structures that differed from the Euro-American nuclear family. According to the theory, the Oedipal conflict occurs during the phallic stage of psychosexual development (approximately ages three to six). Based on observations of nuclear families, Freud hypothesized that a male child experiences an unconscious sexual desire for his mother and aggressive patricidal impulses toward his father, who he sees as a competitor. Among the Trobriand Islanders, the family structure is consanguineal (extended) and matrilineal. In such a structure, a male child inherits from his mother's brother, the maternal uncle, not from his father. Inheritance thus flows from uncle to nephew. The maternal uncle plays the role of father in parenting, while the biological father parents his sisters' children. Malinowski found no evidence of the development of the Oedipal conflict in this type of family configuration.

Fanon (1967a) strongly rejected the universality of the Oedipal conflict, stating that it was virtually nonexistent in Martinique. The population of Martinique, which is of African descent, retains a consanguineal family structure. Fanon (1967b) criticized the ontogeny of psychoanalytical theory. He believed instead in the importance of sociogeny, or "socio-diagnosis," and argued that theories of human behavior need to have a sociohistorical and cultural base.

The way in which people go about learning also may differ across cultures. Gladwin (1964) studied learning cross-culturally by observing the Truk in Micronesia canoe to islands hundreds of miles away using no navigational techniques. How do they get to their destination in the absence of visual cues on the open sea? Is it the feel of a paddle in the ocean currents, the feel of wind currents? Are they responding to proprioceptive stimuli? Because it is assumed that they are not born knowing how to find their way, Western theorists have been puzzled. Similar puzzles exist. For example, the people of the Kalahari bury gourds of water in the desert and return two years later. There are no visual markers because the wind has shifted the sand; however, they find the gourds. Skills Westerners do not even know exist are learned.

The cognitive-development paradigm developed by Jean Piaget (1926) is another model assumed to be a universal. The four factors that Piaget hypothesized influence the development of cognitive functions are biological factors, which account for an invariant sequence of stages; equilibration factors, which arise through interaction with the environment and determine the development of mental operations; general socialization factors, which are identical for all societies; and social factors, which differ from one society to another and include particularly educational and cultural transmission. Since the appearance of Piaget's work, scholars have been examining how much of the variance in cognition can be attributed to each of these or other factors. Volumes of research, including cross-cultural studies, have been generated (Miller 1989). However, because of the difficulties in conducting cross-cultural research, Piaget (1966) was guarded in his interpretation of these data. Mead (1923) considered one aspect of

Piaget's formulation in her study of children in New Guinea. In Western culture, children are read fairy tales and see cartoons that attribute anthropomorphic characteristics to inanimate objects and animals, and they engage in animistic thinking. Mead found among the children in New Guinea no animistic thinking, though at puberty the children were initiated into a religious belief system that involved such thinking.

Some anthropologists, such as Monroe and Monroe (1975), do not consider Piaget's cognitive-development model or Erik Erikson's psychosocial developmental hierarchy universally applicable, except, perhaps, in infancy and early childhood. Even during Piaget's first developmental stage, the sensorimotor period, both African and African American children showed precocious sensorimotor development compared with white children (Werner 1972; Wilson 1978).

Another Euro-American model, Lawrence Kohlberg's (1976; Kohlberg and Kramer 1969) description of six stages in the development of moral judgment from childhood to adulthood, has been criticized for bias in favor of certain moral values that are culturally and class specific. Kohlberg's hierarchy describes moral development as the capacity to abstract a principle rather than as the ability to achieve social change. Accordingly, the highest stage of moral development is identified with the independent thinker, who need not have any involvement in actions for social change (Hampden-Turner 1982). A broader view of moral development than Kohlberg's is needed, one that reconciles the different levels of action. Other anthropological studies, such as those conducted by Gorsuch and Barnes (1973) in various cultures including the Black Caribbean in British Honduras, found no individuals who achieved Kohlberg's "postconventional" level of development. It is questionable that only Westerners achieve high moral development. Not only does Kolhberg's paradigm appear ethnocentric, but others have criticized it for its androcentric inclinations (Gilligan 1982).

Some psychologists utilize a constructivist developmental paradigm that delineates stages of development over the life cycle from infancy through later adulthood, incorporating the thinking of Freud, Erikson, Piaget, Kolhberg, R. Selman, and others (Dorfman 1988). The constructivist developmental paradigm describes what is considered normal development. It assumes developmental stages that are more or less universal and developmental tasks associated with each stage. The stages usually include infancy, childhood, adolescence, and early, middle, and later adulthood. However, early anthropological studies indicate that the stage of adolescence exists only in some societies. In other societies, people are children until puberty, at which time they are considered adults. In many non-Western countries even today, people marry, procreate, do adult work, and fight in wars at puberty.

Some psychologists using the constructivist developmental paradigm, such as Newman and Newman (1987), who use Erikson's eight life stages as a framework, propose specific developmental tasks for each stage. However, specific developmental tasks associated with different stages of the life cycle may differ from culture to culture and, within cultures may differ by social class. For example, career choice, a proposed task of early adulthood, and career management, a purported task of middle adulthood, assume that one is free to make choices (Newman and Newman 1987). In much of the African American community, where there are high rates of unemployment and underemployment, and high numbers of school dropouts and of high school graduates who are minimally literate (Urban League 1990), the freedom to select a career and pursue it does not exist. Life-stage theorists hold that the developmental task of parenthood occurs in early adulthood. However, parenthood can and does occur in early adolescence. Also, in the African American community, where life expectancy is often lower than it is in the white middle-class community, a different expectation about reaching later adulthood affects the time at which people perceive themselves to be at middle adulthood.

Most clinicians would agree that when psychotherapy or counseling is offered, the helping professional and the client must have enough shared reality or similar enough world views for the professional to be able to assume the role of the client and to give an empathetic response. If the implicit world view of the theory being applied in intervention is too dissimilar to that of the client, effective intervention cannot occur. The preceding illustrations demonstrate a few of the ambiguities anthropologists have observed in the cross-cultural application of Euro-American theories of human behavior.

Challenges from the African Diaspora to the Universality of Euro-American Paradigms

Historically social scientists have argued that African Americans have retained nothing of significance from African culture and that the experience of slavery destroyed all remnants of African culture. Until the 1970s a cornucopia of literature described African Americans as culturally deprived or as a group whose culture developed only as an adaptation to slavery and poverty. This view is well represented in the literature on the culture of poverty and the deficit model (Banfield 1977). Opposing views (for example, those that offer evidence of continuity in the cultural traits of black peoples from Africa, Latin America, North America, and the Caribbean) were not well received by the African American community or by the white community.

Herskovits's classic work, *The Myth of the Negro Past* ([1941] 1958), and Jahn's *Muntu* (1979) presented clear evidence of the retention of Africanisms by people of African descent in the diaspora. These authors frequently argued that from the cultural and psychological resources of slaves emerged the diverse and complex life-styles of contemporary African Americans (White 1984). Herskovits (1938–1939:93) once commented:

> We are amazed when we are confronted with psychological studies of race relations made in utter ignorance of characteristic African patterns of motivation and behavior, or with sociological analyses of Negro family life which make not the slightest attempt to take into account even the chance that the phenomena being studied might in some way have been influenced by the carry-over of certain African traditions.

There is, of course, variation in degree of retention. Nevertheless, African Americans cannot be considered either culturally deprived or culturally the same as Euro-Americans. The retention of African culture, or Africanisms, can be found throughout the diaspora. Herskovits offered a list of aspects of African American culture that reflect Africanisms, including African American folklore, funeral ceremonies, ways of dressing, child-rearing practices, child-naming practices, etiquette, and spiritual and religious expressive styles. Words that are now part of the English language reflect Africanisms as well (Harris et al., 1974:6):

African Word	African American Word
Yaw Kay	Okay
Goy	Guy
Banzar	Banjo
Dega	Dig
Hipi	Hip

Africanisms also include African American languages (not dialects, which are mergers of African and European languages), such as the

Haitian language, the so-called Piatio in Lousiana, and that of the Gecchres, who live on the sea islands off the coast of Georgia (Dillard 1972, 1975). The Africanisms reflected in African American music, dance, food, churches, folklore, and family structure are perhaps more commonly recognized than the languages. Some aspects of these Africanisms are reflected in the interpersonal styles of African Americans and are adaptive behavior patterns.

In addition to the previously reviewed literature on the general limitations of Euro-American paradigms of human behavior, African American psychologists and social scientists began in the late 1960s to criticize the use of "white psychology" with African Americans. These social scientists criticized the extent to which theories explained behavior and the application of theory in the provision of mental health and social services. The issues were twofold: the implicit ethnocentrism of theories that label behavior as deviant and psychopathological rather than culturally different: and the extent to which theory blamed victims of oppression for conditions that had their etiology within the socioeconomic system. Ethnocentric and victim-blaming approaches produced literature that was racist in its description of African Americans and in its proposed interventions for them.

An explosion of literature by African American social scientists can be attributed to the publication of the Moynihan Report (Moynihan 1965; Rainwater and Yancey 1967), the racial-consciousness movement, and the struggle for liberation during the 1960s. In addition, information about African history, which had been suppressed in or omitted from the American educational system, enabled the development of a different view of African American psychology.

The Africentric Perspective

Several schools of African American psychology and sociology have emerged since the late 1960s, including the Africentric school (Thomas 1988), which looks at African culture and delineates expressions of African values, social institutions, and behaviors within the African American community. Although there is great variation among groups of people on the African continent, Mbiti (1969) argues that some things are common to almost all people throughout Africa. Africentric writers agree that, in spite of different life experiences, the African American community has retained to some degree a basic African value system.

The principles of the Africentric perspective include the interconnectedness of all things; oneness of mind, body, and spirit; collective identity; consanguineal family structure; consequential morality; analogue thinking; phenomenological time; and spirituality. Though presented here as separate, all are interrelated. "The African world view begins with a holistic conception of the human condition" (White 1984:5).

THE INTERCONNECTION OF ALL THINGS

In African cosmology or philosophy people are perceived as being interconnected to everything in their environment. People are embedded in nature as a part of it and interconnected to all of it, not separate from it. Nature is not something to be conquered or a savage wilderness to be stamped out. Rather, the goal is for people to exist in harmony with nature. This idea of interrelatedness encompasses the entire universe. A series of interlocking systems includes, in hierarchical order, God, humans, animals, plants, and inanimate objects (White 1984). All people are considered interconnected to each other, to those who have died, and to those who are not yet born. The link between people of the past and present is maintained through oral traditions, which help to solidify interdependent relationships and social networks across time and space. Interconnectedness involves the concept of oneness of being with all living things. Being out of harmony with nature, with other people, with oneself is perceived as a cause of illness and other problems. This concept of psychosomatic illness, in which one can become physically ill because of relationships with others, was not introduced into European thinking until relatively recent times by Freud.

ONENESS OF MIND, BODY, AND SPIRIT

The Cartesian mind/body dichotomy in European philosophy contrasts sharply with the African philosophical view that mind, body, and spirit are inseparable (White and Parham 1990). No mind/body dualism exists in African philosophy, which offers a holistic approach to medicine. For example, the traditional African healer was also the priest. Thus, physical and spiritual healing were performed by the same person. An explanation of physical illness embodied a metaphysical explanation as well. To say that an illness was caused by microbes in contaminated water did not explain why only some of the people who drank the water became ill and died. If this question were not addressed, nothing had been explained.

COLLECTIVE IDENTITY
VERSUS INDIVIDUAL IDENTITY

African psychological identity differs from the Eurocentric ideal of individualism in that it is collective. In many African cultures, the tribe, as the basic human unit, sought to ensure its collective survival. This collectively shared psychological identity was also evident in the behaviors of slaves who were together able to generate a sense of worth, dignity, and belonging separate from slave masters (Gutman 1976). The concept of the interconnectedness of all living things is related to this African psychological identity. The unit of identity in Africa is "we" and not "I" as suggested in an Ashanti proverb: "I am because we are, without we I am not. I am because we are; and since we are, therefore I am" (quoted in Mbiti 1969:141). To share a collective identity is to know that one is not alone and that others bear witness to the joys and sorrows of life (White 1984).

Another African proverb depicts aspects of the African psychological identity: The bigger we are, the greater I am. "Whatever happens to the individual happens to the whole group and whatever happens to the whole group happens to the individual." This is a cardinal point in understanding the African view of man (Mbiti 1969:141). Sharing a collective identity suggests that the praise, blame, or shame of an individual is assumed by the group.

A group of people living in Brazil who escaped slavery and went into the interior maintain a way of life virtually identical to their way of life in West Africa. Harmony with each other is considered paramount because if one person is incapacitated or lost, it is thought to diminish the entire group, which cannot afford to lose anyone. Nobles (1977), in discussing collective identity and interdependence, notes that aggression directed toward another person is also aggression against oneself. The concept of collective identity is juxtaposed to the Western ideal of rugged individualism and fierce insistence on individuals being independent as opposed to interdependent.

Children

Shared parenting patterns among African Americans are illustrative of a collective identity. Historically, in the African American community, everyone assumed responsibility for disciplining children. If neighbors saw someone's child misbehaving, they admonished the child and informed the parents later. Raising children was seen as everyone's responsibility (Hill 1972; White and Parham 1990).

"Children are the buds of society and every birth is the arrival of spring when life shouts out and the community thrives" (Mbiti 1969:143). Thus, the birth of a child was the concern of the entire community, especially relatives. A child was considered "our child" rather than "their child." Children were highly valued in African culture, where the concept of an illegitimate child was nonexistent; all children were legitimate. They increased the collective and belonged to the community rather than to the two parents. Polygamy allowed families to have more children, and in an agrarian economy children were a great resource. This tradition continues in Africa today. In Malawi, a central African country, the community comes to thank a woman who has given birth. In Ghana, when an Ashanti woman has had more than ten children, she is given a special title and a ceremonial festival is held.

Africans see their children as a part of their immortality—that is, they live on through their children. According to African folklore, people who have died are considered to live as long as there are people who remember them and who would recognize them if they walked through the door. The more children, the more people to remember. The African American Catholic liturgy pours libation to ancestors to remember them (which should not be mistaken for ancestor worship).

In some African societies, a marriage was not fully recognized or consummated until a wife had given birth (Mbiti 1969). In other parts of Africa, individuals were not considered adults until they had "brought forth" children. Social norms rather than religious doctrine governed sexual behavior. Virginity was very important among some groups and less important among other groups. Nevertheless, if a woman became pregnant before marriage, she was more likely to be valued than stigmatized because a man knew that she was fertile.

Historically, in the African American community, unwed mothers generally suffered less stigma than Euro-American women, who were often ostracized and disowned by their families. African American parents were (and are) less likely to place children for formal adoption. The children were informally adopted and cared for by other members of the family (Hill 1972). African Americans who became pregnant when unmarried were less likely to use abortion as an option compared with white women. Likewise, if parents, single or married, were unable to meet the needs of the children, relatives were willing to accept the responsibility.

Role of Leader

The role of a leader or chief in African culture is to see that the people are provided for or to empower them to meet their needs. An Ashanti proverb speaks to the role of the leader; "If you are a chief, why aren't you feeding me?" This view of a leader as someone who takes responsibility for the well-being of the people is in sharp contrast to the Ronald Reagan-Horatio Alger philosophy: "I got mine; you go get yours. If you can't get yours by your own efforts through hard work, don't look to me for help."

View of Wealth and Resources

Many African economies were historically communal, as were the first Christian monasteries in East Africa; the resources from agriculture were shared by the entire village. The concept of private property did not exist in the same way as it does in the contemporary West. Ownership of land was an alien concept in many African societies. People used the earth but did not own it—a view similar to the American Indian's view of people's relationship to the earth. When the colonists came to build on the land, the American Indians did not understand that the Europeans were actually to own the land forever.

Views of wealth were also different. Self-esteem was not tied to one's wealth. A person in Nigeria could be a pauper but valued for other qualities. Wealth was to be consumed and shared, rather than saved for the sake of saving. This view is in contrast to the archetypal image of the frugal Westerner who dies leaving substantial savings that were never enjoyed or shared.

Authors (for example, Nobles 1974) have discussed the emphasis on conspicuous material consumption in the African American community, referring to people spending a disproportionate amount of their funds on clothes, cars, and other material goods. This type of consumption has usually been attributed to psychological insecurity. However, other factors may be operating.

Consanguineal Family Structure

The interconnectedness and interdependence of living things expressed in collective identity are seen throughout Africa in the consanguineal family. The family as an institution includes all related through the blood line and those related by marriage. The term *extended family* is also used to describe this type of structure (Sudarkasa 1981). *Nuclear ethnocentric* families, in contrast, include only the conjugal unit and its children. From an Africentric perspective, the nuclear unit is not the central or basic unit. The genetic or blood line is the basic unit. Thus, even if the conjugal unit is dissolved, the family remains intact.

African families are either matrilineal, referring to lineage—which is not the same as matriarchal, which refers to authority—or they are patrilineal. They are either matrilocal or patrilocal—referring to where the married couple resides; rarely are they neolocal—that is, independent and separate households.

Being familiar with and keeping track of kinship are extremely important, so much so that people can often name many relatives. Kinship is thus a prominent force in African life. "It governs social relationships between people in the community and how people behave toward each other. It governs the whole life of the tribe. It is extended to cover animals, plants, and nonliving objects through a totemic system. Kinship isn't simply horizontal in the temporal sense, but is vertical, covering those departed and those not yet born" (Mbiti 1969:135–136). There are far more kinship terms in African languages than there are in English. In the diaspora the consanguineal family system has survived. Presently, there are still proportionately more African American than Euro-American families that have a consanguineal structure. The literature on existing African American extended families is discussed in Chapter 4.

Role of Elders

Within the family, and by extension within the clan and community, African elders are treated with great deference. Because they have survived to old age, their opinions are considered of great value. In the role of storyteller, African elders teach children their genealogy, family history, and the history of the tribe. The African view of elders has survived in the West. It can be seen within the African American church, which has structured roles for elders, such as church mothers. A higher percentage of African American families compared with white families keep elderly relatives home rather than place them in nursing homes, even when they have the means for financing nursing-home care (Hill 1972). In consanguineal African American families, decision-making authority is given to elders—generally the oldest males; in the absence of a male figure, the eldest female holds the position in deference to age rather than because the society is matriarchal. Children among some groups are taught to look down and not make eye contact when talking to elders. For African American children who are still taught this practice, problems arise when Euro-Americans read a lack of eye contact as a sign of guilt or a manifestation of psychopathology.

Mother/Son Relationship

The relationship a son has with his mother is given primacy over his relationship with his wife in many African societies. He owes a lifelong loyalty to his mother that supersedes other relationships. In some African American families this mother/son relationship has been retained to some degree. Sons may have strong attachments to their mothers that do not fit the Euro-American norm of autonomy from parents. Continuous interdependence in adulthood is often perceived by Euro-Americans as pathological dependence or as pathological dominance by so-called matriarchical African American women: this phenomenon has been extensively discussed in the social science literature (Bracey, Mier, and Radwick 1977; Staples 1970). The fact that an African son's relationship with his mother is more important than his relationship with his wife is consistent with the consanguineal rather than the conjugal, or nuclear, family being the basic unit of society.

Gender Roles

Male/female roles in both African and African American families are traditionally more flexible than in Euro-American families. This flexibility has been described as a strength by several authors (Hill 1972; Nobles 1974; Staples 1971) but is labeled as pathological in much of the social science literature. Ironically, the feminist movement is now redefining gender roles for white families in the direction of increased flexibility.

The form of marriage in Africa was primarily traditional polygamy, as with Islamic marriages, where up to four wives are allowed. With the introduction of Christianity in West Africa, monogamy was also introduced. (It should be noted that Christianity had been in north and east Africa since the first century.) With colonial rule, monogamous marriage was instituted by civil ordinance. However, traditional polygamy and Islamic marriages still exist. Polygamy is engrained in African culture and is accepted by both men and women. Presently in Africa some African Christian churches allow polygamy as a protest against colonialization (personal communication, A. S. Mohammed, National Institute for Policy and Strategic Studies, Kura, Nigeria, August 15, 1990). It is not unusual also for men in monogamous marriages to have lifelong outside wives and children. The legal wife and her children may even know the outside wife and children. Such arrangements also occur in the African diaspora but on a limited basis.

CONSEQUENTIAL MORALITY

African morality is consequential. Whether an act is good or bad depends on its consequences to oneself or others. This is not a rigid code of absolute do's and don'ts. For example, killing someone to protect one's family could be the moral thing to do, whereas killing under different circumstances would be wrong. African consequential morality is similar to morality in Buddhism or Hinduism, where there are no absolute rights or wrongs; moral judgments depend on the situation.

ANALOGUE VERSUS BINARY THINKING

African analogue thinking and European binary thinking (Jones 1988) differ. Binary thought divides concepts into mutually exclusive, polar opposites, such as good/bad, right/wrong, guilty/innocent. In analogue thought, these concepts are seen as shades of gray rather than black or white; a negative component of a whole that is primarily positive does not negate the whole. Analogue thought is similar to the Eastern concepts of yin and yang. African religions, excluding Christianity, Islam, and Judaism, do not have a figure such as Satan (the personification of evil). The closest thing to a devil is an entity who is more like a malicious trickster.

PHENOMENOLOGICAL TIME
VERSUS MATHEMATICAL TIME

The traditional African concept of time was radically different from the concept of time in Western culture. In the West, time is mathematical, it is future oriented, and it is a commodity people can waste. Most people are time oriented and highly aware of the mathematical reckoning of time, as evidenced by the omnipresence of wrist watches, clocks, calendars, and appointment books. In traditional Africa, with a few exceptions, time is phenomenological. It is present-oriented. And the concept of time as something one can waste is alien.

Operating on mathematical time, a person in London might say, "I will meet you at 7:35 P.M. at Paddington Station," or "I will call you at 7:15 A.M. Pacific Standard Time." Operating on phenomenological time, two people might agree to meet at sunset. Whether the sunset is at 5:00 P.M. or 8:00 p.m. is not important, and it is also understood that the meeting will not necessarily occur precisely at sunset, but within a range of a time before or after sunset. In some rural parts of the United States, people operating on phenomenological time might say that an event occurred around the time the hog died—that is, events are linked to other events.

African time is oriented toward the here and now. Future events are those that are certain to occur within the inevitable cycle of nature in the next few months. The concept of a far away, indefinite future does not exist as it does in the West. Future beyond a couple of years cannot be expressed in some languages because there are no verb tenses for it (Mbiti 1969). For instance, in Swahili, only two terms express the concept of time, the Sasa and the Zambani. The Sasa is the present, the short-term future, and the recent past. The Zambani is the indefinite past. It overlaps with the Sasa. The longer a person has lived, the greater his or her Zambani. Events move backward from the Sasa into the Zambani. With the Westernization of Africa, people have begun to use a future dimension. However, an African individual is much less likely than a Westerner to be focused on the distant future, such as on a forty-year financial plan for retirement.

The idea that time is a commodity one can waste is also a Western concept. From the African perspective, time can be produced or created; simply being in time is not wasting time. In the Caribbean, the word *liming* comes from the act of hanging out with other people under a lime tree. From a Western perspective this activity could be seen as wasting time. From an African perspective it is being in time. On corners in many inner-city African American communities African American men appear to be just standing around (Liebow 1967) and wasting time. However, people in these communities know that if they need someone to mow their lawn or do odd jobs, these men may be available. There is an expression "doing things on colored people's time" (CPT), which is jokingly referred to as being behind white people's time. Americans who have spent time in the Caribbean, Latin America, or Africa notice, sometimes with great frustration, that some people do not share their orientation toward precise time and efficiency.

SPIRITUALITY

Religion in Africa is not simply a set of beliefs one subscribes to and quietly participates in; it is experiential and participatory. It also permeates everyday life. It is known to people through experience in a spiritual, mystical, extrasensory, or consciousness-altering way. This experiential religion can be seen in African American churches, where people spontaneously sway, dance, shout, testify, and give prophecy. The spontaneous call and response between the congregation and the minister also has its origin in African culture (McAdoo 1988). Religion is thus not merely cognitive.

In addition, the parameters of what is considered to be reality are broader in some parts of Africa, even today. Phenomena that Westerners would classify as supernatural, such as seeing people who have died walk through a door and seeing powers of healing channeled through an individual, are considered quite natural (Jones 1990). Retention of beliefs that are correlates of West African religious beliefs are found in Cuba, the Caribbean, Brazil, and the United States, particularly Louisiana. "Root work," for example—the belief that the use of herbs and vegetable roots—is powerful in curing, healing and removing evil spells, casting good luck, and warding off negative forces—is fairly common among some African Americans, especially among older people. It is African in origin and often misunderstood by those in helping professions.

Toward an African American Psychology: Implications of an Africentric View

Some of these Africentric principles have serious consequences for professionals working with African American families. In cultures where there is collective identity rather than individual identity, such as Africa, the developmental tasks of attaining group identity and then individual identity might occur at different points in the life cycle and look different from Western descriptions of these processes. In extended family structures that are either patrilocal or matrilocal, the developmental task of autonomy from parents might be described differently from that in a neolocal nuclear family. Metaparadigms—for example, ecosystems perspective, cybernetic epistemology (Dorfman 1988), or the social-system models—are more congruent with the Africentric perspective than models that look for linear causality. Metaparadigms view phenomena as interconnected and interrelated in a causal network and view individual behavior as something that can be understood only in context. These metatheories, or metaparadigms, are like transparencies that are content free and therefore not subject to ethnocentric bias. This cultural framework of the African American community, along with the historical and contemporary experience of racial oppression, must be acknowledged and taken into consideration in providing and planning social services for African Americans.

The miseducation, economic oppression, limited access to health care, and lack of concern for the welfare of African American children affect the entire nation and its future security. American business and corporations are already experiencing the consequences of benign neglect, as they see a present and future work force ill educated and lacking skills that would allow the United States to remain competitive with other industrialized nations. The interconnectedness and interdependence of all living things, an Africentric concept, would lead us to view the fate and destiny of white American children as inseparable from the fate and destiny of African American children.

References

Banfield, E. C. 1977. *The Unheavenly City Revisited*. Boston: Little, Brown.

Berger, P. L., and T. Luckmann. 1967. *The Social Construction of Reality: A Treatise in the Sociology of Knowledge*. Garden City, N.Y.: Doubleday, Anchor Books.

Bracey, J., A. Mier, and E. Radwick, eds. 1977. *Black Matriarchy: Myth or Reality*. Belmont, Calif.: Wadsworth.

Cole, M., and S. Scribner. 1974. *Culture and Thought: A Psychological Introduction*. New York: Wiley.

Dember, W. 1979. *The Psychology of Perception*. 2d ed. New York: Holt, Rinehart & Winston.

Dillard, J. L. 1972. *Black English*. New York: Random House.

————. 1975. *Perspective on Black English*. The Hague: Mouton.

Dorfman, R. A., ed. 1988. *Paradigms of Clinical Social Work*. New York: Brunner/Mazel.

Fanon, F. 1967a. *Black Skins, White Masks*. New York: Grove Press.

————. 1967b. *The Wretched of the Earth*. Middlesex, England: Penguin Books.

Gilligan, C. 1982. *In a Different Voice*. Cambridge: Harvard University Press.

Gladwin, T. 1964. "Culture and Logical Process." In *Explorations in Cultural Anthropology*, edited by W. H. Goodenough, 167–177. New York: McGraw-Hill.

Gorsuch, K. L., and M. L. Barnes. 1973. "Stages of Ethical Reasoning and Moral Norms of Carob Youth." *Journal of Cross-Cultural Psychology* 4:283–301.

Gutman, H. G. 1976. *The Black Family in Slavery and Freedom, 1750–1925*. New York: Vintage Books, Random House.

Hampden-Turner, C. 1982. *Maps of the Mind*. New York: Colliers.

Harris, M., M. Levitt, R. Furman, and E. Smith. 1974. *The Black Book*. New York: Random House.

Hatch, E. 1985. "Culture." In *The Social Science Encyclopedia*, edited by A. Kuper and J. Kuper, 178–179. Boston: Routledge & Kegan Paul.

Herskovits, M. J. 1938–1939. "The Ancestry of the American Negro." *American Scholar* 8:84–94.

————. [1941] 1958. *The Myth of the Negro Past*. Boston: Beacon Press.

Hill, R. B. 1972. *The Strengths of Black Families*. New York: Emerson Hall.

Jahn, J. 1979. *Muntu*. New York: Grove Press.

Jones, E. 1988. "Black Hebrews." *Journal of Religious Thought*, January, 44:35–49.

————. 1990. *In Search of Zion*. New York: Lang.

Kohlberg, L. 1976. "Moral Stages and Moralization: The Cognitive-Developmental Approach." In *Moral Development and Behavior*, edited by T. Lickona, 31–53. New York: Holt, Rinehart & Winston.

Kohlberg, L., and R. Kramer. 1969. "Continuities and Discontinuities in Child and Adult Moral Development." *Human Development* 12:93–120.

Liebow, E. 1967. *Talley's Corner*. Boston: Little, Brown.

McAdoo, H. P., ed. 1988. *Black Families*. 2d ed. Newbury Park, Calif.: Sage.

Malinowski, B. 1927. *Sex and Repression in Savage Society*. New York: Harcourt Brace Jovanovich.

Mbiti, J. S. 1969. *African Religions and Philosophies*. New York: Praeger.

Mead, M. 1932. "An Investigation of the Thought of Primitive Children with Special Reference to Animism." *Royal Anthropological Institute of Great Britain and Ireland Journal* 62:173–190.

Miller, P. H. 1989. *Theories of Developmental Psychology*. New York: W. H. Freeman.

Monroe, R. L., and R. H. Monroe. 1975. *Cross Cultural Human Development.* Monterey, Calif.: Brooks/Cole.

Moynihan, D. P. 1965. *The Negro Family: The Case for National Action.* Washington, D.C.: Government Printing Office.

Newman, B., and P. Newman. 1987. *Development through the Life Cycle: A Psychosocial Approach.* Chicago: Dorsey Press.

Nobles, W. W., 1974. "African Root and American Fruit: The Black Family." *Journal of Social and Behavioral Sciences* 20:52–64.

———. 1977. "The Rhythmic Impulse: The Issue of Africanity in Black Family Dynamics." Paper presented at 2d annual Symposium on Black Psychology, Ann Arbor, Michigan.

Piaget, J. 1926. *The Language and Thought of the Child.* New York: Harcourt Brace.

———. 1966. "Need and Significance of Cross-Cultural Studies in Genetic Psychology." *International Journal of Psychology* 1 (1):3–13.

Rainwater, L., and W. Yancey, eds. 1967. *The Moynihan Report and the Politics of Controversy.* Cambridge: MIT Press.

Sapir, E. 1933. "Language." In *Encyclopedia of Social Sciences,* vol. 9, 115–169. Boston: Routledge & Kegan Paul.

Segall, M. H. 1979. *Cross-Cultural Psychology: Human Behavior in a Global Perspective.* Monterey, Calif.: Brooks/Cole.

Segall, M. H., D. T., Campbell, and M. J. Herskovitz. 1966. *The Influence of Culture on Visual Perception.* Indianopolis: Bobbs-Merrill.

Seidman, E., and J. Rappaport, eds. 1986. *Redefining Social Problems.* New York: Plenum.

Staples, R. 1970. "The Myth of the Black Matriarchy." *Black Scholar* 1:8–16.

———. ed. 1971. *The Black Family.* Belmont, Calif.: Wadsworth.

Sudarkasa, N. 1981. "Interpreting the African Heritage in Afro-American Family Organization." In *Black Families,* edited by H. P. McAdoo, 37–53. Beverly Hills, Calif.: Sage.

Thomas, C. 1988. Untitled. Presentation at the annual conference of the Association of Black Psychologists, Washington, D.C.

Urban League. 1990. *The State of Black America.* New York: Urban League.

Werner, E. E. 1972. Infants around the World: Cross-Cultural Studies of Psychomotor Development from Birth to Two Years." *Journal of Cross Cultural Psychology* 32:111–134.

White, J. L. 1984. *The Psychology of Blacks: An Afro-American Perspective.* Englewood Cliffs, N.J.: Prentice-Hall.

White, J. L., and T. A. Parham. 1990. *The Psychology of Blacks: An African American Perspective,* 2d ed. Englewood Cliffs, N.J.: Prentice-Hall.

Whorf, R. J. 1956. *Language, Thought, and Reality.* New York: Wiley.

Wilson, A. 1978. *The Developmental Psychology of the Black Child.* New York: Africana Research Publications.

KETAYUN H. GOULD

Limiting Damage Is Not Enough: A Minority Perspective on Child Welfare Issues

Open thou the door of opportunity to little children of every race and condition and let them know the world they live in and its possibilities.
—W.E.B. DU BOIS,
Prayers for Dark People

From its beginnings, the child welfare field's mandate of providing services to children whose parents are unable to fulfill child-rearing responsibilities has opened the possibility that societal and professional ideologies will be thrust too easily into family systems. This outcome is possible with all families within the child welfare structure but never more surely than when families are racially different from the majority population. In fact, the fate of all minorities of color within the service-delivery system has been inextricably affected by negative professional judgments regarding their functioning.

Child welfare workers have generally displayed an inability to master two measures that Solomon (1985:11) considers important in describing a population: "a measure of central tendency and a measure of dispersion." Solomon uses these statistical terms to convey the idea that professionals need knowledge to predict within a certain range of probability that some groups are more likely than others to demonstrate specific characteristics. In addition, she stresses that it is just as essential that social workers understand the variations—the characteristics of those individuals and families who might be described as falling on the edges of the normal curve. Despite these suggestions, the prevailing situation within the child welfare system is that workers use their professional power to impose the dominant society's mores on minorities of color. A variation of this theme is the proclivity to view minorities as a monolith—either as negative or positive stereotypes or as all victims or as all survivors. The extremely biased nature of workers' caseloads, which consists of poor minority clients, plus the nature of child welfare work further deter the possibility that professional judgments will be based on exposure to a wide variety of minority life-styles, unless workers have had previous contact with minority communities.

The systematic failure to make an accurate assessment of the plight of minorities of color has resulted in minority children receiving insufficient, inadequate, and often inappropriate and damaging child welfare services. Research in this area has demonstrated clearly that minority children of color enter the welfare system in disproportionate numbers, remain in the system longer than white children, do not receive as many in-home services as white children, and have a disproportionate number of undesirable experiences in the system (Billingsley and Giovannoni 1972; Fanshel and Shinn 1978; Knitzer, Allen, and McGowan 1978; Mech 1985; Shyne and Schroeder 1978; Stehno 1982). Moreover, African American children fare worse than white children or any other minority children of color on all measures of service delivery and evaluation, such as recommended versus actual length of placement, placement time and number of services, provision of adoption services, and worker contact with child and principal child-caring persons (Mech 1985).

The professional community has responded to these findings by recognizing the need for a minority perspective on child welfare issues (Billingsley and Giovannoni 1972; Chestang 1978; Costin and Rapp 1984; Gould 1985; Edelman 1987; Grey, Hartman, and Saalberg 1985; Montalvo, Lasater, and Valdez 1982; National Black Child Development Institute 1981; Washington 1987; Wilson and Green 1983). Although the minority perspective has gained some acceptance in social work education and practice, little attention has been devoted to a theoretical analysis that examines the main ideological assumptions and values of this conceptual framework (Montiel and Wong 1983).

This type of evaluation is particularly significant in the context of this book because the book utilizes an Africentric perspective to understand the impact of child welfare policies and practices on African Americans. The questions that arise as a result of the juxtaposition of these two concepts—minority and Africentric—are the following: Are these two perspectives interchangeable, separate, or overlapping? How are these perspectives to be defined theoretically or put into practice empirically in the child welfare field? Is it possible to provide effective service to African Americans in the child welfare system if only one of these perspectives is incorporated into practice? What other perspectives need to be included in the child welfare framework to qualify the model as an effective conceptual approach for work with African Americans? What are the implications of this theoretical analysis for social work education and practice in the child welfare field?

This chapter, therefore, undertakes a theoretical analysis of the minority and Africentric perspectives, examining the basic assumptions and values of the two frameworks to determine their applicability to child welfare policies and practices for African Americans. Although the focus is on African American children and families, the practice and policy implications may relate equally to children and families of other minorities of color whose social circumstances are similar. The chapter further provides illustrations of these ideas from the different areas of this field of practice and the minority feminist perspective. Finally, the chapter explores the implications for social work education and practice of using the minority and Africentric perspectives.

Minority Perspective

To place the minority perspective within the child welfare framework, the first step is the delineation of the basic principles that will guide the analysis. A definition of the minority world view is needed and an explanation of how this perspective might be applied to draw the boundaries and service-delivery functions of the child welfare system.

Fundamentally, a minority world view is a structural understanding of the system of societal stratification from the viewpoint of the underprivileged. The focus of attention is the structure of social arrangements, particularly the economic, political, and social constraints that operate to maintain the balance of power between the dominant and subordinate groups in society. The level of analysis, however, is not confined to the social environment—the macro and mezzo levels, as these layers are commonly defined in the social work literature.

Rather, a person-in-society approach (Gould 1987b, 1988) is utilized to make the transition from the societal to the individual level—to apply the societal perspective to demonstrate concretely the connections between personal experiences and structural realities. The emphasis here is on both the externally imposed system and its concomitant internalized subsystem of victimization.

This line of reasoning does not minimize the fact that faulty social arrangements are largely responsible for the plight of the underprivileged in society. Moreover, the basic argument for using the term *person in society* rather than the more popular social work phrase *person in environment* is to stress the idea that the popular concept does not provide a realistic understanding of the situation for minorities of color. Efforts to remedy this lack of understanding by expanding the definition of the term *environment* to include physical, social, interpersonal, and organizational components (Germain and Gitterman 1980) do not capture the fact that the primary stressors for minorities of color are created by societal inequalities. In this respect, the person-in-society approach is in tune with a minority world view because it does not address only those aspects of the environment that are considered amenable to social work intervention. By looking at the broad societal picture, the person-in-society approach evaluates the potential of the system to respond positively to minority needs and the ability of the profession to produce such a response. Moreover, the person-in-society perspective does not avoid the conclusion that, under certain conditions, striving for an adaptive balance between the person and the environment is not always desirable for minorities of color, especially when the basic goal is the transformation of institutions to ensure a just society (Gould 1978 b, 1988).

The foregoing discussion argues for the minority perspective as a framework that informs thinking and not just as a model that provides specific strategies for transforming child welfare policies and practices. The perspective provides a profound critique of societal and professional ideologies because it does not assume that the vision of society expounded by the existing establishment is sound. In this respect, the perspective serves as an "instrument of idea formation" (Asante 1980:38) because it is not confined within the societal and disciplinary structures to which it reacts.

To apply these ideas to child welfare policies and practice, the foremost consideration should be to establish child welfare not as a subsystem of the welfare system but as an integral part of societal systems as a whole—the political system, the economic system, and the law-enforcement system (Billingsley and Giovannoni 1972; Costin and Rapp 1984). Only then is it possible to evaluate the effects of societal forces on child welfare policies for African Americans within the large social arena—within those institutional structures that are broadly defined as serving child welfare needs. Otherwise, the "potential inherent within these systems for good and ill of Black American children is not appreciated" (Billingsley and Giovannoni 1972:6). Moreover, single and fragmentary strategic responses to the complex problems of African Americans in the child welfare system can create as many problems as they solve.

The evaluation process, however, must begin with an examination of the child welfare bureaucracy and its past performance in serving African American children. Otherwise, the tendency might be to advocate changes that do not differ from past approaches. It is apparent, however, that in this area of service delivery, the predominant picture is one of deficiencies, gaps, and a lack of commitment to adopt a pluralistic, multiethnic concept of child welfare services (Billingsley and Giovannoni 1972; Chestang 1978; Grey, Hartman, and Saalberg 1985; National Black Child Development Institute 1981; Stehno 1982). There is no absence of research in this area. A review of the child welfare literature for the 1980s, however, revealed few articles that addressed the question of a minority perspective, although some attention has been given to staff sensitivity in serving African American children (Jones 1983; Katz 1976). Still, the data that are available consistently support the move toward a pluralistic system by demonstrating that there is no single definition that completely fits every cultural group's conception of an "American standard of child care" (Polansky, Ammons, and Weatherby 1983).

A few examples from the literature illustrate the necessity for critiquing the professional stance toward serving African Americans in the child welfare system. One issue is the belief that standardizing procedures and regulations, policies, and role expectations will guarantee that professional and organizational prejudices will not affect service delivery to minorities of color. In fact, as Solomon (1976) points out, the resulting form of discrimination that is evident—institutional racism—results from the fact that "standardization is done along lines consistent with the values, norms, life styles etc. of the dominant group" (p. 14). For instance, there has been increased interest in and attention to the concept of preventive services in the child welfare field (Costin and Rapp 1984; Gray, Hartman, and Saalberg 1985). Undoubtedly, this trend has produced many positive outcomes, demonstrating to workers the value of acting swiftly to prevent the development of conditions that might require drastic action.

This concept, however, needs to be evaluated to see how it affects African Americans specifically. A report from the National Black Child Development Institute (1981:25) reveals that "only [10 percent] of all placements into foster care result from actual determinations of abuse and neglect; the remainder are placed as preventive measures against a possibility of harm. . . . Given the focus and structure of such policies, then, poor Black families cannot help but be at the mercy of the child welfare system." The example illustrates the failure of the social work profession to integrate theories on prevention and permanency planning with an Africentric perspective (which will be discussed later). Such integration is needed to arrive at a minority world view that might immediately alert child welfare workers to the implications of these practices for African Americans.

Furthermore, it is evident that child welfare policies and practices have been designed to perpetuate the system (Seligsen 1988). Thus, despite the clear hazards of long-term foster care, research reveals that the cumulative placement time of 61.6 months for African American children was significantly higher than for both white (36.8 months) and Hispanic (36 months) children. The most significant deviation from a recommended placement plan was noted in the case of the African American community (Mech 1985:161–162):

> Placements of 12 months or less were recommended for 45 percent of the black children placed, yet only 18.6 percent actually were in placement 12 months or less. The largest discrepancy between recommended and actual placement length was in the long-term placement group, that is, four years and over. Approximately 37 percent were recommended to receive placement for a period of four years or more, but 50 percent of black children were in placement for longer than four years.

The National Black Child Development Institute (1981) hypothesizes that this phenomenon is due to the fact that state agencies are eager to retain a source of income by keeping children in foster care where they are eligible for federal subsidies. Adoption subsidies and costly services are perceived as burdens that the state might have to bear, as against a guaranteed federal subsidy for keeping the child in foster care and institutions.[1]

The situation is complicated further by the fact that child welfare cases are likely to be handled by white workers, who might not have had an opportunity to develop a minority world view. Some scholars, however, like Billingsley and Giovannoni (1972), charge that the root of this problem is the fact that racism persists in the present operation of child welfare bureaucracies. It is hard to deny these allegations given the following findings from Mech's (1985:164) analyses of a national data set: African American children were more likely to have no contact with workers than white or Hispanic children; in cases where children were legally available for adoption, no homes had been found for 63 percent of the African American children versus 51 percent of Hispanic and 46 percent of white children; and "regardless of the reason for referral or problem category, black children were consistently in placement for longer periods of time than Hispanic or white children." Again, the research provides a clear indication that the social work profession needs to undertake a critique of its service-delivery performance with African Americans without feeling the necessity to justify the rightness of the existing system.

The evaluation of the professional bureaucracy cannot be undertaken without examining the societal context that enhances the chances of developing racist practices (National Urban League 1988). For child welfare, a minority world view might raise the following questions: Why did the dominant society fail to recognize the seriousness of the problem of unmarried teenage parents until its "own" were affected by the situation? (Gould 1985). Why are professionals generally unaware that "even if black and white women had equivalent levels of contraceptive use, sexual activity and recourse to abortion, there would still be substantial racial differences in nonmarital fertility rates because of the greater propensity among whites to legitimate premaritally conceived births" (Cutright and Smith 1988:119)? Why does the social work literature generally not report—except for one article by Nichols-Casebolt (1988)—that the rise in African American families headed by women is "due in part to the increasing economic anomie of Black men" (Joe and Yu 1986:235) rather than to an erosion of traditional family values? The connection between the societal and professional stance toward African Americans is self-evident. Meyer explained this link when she stated that "one of the most important qualities of social work is that it, perhaps more than any field of practice, is systematically related to the social scene. . . . When these social forces turn inward and become reactionary, social work as one of society's institutions will also follow that course" (1970:3).

A minority world view seeks to challenge the child welfare system's predilection to adopt the dominant society's definitions of child care. Some practitioners may have difficulty accepting the need for changing this orientation because efforts up to now have been expended on integrating minority children into a standardized system of child welfare policies and regulations. A minority perspective stresses that priority has to be given to developing a multiethnic concept of child welfare services—a move away from forcing minority children's integration *into* an existing system and toward minority children's integration *with* the system.

The minority perspective, as a critique of society from the viewpoint of the underprivileged, is not exclusive to any particular minority of color. Neither is a minority world view a straightforward summation of the experiences of all minorities of color. (This is not to deny the contribution of minority perspectives to child welfare issues. They provide the experiential basis of models that recapitulate as theory the practical reality of the lives of oppressed groups in society.) A minority world view politicizes such culturally centered perspectives as the Africentric and, therefore, can be conceptualized as the political arm of any single minority of color's cultural framework. Thus, professionals working with African Americans in the child welfare system cannot take for granted that an Africentric perspective will reflect a minority world view automatically. For this amalgamation to take place, one has to take an extra step beyond the cultural: politicizing the dialogue.

Some examples from the social work literature may illustrate the point. For instance, the "cultural-awareness" and "staff-sensitivity" literature in child welfare (Jones 1983; Montalvo, Lasater, and Valdez 1983; Wilson and Green 1983) places heavy emphasis on disseminating knowledge about minority cultures for only one reason: so that professionals can engage in "ethnic-sensitive practice" (Devore and Schlesinger 1987; Dodson 1983; Lum 1986). The same limitation applies to the literature on cross-cultural practice, where the "political implications are rarely discussed" (Montiel and Wong 1983:112). Thus, an amalgamation of the Africentric and minority perspectives is not a foregone conclusion, although it can be argued that without this combined lens it is impossible to have a realistic comprehension of the African Americans' world as an operating social system. A convergence needs to take place so that ethnic-sensitive child welfare practice is firmly anchored in the context of an understanding of unequal societal relationships. If professional practice is to help African Americans gain control over their lives, it has to follow a model of service that does not perceive a dichotomy between those who deal with individual problems and those who deal with systems.

Africentric Perspective

The Africentric perspective moves the discussion on the minority perspective from the procedural to the substantive level because it provides the basic knowledge to "develop the capacity to look *into* the lives of Black Americans, *not at* the lives of Black Americans" (Leigh 1983:118). The perspective provides specific constructs that can help child welfare workers understand the individual elements that come together to constitute what can be described as the African American experience. These constructs, however, are not specific to the African American community and may apply to the life-styles of other minorities of color who share the same ethnic values (Lum 1986). Moreover, the extent to which any individual member of the African American community adheres to the norms, beliefs, and traditions encompassed by this perspective should be a matter of empirical investigation rather than an assumption (DeVore and Schlesinger 1987; Dodson 1983).

Before assessing the extent to which child welfare policies and practices with African American children can be guided by specific constructs of the Africentric perspective, it is worthwhile to examine how the main ideological assumptions and prescriptions of this framework might influence child welfare workers to rethink their practices with African Americans. It is important to stress that just as the Africentric perspective cannot be assumed to reflect a minority world view, talking about African American issues does not guarantee that the discourse will be Africentric (Asante 1987). To be so, the discussion must be based on an attempt to develop a structural understanding of the collective experience—the collective aspirations that are culturally rooted in African heritage and the experiences of African Americans in this country. For child welfare workers, who deliver services on a case-by-case basis, this model provides the insight that the minority status of their clients sharpens the necessity of fostering group consciousness in order to develop a strong personal identity.

The Africentric perspective supports two slightly varied approaches to the issue of minority identity. Chestang's (1984) conceptualization is an example of the first approach—that participation in a collectivity can build racial identity through identification with the alienation that members of one's group experience in the wider society. Chestang also emphasizes that participation in a collectivity can build personal identity, which involves the effort to reach beyond racial pride to assert one's dignity.

Gurin and Epps (1975), however, suggest a somewhat different approach to the topic of personal identity. They raise a provocative point when they ask why so much stress has been put on the negative implications of minority status. In their view, minority status can be an enormous asset in the formation of personal identity as one develops "a sense of history and connectedness to past and future that is crucial" (p. 4). These authors also provide a valuable societal explanation that can *help* aid in the rethinking of child welfare policies for African Americans: Racial group membership is not viewed as an asset in identity formation for African Americans because "racial identity among black youngsters is seen as acceptance of oneself in a devalued group" (p. 5). Any discussion of child welfare policies and practices aimed at African Americans should incorporate the Africentric perspective on personal and racial identity.

Articulation of an Africentric perspective that is informed by a minority world view can serve several important functions: (1) It can greatly enhance the chances that a true account of the reality of African Americans' lives will be presented; (2) it can serve as an empowering experience that might help create a self-determining individual and community; and (3) it can divorce the experience of African Americans from the meaning attributed to it by powerful outsiders, thus minimizing the internalization of destructive self-concepts that encourage victimization.

The modification of child welfare policies and practices to enhance the well-being of African American and other minority children is a complex task. It requires skill in assessing at what point workers are "dealing with universalities and at what point they are dealing with unique issues," how African American children and families are "simultaneously like every family in this country, like some other families, and like no other families at all" (Solomon 1985:10). It also

requires judgment in determining at what level child welfare policies
and practices can be analyzed for their impact on all minority children,
as if they are a social unit, while at the same time recognizing that for
all practical purposes the minority category is not a monolith but a
"medley of groups with widely different needs and interests" (Walters
1982:27). At the intragroup level, modification of child welfare policies and practices requires determining the degree to which the Africentric view of African American experiences takes into account or
incorporates the ethnic reality of all social classes, keeping in mind that
current indicators of social class cannot be applied whole cloth to African Americans to derive an accurate picture of status hierarchies (Billingsley 1968; Devore and Schlesinger 1987; Dodson 1981).

If one keeps these conditions in mind, it is worthwhile to delineate
how an understanding of some of the major constructs of the Africentric perspective suggests a critique and a modification of current child
welfare policies and practices for African Americans. In addition, the
impact of some of the key elements of the major constructs on policy and practice are analyzed here through the lens of a minority
world view.

EXTENDED AND FLEXIBLE
KINSHIP BONDS

The welfare of African American children cannot be understood
outside the context of the African American family. The African
American family in the child welfare system cannot be understood
outside the context of the African American community and its relationship to the wider society. Despite this truism, it is fair to state that
the contexts have not been used to mold child welfare policies and
practices for African Americans (Billingsley and Giovannoni 1972).
The "Anglo Conformity doctrine" (Billingsley 1968: 155) still domi-
nates the definition of the parameters of a traditional family system.
Social workers, under the influence of the systems perspective, might
have made strides in understanding the interaction of a subsystem
with the total environment, such as the interaction of the nuclear
family with other such families or community structures. This eco-
map, however, would not capture the reality of many African American families. To do so, the diagram would have to reflect one inclusive
boundary around a system that might include extended family, members beyond the extended family, and fictive kin (Billingsley 1968;

Stack 1974). The viability of this family structure can be appreciated fully only when it is examined within the societal context where trends for African Americans—the fragile nature of legal ties (for example)—have only foreshadowed trends for whites (Farley and Allen 1987). Examples of how effectively the African American extended family functions in its natural environment are provided by Martin and Martin (1978) and Hill (1972), who stress the security and welfare that this system provides for dependent family members.

Because many of the modifications in child welfare policies and practices for African American children should build on the strength of African American families, a few ideas from the child welfare literature might provide some guidelines. Workers should learn to redefine the professional role so that it fits the ethos of the African American family. Because networking and affiliative mutual aid are the natural helping and help-seeking strategies of African American families, child welfare workers can utilize these existing mediating structures to provide services rather than being compelled to be the direct service providers in all situations. In other words, a worker can carry the reciprocity inherent in the family system a step further by "acting as the enabler and facilitator with the helping process going on elsewhere" (Hartman 1985:78; Solomon 1985). Leigh (1985) further elaborates the use of indigenous structures when he suggests the possibility of using some African American families as role models for others. In this context, workers need to rethink their stance on confidentiality and determine how cultural contradictions dictate the necessity of adapting professional principles to fit community patterns. In fact, role modeling by some families can be seen as a way to tap into the benefits of extended family systems—existent and created—to integrate families that might be isolated, such as female-headed households (Gould 1985).

This emphasis on extended kinship and support systems is not used here as an excuse to neglect the provision of needed family-based services, nor is it assumed that the existence or creation of such a kinship system is a foregone conclusion (Rosentraub and Harlow 1983). Moreover, it is not assumed that all family needs should be fulfilled by an extended kinship network. Professionals should reexamine the cultural contradictions in definitions of parental and children's roles, especially as they relate to latchkey children. Many individuals, including older siblings and significant others, are capable of assuming responsible parenting roles (Chestang 1978). Child welfare workers have to recognize that there is a spectrum of parental responsibilities, and they all do not have to be fulfilled by the biological parent (Rutter 1974).

COMMUNAL IDENTITY AND SURVIVAL

Communal (collective) identity was alluded to in the discussion of the ideological assumptions of the Africentric perspective in Chapter 2. However, the term needs further elaboration because of its importance in integrating the Africentric perspective into a minority world view. Chestang (1983) explains that the function of communal identity is to mitigate the assaults made by poverty and racism on the survival, security, and self-esteem of African Americans. Given the fact that African Americans have to survive within the wider society, where they constantly face social inequalities and injustices, the consistent aspect of their lives is the binding together within the boundaries of the African American community. Thus, African Americans relate instrumentally to their sustaining environment (the wider society) and affectively to their nurturing environment (the black American community). This sustaining quality of African American culture, which helps individuals cope with oppression, is the key element that transforms the Africentric perspective into a minority world view.

At the heart of the child welfare system's failure to serve the needs of African American children is its inability to understand, utilize, or replicate the manner in which communal identity operates in the natural environment to take care of its members. Perhaps child welfare workers are caught up in their own rescue fantasies, which may stop them from examining indigenous, alternative approaches to removing children from their own homes. They may also harbor professional biases and ethnocentric views that prevent them from accepting findings that demonstrate that African American children are informally adopted under a variety of circumstances—death or illness of parents, divorce, "immaturity" of parent, proximity of adopting parent to school, or a simple desire on the part of the adopting parent to raise a child (Hill and Shackleford 1986). Workers who have been inculcated with the idea of "hard-to-place" children naturally might be reluctant to invest valuable time and energy in recruitment, outreach, and community involvement, which have proven to be so successful in programs like Homes for Black Children and One Church, One Child (Lewin 1988; Moffett 1985; Washington 1987). In addition, as we have seen, the need for subsidies, which are entailed in about 52 percent of agency-arranged adoptions of African American children (Mech 1985), is an impediment if workers are already reticent to involve themselves with "nonroutine" adoptions.

SELF-HELP

The tradition of self-help, as embodied in a cooperative life-style built on exchange and reciprocity, is an active pattern in many minority communities (Lum 1986). Although the survival function of this tradition is undeniable given the precarious economic status of many minorities of color (Stack 1974), it would be short-sighted if child welfare workers failed to realize that racial consciousness plays a significant role in the establishment of these networks. Martin and Martin (1985) theorize that the African American helping tradition originated in the African American extended family, particularly the emphasis on cooperation between men and women, and among people of different social classes. That child welfare has not recognized the value of incorporating such a long-established tradition in its service delivery is another example of the dominant society's tendency to devalue minority endeavors. Martin and Martin (1985) and Platt and Chandler (1988) have demonstrated how social work has overlooked the legacy of African American helping traditions and the struggles against racism.

Several authors have pointed out how application of the self-help tradition can modify child welfare service delivery. Solomon (1985) and Leigh (1985) discuss how clients—some who had terminated and others who were active—were used as collaborators in the helping process after they offered to do things for the agency as a way to establish a two-way relationship. In fact, Solomon (1976) sees "peer collaboration" as an empowering strategy for clients. Services included babysitting abused children when the parents came for counseling, doing the receptionist's job to help out agency personnel, and helping with other office jobs such as checking out materials used in play therapy.

Leigh (1985) presents another idea that might also warrant a reexamination of professional notions of confidentiality: putting clients in touch with other clients who have solved similar problems successfully. He sees this approach as an elaboration of an indigenous African American family pattern—the tendency to collect specific information for problem solving from a variety of people. The professional's role in this case is to direct the client to talk with community members who can articulate certain perspectives and points of view that are unavailable from the worker. The search can lead to the client's collecting the information and sorting out the facts with the worker.

A related program described by Leigh (1985) is the professional use of persons who know the needs of the African American community well enough to serve as "cultural amplifiers." These people are seen as repositories of innovative ideas for creating a viable community. But they are also perceived as needing "technical assistance" to translate their ideas into practice. Again, the professional is an enabler and facilitator, translating ideas into viable services. The benefits of this view of professional responsibility are clarified by Moffett (1985), who conceptualizes it as a two-way street to help the community and to help the worker. Professionals, who otherwise feel powerless in the face of inordinate problems, can share the burdens of responsibility while empowering the community to seek its own solutions.

Incorporation of the Minority
Feminist Perspective

The field of child welfare has traditionally accepted the "maternal code"—that women will bear chief responsibility for the nurturance of children—in developing policy and practice guidelines for services to families and children (Costin 1985). Consequently, there have always been a disproportionate number of women among the clients of child welfare agencies. Given this fact, it is imperative that an Africentric perspective reflect a minority world view that is informed by a minority feminist perspective (Gould 1987a). The rationale for this viewpoint is simple: Racism and sexism interact in society and the child welfare system to produce gender-specific race effects that need to be examined apart from the other effects of racism (Smith and Stewart 1973). Otherwise, there might be a feeling that addressing the issue of racism in society and the child welfare system is sufficient for understanding the impact professional policies and practices have had on all African Americans. The minority feminist framework, however, does not exclude the independent effects of racism in African American women's lives. It only asserts that a realistic comprehension of the African American woman's world as an operating social system is best provided by an interactional model because race and sex are both inherent facets of her destiny.

Numerous examples from the child welfare field illustrate the value of such a perspective: the need to unravel the dual myths of racism and sexism that surround the child welfare debate on reasons for the rise in birthrates among African American unwed teenagers, especially the causes of the drop in teenage marriage rates; the need to evaluate why the politics of both the African American and white communities determine the stance on whether the African American unwed teenage birthrate is a critical issue (Jacob 1983–1984); and the need to sort out the reasons for the ideological positions that inform the child welfare debate about the "strength" of African American women (Hooks 1981). Asante (1987) provides the closing thought for this discussion when he states that the feminist critique of society is close to the Africentric line of reasoning; it provides a post-Eurocentric idea where true transcultural analysis is possible. The objective of both discourses is the establishment of a world view that speaks to the concerns of oppressed people.

Implications

In an editorial, Hopps (1988) commented that twenty years after the President's Advisory Commission on Civil Disorders stated that the United States was moving toward two societies, one African American, one white, separate and unequal, we are still facing the specter of a polarized nation. It is illuminating, however, to reread the minority perspective that Billingsley (1968: 193) provided on the same statement:

> The report of the President's Advisory Commission on Civil Disorders concluded in 1968 that we are moving toward two societies. . . . This is in fact a gross understatement of the situation. We have and have always had two separate and unequal societies. What is new is a recognition on the part of the white society that these two societies exist and a determination on the part of the black society that they should no longer exist.

If one accepts the implications of Billingsley's comment, the social work curriculum in this field, as well as child welfare policies and practices in agencies, will have to forcefully present a minority world view. The first item on the agenda has to be a societal perspective, which has so far been considered only peripherally. Variations in the cultural roots of African Americans from those of the dominant group encourage a tendency in the child welfare area to teach from a strictly ethnocultural perspective. This treatment of the Africentric framework as a culturally relevant perspective on welfare policies and practices for African American children is a basic step because African Americans have to function in at least two environments—their own and that of the mainstream society.

In addition, however, the child welfare curriculum has to stress that an "explanation of ethnic and community behavior will be found in the relationship of the ethnic community to the larger macroscopic structure of the society" (Yancey, Eriksen, and Juliani 1976:399). In other words, cultural differences (the Africentric perspective) and minority-group structure (the minority feminist perspective and the minority world view) need to be examined jointly if child welfare workers are to understand what Hartman (1985: 80) calls the African Americans' "normative relationships with the environment." To avoid teaching about African Americans exclusively from a victimization perspective, emphasis should be placed also on the resources that empower African American children to cope with stressful life situations—"the world of supportive institutions within the Black community" (Chestang 1983:19) that serve as a haven against the assaults of the wider society. A minority perspective based on empowerment (Solomon 1976) can reinforce the idea that "various groups [are] creators of their own histories," and such a perspective does not assume that the "social and psycho-social behavior of minorities is merely a response to oppression" (Montiel and Wong 1983:116).

Similarly, the Africentric framework has to serve as the knowledge base to build a nondeficit model of child welfare policies and practices for African Americans (Dodson 1983). Again, in addition, the professional stance has to be that "we are going to have to look not only at what information people need in order to make skilled assessments, but at what kinds of organizational environments are required if they are going to be able to do it" (Solomon 1985:19). In other words, innovations in service delivery to African American children require modifications in the knowledge base and also in multiple, interacting forces operating at the individual, professional, organizational, and societal levels.

"Managing the contradictions" (Hartman 1985:97) involves the following tasks: managing racial gender-based, and cultural differences in world views that might lead to nonsupport of the ideological assumptions and values of the Africentric perspective; managing the tensions created by the fact that the professional culture socializes workers to be formal and nonrevealing in official interactions while the ethnic culture teaches clients to respond favorably to an informal, personal, collaborative style of service delivery; managing the organizational demands for system maintenance and the client's demands for individual and community advocacy; and managing the contradictions in society that preaches cultural pluralism and the worth of every individual but practices institutional racism and sexism.

None of these strategies, in isolation, is a guarantee that the child welfare system will be able to see its way clear to reexamine and reinterpret current policies and practices for African Americans. However, one thing is clear. The fundamental problems that have led to the disproportionate involvement of African American children in the welfare system are not going to be solved by just tinkering with solutions like an increase in services or delivery of services in a culturally sensitive manner. The time has come when limiting damage is not enough.

Notes

1. The adoption maintenance subsidy, as an incentive to increase adoptive placements for special-needs children, was recommended by the Child Welfare League of America as early as 1958. In 1968 New York became the first state to enact such legislation. Within the next ten years, forty-one states and the District of Columbia adopted the program. Uniformity in subsidy legislation was mandated by the Adoption Assistance and Child Welfare Act of 1980, P.L. 96–272. All states except Hawaii now have subsidy legislation, and Hawaii's regulations are covered by an administrative rule (Kadushin and Martin 1988:640–643).

References

Asante, M. K. 1980. *Afrocentricity: The Theory of Social Change.* Buffalo, N.Y.: Amuleji.
———. 1987. *The Afrocentric Ideal.* Philadelphia: Temple University Press.
Billingsley, A. 1968. *Black Families in White America.* Englewood Cliffs, N.J.: Prentice-Hall.
Billingsley, A., and J. M. Giovannoni. 1972. *Children of the Storm: Black Children and American Child Welfare.* New York: Harcourt Brace Jovanovich.
Chestang, L. 1978. "The Delivery of Child Welfare Services to Minority

Group Children and Their Families." In *Child Welfare Strategy in the Coming Years: An Overview,* edited by A. Kadushin, 169–194. Washington, D.C.: U.S. Department of Health, Education and Welfare.

———. 1983. "The Policies and Politics of Health and Human Services: A Black Perspective." In *The Black Experience: Considerations for Health and Human Services,* edited by A. E. Johnson, 13–25. Davis, Calif.: International Dialogue Press.

———. 1984. "Racial and Personal Identity in the Black Experience." In *Color in a White Society,* edited by B. W. White, 83–94. Silver Spring, Md.: National Association of Social Workers.

Costin, L. B. 1985. Editorial. *Child Welfare* 64:197–201.

Costin, L. B., and C. A. Rapp. 1984. *Child Welfare: Policies and Practice.* 3d ed. New York: McGraw-Hill.

Cutright, P., and H. L. Smith. 1988. "Intermediate Determinants of Racial Differences in 1980 U.S. Nonmarital Fertility Rates." *Family Planning Perspectives* 20:119–127.

Devore, E., and E. G. Schlesinger. 1987. *Ethnic-Sensitive Social Work Practice.* 2d ed. Columbus, Ohio: Merrill.

Dodson, J. E. 1981. "Conceptualizations of Black Families." In *Black Families,* edited by H. P. McAdoo, 23–36. Beverly Hills, Calif.: Sage.

———. 1983. *An Afrocentric Educational Manual: Toward a Non-Deficit Perspective.* Knoxville: University of Tennessee School of Social Work.

Edelman, M. W. 1987. *Families in Peril: An Agenda for Social Change.* Cambridge: Harvard University Press.

Fanshel, D., and E. Shinn. 1978. *Children in Foster Care: A Longitudinal Investigation.* New York: Columbia University Press.

Farley, R., and W. R. Allen. 1987. *The Color Line and the Quality of Life in America.* New York: Russell Sage Foundation.

Germain, C. B., and A. Gitterman. 1980. *The Life Model of Social Work Practice.* New York: Columbia University Press.

Gould, K. H. 1985. "A Minority-Feminist Perspective on Child Welfare Issues." *Child Welfare* 64:291–305.

———. 1987a. "Feminist Principles and Minority Concerns: Contributions, Problems, and Solutions." *Affilia: Journal of Women and Social Work* 2(3):6–19.

———. 1987b. "Life Model versus Conflict Model: A Feminist Perspective." *Social Work* 32:346–351.

———. 1988. "Asian and Pacific Islanders: Myth and Reality." *Social Work* 33:142–147.

Grey, S. S., A. Hartman, and E. S. Saalberg, eds. 1985. *Empowering the Black Family.* Ann Arbor, Mich.: National Child Welfare Training Center.

Gurin, P., and E. Epps. 1975. *Black Consciousness, Identity, and Achievement.* New York: Wiley.

Hartman, A. 1985. "The Roundtable" and "Summing Up." In *Empowering the Black Family,* edited by S. S. Gray, A. Hartman, and E. S. Saalberg,

69–107. Ann Arbor, Mich.: National Child Welfare Training Center.

Hill, R. B. 1972. *The Strengths of Black Families*. New York: Emerson Hall.

Hill, R. B., and L. Shackleford. 1986. "The Black Extended Family Revisited." In *The Black Family: Essays and Studies*. 3d ed., edited by R. Staples, 194–200. Belmont, Calif.: Wadsworth.

Hooks, B. 1981. *Ain't I a Woman: Black Women and Feminism*. Boston; South End Press.

Hopps, J. G. 1988. "Deja Vu or New View?" *Social Work* 33:291–292.

Jacob, J. E. 1983–1984. "Teen Pregnancy: A Misunderstood Problem." *Planned Parenthood Review* 3 (Winter):10.

Joe, T., and P. Yu. 1986. "The 'Flip-Side' of Black Families Headed by Women: The Economic Status of Black Men." In *The Black Family: Essays and Studies*, 3d ed., edited by R. Staples, 232–238. Belmont, Calif.: Wadsworth.

Jones, R. L. 1983. "Increasing Staff Sensitivity to the Black Client." *Social Casework* 64:419–425.

Kadushin, A., and J. A. Martin. 1988. *Child Welfare Services*. 4th ed. New York: Macmillan.

Katz, E. 1976. "Can Agencies Train for Racial Awareness?" *Child Welfare* 55:547–551.

Knitzer, J., M. L. Allen, and B. McGowan. 1978. *Children without Homes*. Washington, D.C.: Children's Defense Fund.

Leigh, J. 1983. "The Black Experience with Health Care Delivery Systems: A Focus on the Practitioners." In *The Black Experience: Considerations for Health and Human Services*, edited by A. E. Johnson, 115–129. Davis, Calif.: International Dialogue Press.

———. 1985. "Primary Prevention Approaches" and "The Roundtable." In *Empowering the Black Family*, edited by S. S. Gray, A. Hartman, and E. S. Saalberg, 41–55, 69–102. Ann Arbor, Mich.: National Child Welfare Training Center.

Lewin, T. 1988. "Black Churches: New Mission on Family." *New York Times*, August 24.

Lum, D. 1986. *Social Work Practice and People of Color: A Process-Stage Approach*. Monterey, Calif.: Brooks/Cole.

Martin, E. P., and J. M. Martin. 1978. *The Black Extended Family*. Chicago: University of Chicago Press.

Martin, J. M., and E. P. Martin. 1985. *The Helping Tradition in the Black Family and Community*. Silver Spring, Md.: National Association of Social Workers.

Mech, E. V. 1985. "Public Social Services to Minority Children and Their Families." In *Children in Need of Roots*, edited by R. O. Washington and J. Boros-Van Hull, 133–186. Davis, Calif.: International Dialogue Press.

Meyers, C. H. 1970. *Social Work Practice: A Response to the Urban Crisis*. New York: Free Press.

Moffett, J. A. 1985. "Practice with Black Families." In *Empowering the Black*

Family, edited by S. S. Gray, A. Hartman, and E. S. Saalberg, 57–78. Ann Arbor, Mich.: National Child Welfare Training Center.

Montalvo, F. F., T. T. Lasater, and N. G. Valdez. 1982. "Training Child Welfare Workers for Cultural Awareness." *Child Welfare* 61:341–352.

Montiel, M., and P. Wong. 1983. "A Theoretical Critique of the Minority Perspective." *Social Casework* 64:112–117.

National Black Child Development Institute. 1981. *The Status of Black Children in 1980.* Washington, D.C.

National Urban League. 1988 *The State of Black America, 1988.* New York.

Nichols-Casebolt, A. M. 1988. "Black Families Headed by Single Mothers: Growing Numbers and Increasing Poverty." *Social Work* 33:306–313.

Platt, T., and S. Chandler S. 1988. "Constant Struggle: E. Franklin Frazier and Black Social Work in the 1920s." *Social Work* 33:293–297.

Polansky, N. A., P. W. Ammons, and B. L. Weatherby. 1983. "Is There an American Standard of Child Care?" *Social Work* 28:341–346.

Rosentraub, M. S., and K. S. Harlow. 1983. "Child Care Needs and Policy Issues: Implications from Texas Surveys." *Social Work* 28:354–359.

Rutter, M. 1974. *The Qualities of Mothering: Maternal Deprivation Reassessed.* New York: Aronson.

Seligsen, T. 1988. "Wanted: A Permanent Home." *Parade Magazine,* July 31.

Shyne, A. W., and A. G. Schroeder. 1978. *National Study of Social Services to Children and Their Families.* Washington, D.C.: Government Printing Office.

Smith, A., and A. J. Stewart. 1973. "Approaches to Studying Racism and Sexism in Black Women's Lives." *Journal of Social Issues* 39:1–15.

Solomon, B. B. 1976. *Black Empowerment: Social Work in Oppressed Communities.* New York: Columbia University Press.

———. 1985. "Assessment, Service, and Black Families" and "The Roundtable." In *Empowering the Black Family,* edited by S. S. Gray, A. Hartman, and E. S. Saalberg, 9–20, 69–102. Ann Arbor, Mich.: National Child Welfare Training Center.

Stack, C. B. 1974. *All Our Kin: Strategies for Survival in a Black Community.* New York: Harper & Row.

Stehno, S. M. 1982. "Differential Treatment of Minority Children in Service Systems." *Social Work* 27:39–45.

Walters, R. W. 1982. "Race, Resources, Conflict." *Social Work* 27:24–30.

Washington, V. 1987. "Community Involvement in Recruiting Adoptive Homes for Black Children." *Child Welfare* 66:57–68.

Wilson, L., and J. W. Green. 1983. "An Experiential Approach to Cultural Awareness in Child Welfare." *Child Welfare* 62:303–311.

Yancey, W. L., E. P. Eriksen, and R. N. Juliani. 1976. "Emergent Ethnicity: A Review and Reformulation." *American Sociological Review* 41:391–403.

TWO
Understanding Families and Child Rearing

B U I L D I N G   O N   T H E   C O N C E P T S and values underlying the Africentric perspective, the following chapters examine the cultural heritage and experiences of African American families and children. Although each chapter emphasizes a different aspect of family life, each has one or more of three common themes: the diversity among African American families; the centrality of the kinship-based system of support for family functioning; and the unavoidable necessity of negotiating the interface between individuals and institutions.

Any assumptions of homogeneity among African American families ignore the variations in social environments, cultural experiences, and life-styles that constitute the social reality and legacy of these families. The cultural diversity among African American families created by regional, geographic, ethnocultural (for example, Haitian, Creole-speaking, West Indian), socioeconomic, and personality factors defies categorization and stereotyping (Bell-Scott 1990). The effects of these factors are observed in the child-rearing practices, help-seeking behaviors, and family dynamics of African Americans and are given expression through their perceptions of and adaptations to life circumstances.

In spite of the diversity however, some cultural similarities do prevail. One similarity is the development and utilization of extensive kinship-based support systems as a "natural" coping mechanism and resource for families. These primary group support systems enable the exchange of goods and services, the sharing of emotional life, and the protection of members. Increasingly, kinship support systems are affected by, and in turn affect, relationships between individuals and institutions. Negotiating relationships with the school, the workplace, the health-care system, the child welfare system, and other institutions is a critical task for African American parents. A lack of skill in navigating pathways through bureaucratic mazes can have deterimental effects on the growth and development of children.

Failure to understand how African American and other families of color are organized and function and how children in them are reared, grow, and develop belief systems and helping response patterns can result in a dehumanizing and degrading child welfare system. Having knowledge about cultural and racial differences does not, however, ensure ethnically sensitive practice. Too many African American children enter the welfare system because of inadequate knowledge about and understanding of their culture, especially the structure and quality of support provided by their families. Ethnically sensitive practice hinges on the practitioner's ability to carefully adapt and integrate the special features of African American family structure and functioning into the delivery of organized child welfare services. Gaining knowledge and understanding of African American families, particularly extended families, child-rearing patterns, and child development, is the primary focus of this part of the book.

Wilson begins Part Two with a description of contextual factors—that is, the values, beliefs, structure, composition, and functions of the African American family and the roles within it. The family as the primary institution for the care, protection, growth, and development of children transmits a distinctive set of cultural values and traditions and is influenced by the larger society. Wilson presents a historical view of the African American family as extended, consisting of kin and nonkin who transmit values, beliefs, and cultural traditions that were in evidence even during slavery. Extended families are cooperative and enduring units in which affection is not contingent on performance; rather, feeling and morality govern the relationships among its members. Despite years of bondage, the unfaltering spiritual beliefs of African American slaves and freedmen fostered interdependence and collective responsibility for family well-being. Informal adoption is one manifestation of this collective responsibility. As a kinship help system, extended families attend to the expressive and instrumental needs of their members, becoming mechanisms for coping with the exigencies of life.

African American families as currently constructed are viewed as models of resilience and survival in Wilson's chapter. Family survival depends on the interchangeability of parental roles and functions among adult family members, particularly grandmothers. As "guardians of generations" (Frazier 1966), grandmothers hold a special status within African American families. Grandmothers are especially valued as storehouses of the oral tradition and provide continuity and consistency. The role and functions of the grandmother are defined in large part by culture, sociohistorical context, and family dependence. With rapid and continuing shifts in the composition of families and households throughout the country, Wilson argues for an expanded definition of family and the protection and support of one-parent and extended-family units through public policy and the delivery of clinical services.

Child rearing in African American families is the subject of the next chapter. Taylor examines the complex processes of child rearing by commenting on the contradictory images of the socialization and psychosocial development of the African American child as portrayed in comparative studies of child-rearing practices among African American and white families. His critique of the sociological and psychological literature on African American socialization, including descriptions of parental and family characteristics, uncovers many of the gaps and limitations of previous studies. Despite regional, socioeconomic, and religious diversity among African American families, Taylor stresses the special features of the socialization of children of color for a bicultural existence—for creating a buffer from racism and discrimination. He further examines the role of parents and others in the development of self-concept, self-esteem, and intellectual competence, and in the encouragement of scholastic performance. Because African American children are socialized to cultural styles and motifs rather than to culturally specific and value-based behaviors, Taylor recommends a multidimensional approach to child development that includes consideration of socioeconomic status, life-style, values, religious beliefs and practices, and the interaction of these and other factors in the process of child socialization.

For the African American child, mastering normal developmental tasks in an environment of racism, poverty, oppression, and discrimination is a challenge. Utilizing the theories of Erik Erikson and Jean Piaget, Gomes and Mabry provide in Chapter 6 an overview of the stages of child development and isolate some of the critical and unique features of growth among African American children. The African American family and the community, which form a buffer around the child, are described as essential in facilitating bicultural socialization. More importantly, the difficulties children may experience within school settings, the place where they spend most of their time, are discussed.

The mastery of normal developmental tasks is a challenging journey for all children and families, especially those entangled with the child welfare system. Yet a quick look at the structure of child welfare services indicates little regard for child-development issues. Services are organized to accommodate the developmental needs of children from infancy to middle childhood, but children in late childhood and adolescence are often shifted away from the protective shield of child welfare services into the juvenile justice system. A major change in the auspices of the care and protection of children at this particular stage of development, puberty, disrupts the security and stability needed to ensure healthy growth and competent coping skills.

Moreover, treatment for children in care regardless of agency auspices frequently omits direct service to the child unless behavioral problems are evident. Instead, the intervention focus is on the parent, who is likely to receive concrete services, family therapy, group services, and individual counseling (Wald, Carlsmith, and Leiderman 1988). Children we assume are adaptable, but we know little of the particular effect a sudden and abrupt loss of familiar family and community surroundings has on children of color. Mastery of childhood developmental tasks may be interrupted by removal and placement. Without a stable, consistent, and secure family environment African American children become vulnerable to such settings as the schools, and community, with their potentially debilitating effects on psychosocial development.

References

Bell-Scott, P. 1990. "Introduction." In *Black Adolescence: Current Issues and Annotated Bibliography,* edited by the Consortium for Research on Black Adolescence, 1–3. Boston: Hall.

Frazier, E. F. 1966. *The Negro Family in the United States.* Rev. ed. Chicago: University of Chicago Press.

Wald, M. S., J. M. Carlsmith, and P. H. Leiderman. 1988. *Protecting Abused and Neglected Children.* Stanford, Calif.: Stanford University Press.

4

MELVIN N. WILSON

The Context of the African American Family

Train up a child in the way he should go; and when he is old, he will no. depart from it.
—PROVERBS 22:6

A family is a functional group with opportunities for at least economic and instrumental cooperation, informal communications, and reciprocated social and emotional obligations among its members. Family interaction and living provide the context for physical maintenance, affection, and social control of family members. Most important, however, family involves the bearing and rearing of and caring for children. Thus, it is important to consider family context because it reflects an important human characteristic—our nature as social beings. This chapter considers the context of the African American family—that is, family values and beliefs, family structure and composition, family functions and roles. However, before we consider the context of the African American family, several assumptions about family life must be clarified.

First, although the origin of the family is not known, sociobiological evidence suggests increasingly that the prolonged periods of lactation and juvenile dependence are primary factors (Hughes 1982; Lee 1977). The vulnerability of lactating mothers and immature children corrals wandering men and forms the cultural unit of family (Daly, Wilson, and Weghorst 1982; Hughes 1982, 1984; Lee 1977). The well-being of children, and ultimately of the human species, is a central factor in the development of the family. Moreover, many believe that family organization serves as the model for other forms of human organization and is a resource for child welfare services (Lee 1977).

Second, the family is a naturally occurring entity that is influenced by the larger social context (Myers 1982). In the case of the African American family, its unique cultural experience is shaped by traditional values, history, and the current social status of African Americans. This cultural experience is different from those of other Americans. The family system among African Americans has been shaped not only by adaptation to the American historical and contemporary social experiences but also by a rich African heritage (Akbar 1976; Aschenbrenner 1978; Gutman 1976; Genovese 1976; Hale 1982; Herskovits [1941] 1958; Nobles 1978, 1980; Otto and Burns 1983).

Third, the African American family is characterized by cultural values and beliefs that are distinct from those of the white American family (Foster 1983; Myers 1982; Nobles 1974, 1980). The most interesting distinction between the African American and white American family is their relationship to nonimmediate family members (Adams 1970; Hale 1982; Martin and Martin 1978; McAdoo 1978; Myers 1982; Stack 1974; Staples 1978; Wilson 1984). Whereas white Americans view family as composed of immediate members, African Americans include nuclear, consanguineal, affinal, and fictive relations (Foster 1983). The African American family includes both a tangible family unit of kin and nonkin and a cohesive group in the African American community (Martin and Martin 1978; Nobles 1974, 1980; Stack 1974). African American family structures also vary according to demographic, situational, and personal factors (McAdoo 1978; Myers 1982; Wilson 1984). "Important differences are due to geographic location of residence, as well as to location of origin, . . . nationality, ethnocultural language, and, of course, socioeconomic status" (Myers 1982:41).

In general, the welfare of the child is the responsibility of the family and, especially, the parents (Billingsley and Giovannoni 1972). When the child's needs are not met by the family, then it becomes necessary for society to assume responsibility through special programs (Billingsley and Giovannoni 1972). A critical consideration for agencies and professionals involved in the care of and advocacy for African American children is that the most important influence on the child's development is the family. Therefore, child welfare programs that ignore the context of African American family life will not be successful and will run a grave risk of failing to help those children they were designed for (Billingsley and Giovannoni 1972).

Traditional Values

Nobles (1974) and Herskovits [1941] (1958) have discussed the basic values of spirituality and collectivism that exist in varying degrees in most African American communities. Spirituality refers to the belief that the universe is basically one nonmaterial and interconnected element (McCombs 1985). Spiritual values are the moral and religious influences on behavior that lead a person to be respectful of life, harmonious with nature, and connected with others. Collectivism refers to the belief that human survival depends on the group as opposed to the individual. The basis of collectivism lies in the notion that the individual owes his or her existence to other members of the family (Nobles 1980). The individual does not exist unless he or she is "an integral part of the collective unity" (Nobles (1980:29). Along with spirituality, collectivism facilitates helping responses and a sense of responsibility for individuals and communities. Child welfare policies and practices should recognize and integrate these resilient and protective aspects of African American community life.

The best manifestation of collectivism and spirituality is the attitudes of African American families toward motherhood and children. In her anthropological analysis of African American child socialization, Young (1970, 1974) suggests that the African American family views child rearing and marital responsibilities as independent activities and tasks. In her study of Georgian families, Young found the sexual and marital attitudes of African American adolescents to be different from those of their white counterparts. Premarital sex, premarital pregnancy, and marriage were viewed as independent activities. An adult or adolescent female was not perceived as precluded from marriage because of prior sexual or birthing activities. Other researchers (Hale 1982: Hill 1972) have reported similar findings. Hale (1982) found that African American grandmothers differed from white grandmothers in that they did not recommend either abortion or marriage. Her sample was "oriented toward girls keeping their baby and rearing it with support from her mother [her family] and baby's father" (p. 142).

HISTORICAL DEVELOPMENT
OF FAMILY LIFE

The development of the African American extended family can be traced to the time of slavery. Several studies report an African American familial tradition that existed throughout this period (Agresti 1978; Billingsley 1968; Fogel and Engelman 1974; Genovese 1976; Gutman 1976; Martin and Martin 1978; Meacham 1983). Others go even further back and point to similarities in the family structure and values of African Americans and Africans (Hale 1982; Nobles 1974, 1978; Staples 1978).

Gutman's (1976) historical analysis shows that during the period before and after the Civil War, an average of seven out of ten slave and ex-slave children were born of conjugal relationships that were long-enduring. Although not legally sanctioned, marital arrangements were recognized and practiced by slaves. Gutman notes that the planters encouraged these unions because capital investment and productivity were enhanced. These early unions were not decided on by the planter but by the slaves (Billingsley 1968; Genovese 1976; Gutman 1976; Meacham 1983). Thus, a network of adults and children related by marriage developed from these first families.

Gutman (1976) hypothesizes that family and kinship patterns associated with traditional West African societies existed among those enslaved. Although the slave trade and initial enslavement experience destroyed traditional kinship and family patterns, the newly enslaved Africans invested nonkin with symbolic kin status, establishing fictive kin relationships. As a result, an African American family and related kin groups emerged from the initial disruptions associated with enslavement and the early creation of symbolic kin networks. The development of inter- and intragenerational links among slave families was accompanied by obligations of mutual support and assistance. The best demonstration of familial ties among slaves was the existence of an exogamy rule that restricted conjugal unions between blood relatives (Blassingame 1979; Foster 1983; Genovese 1976; Gutman 1976). Thus, the institution of the family was not destroyed during slavery; it existed as a mechanism for coping and surviving (Foster 1983; Genovese 1976; Gutman 1976; Meacham 1983). The historical data have been supported by archeological analyses of slave quarters (Otto and Burns 1983). Household and work artifacts were unearthed that appear to document the existence of family units.

The emancipation of slaves, which started in 1861 by military and presidential proclamation and was finalized in 1865 by the enactment of the Thirteenth Amendment, witnessed the emergence not of isolated individuals but of whole multigenerational and extranuclear families (Agresti 1978; Fogel and Engelman 1974; Genovese 1976; Gutman 1976; Lammermeire 1973; Meacham 1983). During this period, two activities occurred with increased frequency and intensity: marital ceremonies legitimizing the unions of former slaves, and the phenomenon of former slaves returning to their plantation of origin in search of separated family members. These activities occurred because the concept of family was transmitted during slavery.

Like slavery and emancipation, the rural-to-urban migration that began around the 1920s and continued until the 1950s (Franklin 1967) put intense pressure on the African American family. Several researchers (Aoyagi 1978; Flanagan 1978; Martin and Martin 1978) have suggested that the urban transition did not deter the development of the family. Specifically, the role played by the extended family involved three phases (Flanagan 1978). First, extended families sponsored the rural-to-urban migration of its individual members (Aoyagi 1978; Flanagan 1978; Holloman and Lewis 1978). For instance, a family member would be sent to obtain work in a city in order to earn money for the family. In other circumstances, a rural family member would join urban family or kin. After a period, whole families of several adults and children would reside in a particular urban area. Second, the families established a social welfare system that allowed for the care of dependent children and adults. Because obtaining a job was difficult even in the cities, many adults relied temporarily on extended family for food, care, and shelter (Flanagan 1978). Finally, a channel of income distribution was developed with less fortunate urban family members being subsidized by others in the kin network (Flanagan 1978).

Slavery, emancipation, and rural-to-urban migration, which have often been thought of as sources of familial instability and disorganization, were thus periods of intense development for the African American extended family (Flanagan 1978; Genovese 1976; Gutman 1976). The patterns of organization that developed during these periods have evolved as keystones of African American familism.

CURRENT STATUS OF THE FAMILY

Although the question of slavery has been long since resolved, current economic and social problems of African Americans existing in white American society have reinforced the reliance of African Americans on their familial network. Although most are not poor, there has always been a higher proportion of African American families living below poverty levels than white families (Duncan 1968; Reid 1982). Since 1960 the average rate of poverty for African American families has been 30.6 percent, an average 3.5 times higher than that for white American families (Reid 1982; U.S. Bureau of the Census 1989). In 1988, 31 percent of all African American families as opposed to 9 percent of white families lived in poverty (Reid 1982; U.S. Bureau of the Census 1989). Among one-parent families, poverty is particularly evident; 56.9 percent of one-parent African American families and 27.4 percent of one-parent white families were classified as poor in 1988.

Duncan (1968) attributed the poverty rate of African American families to past discrimination and limitations placed on certain factors—for example, level of income, educational opportunities, and occupational achievement. However, even when African Americans have attained a favorable socioeconomic level, their children's ability to maintain a comparable socioeconomic level is less than that of their white counterparts (Duncan 1968; Lieberson 1980; Lieberson and Carter 1979; McAdoo 1978; Reid 1982). This discrepancy may result from economic conditions that have culture-specific effects (Duncan 1968; Glick 1981; Lieberson and Carter 1979; Reid 1982) In other words, white and African American families of similar status are affected differently because of racial and cultural differences. For example, in African American families more people depend on the family income, and they are more likely to be dual-worker families than are white families. Also, past social inequities that prevented open housing forced many African American families into expensive areas.

The rate of poverty is highly correlated with family size and family composition (Allen 1979; Angel and Tienda 1982; Cutright 1971; Hofferth 1984). Allen (1979) and Hofferth (1984) found that when race and marital status were controlled, socioeconomic status was highly predictive of family formation in both African American and white families. However, although differences were small, Hofferth's and Allen's data supported the greater likelihood that African American families were involved in coresidential sharing as a way of reducing the effects of low income. Comparing the propensity to extend among African, Hispanic, and Anglo American families, Tienda and Angel (1982; Angel and Tienda 1982) demonstrated that African American family formation was also a group-specific difference. Tienda and Angel (1982) found that African and Hispanic Americans were more likely than Anglo Americans to share residence with extranuclear members who were contributing to the overall household income. In Anglo households extranuclear family members did not significantly contribute to the generation of household income; on the contrary, they were more often the beneficiaries of household income.

Several researchers have suggested that race-specific effects exist not only at the poverty level but at each socioeconomic level (Cutright 1971; Lieberson 1980; Lieberson and Carter 1979). For example, African American families consistently have had relatively lower incomes compared with whites (Cutright 1971; Duncan 1968; Lieberson 1980; Lieberson and Carter 1979; Reid 1982); and the consumable income (income per family member) of African American working- and middle-class families has typically been affected by the greater likelihood that they will have additional children and adult household members (Cutright 1971; Glick and Norton 1979; Reid 1982).

Lieberson (1980) observes that the African American situation in the United States is unique in comparison not only with white immigrant groups but with other nonwhite groups as well. Specifically, Lieberson states that the slavery issue was not present for other nonwhite groups and the economic threat was not as severe. Moreover, the usual controls placed on the population growth among African Americans were more difficult to apply than those imposed on immigrant groups. For example, when it appeared that the number of Asian immigrants was increasing too rapidly, immigration laws were changed to exclude them and, thus, control their presence in this country (Kamin 1974; Lieberson 1980). Likewise, Native Americans were militarily relocated and restricted to reservations (Johnson and Campbell 1981). African American immigration was, however, forced and proceeded under the assumption that slave status would continue indefinitely.

With manumission, Billingsley and Giovannoni (1972) suggest that the government would attempt to fulfill African Americans' specific needs in a universal fashion; consequently, many of the particular issues of the African American community would be ignored and reduced to the least common denominator of the larger society. But, in order to improve child welfare services, race-specific factors affecting the socioeconomics of the African American community must be considered. Billingsley and Giovannoni stress the importance of having services conceived, designed, managed, and staffed "to serve the specific needs of Black children in the context of Black families and the Black community" (1972:229).

Structure and Composition

The African American family has been described as involving various combinations of primary family units—that is, immediate family members—and secondary family members, or extranuclear family members (Hill and Shackleford 1977; Reid 1982). The three categories of primary family units are (1) husband/wife families with no children, "incipient family units" (Hill and Shackleford 1977), who constitute 24 percent of African American families (Reid 1982); (2) husband/wife families with a child or children under eighteen, "nuclear family units" (Hill and Shackleford 1977), who constitute 31 percent of African American families (Reid 1982); and (3) single-parent families with a child or children under eighteen, "attenuated family units" (Hill and Shackleford 1977), who constitute 30 percent of African American families (Reid 1982). The remaining family units, 15 percent, are classified as "other families" and consist of combinations of "grandparents living with grandchildren or brothers and sisters living alone" (Reid 1982:12).

Secondary family members are other relatives who are absorbed into the African American family. There are four types of secondary members: (1) relatives who are minors, including grandchildren, nieces, nephews, and cousins under eighteen (Hill and Shackleford 1977), who constitute 14 percent of African American children (Reid 1982); (2) peers of the primary parents, including adult siblings and cousins (Hill and Shackleford 1977), who constitute 35 percent of African American adults (Sweet 1977); (3) elders of the primary parents, particularly aunts and uncles (Hill and Shackleford 1977); and (4) parents of the primary family members (Hill and Shackleford 1977; Martin and Martin 1978). The latter two groups represent 53 percent of all African American elderly people (Beck and Beck 1989; Soldo and Lauriat 1976).

Attenuated family units with the mother as single parent (including those who are divorced, separated, widowed, and never married) include 94 percent of all African American single parents (Reid 1982). When we compare single mothers on age, number of children, income, and migrant vs. nonmigrant status, older mothers, mothers with larger numbers of children, mothers with higher incomes, and migrant mothers are more likely to live as single parents (Reid 1982; Sweet 1977). A younger, never-married mother is less likely than an older, previously married mother to live as an only adult in a household and more likely to share a residence with another adult family member, frequently her mother (Reid 1982; Soldo and Lauriat 1976; Sweet 1977). The age of the child and the educational level of the mother also affect the nature of the single mother's living arrangements. Mothers with younger children and less education are less likely to live as only adults in a household (Sweet 1977).

Because elderly African American relatives are frequently part of households that include children, it is important to consider the living arrangements of this group. As Langston (1980) reported, 85 percent of her African American elderly sample shared their residence with a spouse, an adult child, or a grandchild. Nationally, panel and census data (Beck and Beck 1989; Sweet 1977) indicate that 51 percent of the African American elderly population share a residence with a relative, as compared with 40 percent of the white elderly population (Beck and Beck 1989; Sweet 1977). In fact, about 10 percent of African American children below eighteen live with their grandparents, and 25 percent of young African American adults between eighteen and twenty-six live with their parents (Beck and Beck 1984, 1989; Sweet 1977). Three times as many African American children as white children under eighteen live with grandparents, while the proportion of African American and white adults living with parents is about equal (Soldo and Lauriat 1976; U.S. Bureau of the Census 1989).

Overall, we can single out several unique living arrangements that are characteristic of African American families. First, African American children are more likely than white children to be living in a single-parent household or with grandparents. Second, elderly African Americans are more likely to be living with grandchildren than are their white counterparts. Moreover, African American elderly persons are more likely to share a residence with an unrelated person than are white elderly persons. Finally, young, low-income single mothers are more likely to be sharing a residence with other family members than are older, middle-income single mothers. Clearly, when working with African American families, it is important to carefully record household members and each person's role and relationship to the focal member. Household composition and various relationships can serve as a resource in child welfare; professionals must be keenly aware of these structural variations and their impacts on the planning and implementation of child welfare services.

Besides these structural variations in African American families, variations attributable to geographical location require similar sensitivity on the part of child welfare professionals. For example, Stack (1974) described extensive networks of attenuated family units and fictive kin who lived in the same section of a small urban community. Martin and Martin (1978) described combinations of nuclear and attenuated family units in which some members shared residences while others lived in close proximity to a main household. Units of African American families living in the rural South usually reside on adjoining properties, while families living in the urban North usually live in separate households scattered throughout a particular section of the city (Shimkin, Shimkin, and Frate 1978).

Changes in household membership are another characteristic that influences structural variations of African American extended families. Several researchers (Kellam et al. 1982; Slesinger 1980; Stack 1974) indicate that lower-income and single-parent families are more likely to make frequent changes in their living arrangements than their respective counterparts. Slesinger (1980) compared intact, extended, and single-parent families during an eighteen-month period. She found that 83 percent of intact families, 30 percent of extended families, and 15 percent of single-parent families maintained the same household composition. Similarly, Stack (1974) found dramatic composition changes in the families she observed over a two-year period. One single mother moved seven times in one year among various relatives and friends.

Demographic and census analyses have indicated that compositional changes in African American families are greatly influenced by marital status and age of mother. For example, in 1988, 67 percent of African American adults who were parents were divorced, separated, widowed, or never married, as opposed to 31 percent of white adult parents; 55 percent of African American births were to unmarried mothers as opposed to 11 percent of white births; 28 percent of African American births were to adolescents as opposed to 14 percent of white births (U.S. Bureau of the Census 1989).

These rates suggest a fluidity in the form of African American families that is typically not present in white families. Several researchers (Furstenberg 1980; Slesinger 1980; Smith 1980; Stack 1974) have indicated that African American low-income, extended, and one-parent families are more likely to make frequent changes in their living arrangements than their respective counterparts. For example, the residential patterns of adolescent mothers (Furstenberg 1980; Furstenberg and Crawford 1978) and single adult mothers (Slesinger 1980: Smith 1980; Stack 1974) indicate frequent changes from independent living to cohabitation to marriage and ultimately to living with families of origin (Furstenberg 1980; Slesinger 1980). The pattern is mostly that of adding family members and developing extended families. In the case of two-parent families, the change is toward deleting a family member, usually through marital dissolution (Smith 1980).

Generally, the increase in extended-family contact among single mothers was attributed to several factors including single mothers' feelings of aloneness, powerlessness, and alienation (Smith 1980). In a national sample of one- and two-parent families, Smith found that household changes in one-parent families were related to the adult's need for psychological support and affiliation. Although two-parent families were often dissolving marital relations, Smith did find a greater likelihood for the one-parent families to experience more frequent household changes than two-parent families.

Many child welfare agencies and professionals do not consider these rapid changes within African American families in planning and implementing programs. Such changes suggest that the extended family is fluid and flexible and is also quite able to respond to crises and emergencies. In order to provide group-specific services, child welfare professionals must have an appreciation and understanding of these dynamics of African American family life.

Roles and Functions

PURPOSES

Like any family organization, the African American family has two purposes: to promote the welfare of dependent family members in dealing with normal and crisis life events; and to provide leadership by giving its members a sense of security, identity, and direction (Martin and Martin 1978).

Promoting family welfare and providing security takes on added meaning in African American families because of the large number of children in single-parent homes. As we have seen, many studies indicate that African American mothers who are rearing children alone live within an extended family (Ladner 1971; Martin and Martin 1978; H. P. McAdoo 1981; Stack 1974; Wilson 1984). In these cases, the detrimental effects of rearing children in single-parent homes are reportedly minimized by the support from the extended family, which offsets the absence of the father (Heiss 1977; Peters and deFord 1978; Rubin 1974; Savage, Adair, and Friedman 1978).

Giving advice and guidance to adults occurs frequently in African American families (Martin and Martin 1978; H. P. McAdoo 1981; Stack 1974). Family members often turn to their elders for counsel on job choices, major purchases, and decisions concerning children (Martin and Martin 1978; McAdoo 1978; Stack 1974). This process is significantly different from the modal way decisions are made in white families. The African American adult involves both conjugal and extended-family members, while the white adult relies heavily on his or her spouse. The egalitarian style of decision making and communication found among African American couples (Landry and Jendrek 1978) is conducive to involving extended-family members. This type of decision making occurs easily within African American families because the modal style is consistent with the structure of the family and respect for adult authority. With a little ingenuity, child welfare services and professionals can incorporate into their traditional programming this alternative advice-giving system.

ROLES OF FAMILY MEMBERS

Mothers

It has long been recognized that the mother's role is crucial for family and child development. Mothers are largely responsible for child and family care and household maintenance (Gecas 1976). The early relationship with and attachment to the mother facilitates the infant's development of feelings of security (Ainsworth 1979) and the school-age child's social maturity and cognitive-motivational competence (Baumrind 1971; Belsky, Robins, and Gamble 1984). Research has supported the description of the mother as expressive, nurturing, and caring (Ainsworth 1979; Gecas 1976; Nye 1976). Indeed, motherhood is seen as a major period in the life of a woman. Gecas (1976) has observed that in spite of the increasingly androgenous family roles of men and women, the persistent social norm is that childcare and socialization are the responsibility of the mother rather than the father.

Nevertheless, research suggests that child rearing is best accomplished as a cooperative venture of at least two adults (Kellam et al. 1982; Tolson and Wilson 1990; Wilson and Tolson 1986). Consistent with research on other groups, the African American mother's role has been independently and repeatedly demonstrated to be most salient in child-rearing activities and in general family functioning (Field and Ignatoff 1981; Slaughter and Dilworth-Anderson 1988; Wilson 1984; Wilson et al. 1989).

Fathers

After the mother, the adult family members most likely to be involved in childcare are the father and the grandmother, respectively (Slaughter and Dilworth-Anderson 1988). Although grandmother and aunt provided the mother with more instrumental assistance in caring for a sick child than did the father, mothers reported a preference for the child's father over the child's grandmother and aunt. More importantly, preference for the father's assistance in childcare was independent of marital status (Slaughter and Dilworth-Anderson 1988).

The father's role in childcare and socialization has undergone changes. No longer are fathers exclusively responsible for the family's economic and material comfort (Cazenave 1979; J. McAdoo 1981; Scanzoni and Scanzoni 1981). Mothers are increasingly entering the work force, and families are depending on the wages of both parents. However, as researchers have documented, maternal employment may be only one of many reasons for the father's increased role in the nurturance and socialization of children (Lamb and Elster 1985; J. McAdoo 1981; Power 1985; Ventura and Stevenson 1986). J. McAdoo (1981) suggests that fathers' increased interactions with their children may reflect their desire to have an increased part in the development of their children. Especially in African American families, fathers have been reported as providing significant childcare and household-task assistance (J. McAdoo 1981).

Grandmothers

Seen as experienced, able, and self-sacrificing, the grandmother is an important part of the African American family. Grandmothers are depended on both in crises and in daily routine matters (Jackson 1974; Martin and Martin 1978; Stack 1974). A major reason for the more active involvement of grandmothers than grandfathers is the high mortality of African American men, who have the lowest life expectancy of the four race/sex groups (Reid 1982). In contrast to seventy-eight years for white women, seventy-four years for white men, and seventy-one years for African American women, African American men are expected to live about sixty-six years (Reid 1982). At all ages African American males have the highest mortality. Although overall the number of men and women in the African American community is about equal, 985 men per 1,000 women, the number of men per women decreases as the cohort becomes older (Reid 1982; Rodgers-Rose 1980).

Another reason for grandmothers' importance in the African American family is basic differences in the family roles of men and women. Comparing grandmothers and grandfathers on the frequency of familial interactions and contacts, Jackson (1970) concluded that the grandmother's presence in the extended family was more vivid and active than the grandfather's. Grandmothers were more involved with grandchildren than were grandfathers. The bonds were closer among grandmothers, daughters, and grandchildren than among grandfathers, sons, and grandchildren. The grandchildren seen most often by the grandmother were the daughter's, rather than the son's.

Jackson's (1970) research also revealed other facets of African American grandparents' roles. Younger grandparents were more likely to report home visits from grandchildren, while older grandparents were more likely to pursue communication. Older grandparents reported engaging less frequently in church activities with grandchildren than their younger counterparts did. Interestingly, the majority of grandparents received expressive rather than instrumental assistance from grandchildren, while the modal form of aid donated by the grandparents was childcare. However, younger grandparents provided more financial assistance than did their older counterparts. The common anecdotal statement made by the grandparents was that obligatory ties were important; it was important to "keep in touch."

Several researchers indicate that the grandmother's role in the African American family is probably a function of her proximity to her adult children and their families (Guthrie 1979; Hale 1982; Jackson 1971; Wilson 1984). Jackson (1971) found that fewer African American than white elderly women were institutionalized and isolated from their families. African American elderly women who lived at home were more likely to be living with an adult child and, when they lived alone, were more likely to be within close proximity to at least one of their adult children than their white counterparts. African American elderly women maintained more frequent contact with and were more dependent on their adult children or other relatives for instrumental assistance and companionship than whites. Generally, Jackson indicated that unlike the activities of the white elderly sample, those of African American elderly women could be best understood in the context of familial relationships.

Finally, Jackson (1971) noted that socioeconomic level was a factor in the kind of relationship African American elderly women had with adult children. Specifically, lower-class grandmothers were more likely to be the donors of instrumental aid, such as childcare, transportation, crisis counseling, and financial support, while middle-class grandmothers were more likely to be the recipients of instrumental aid, such as transportation, medical assistance, shopping trips, and financial support.

In summary, the African American grandmother appears to be critical in the extended family (Frazier 1966; Jackson 1980; Martin and Martin 1978; Stack 1974). As a revered member, the grandmother is the source of guidance, nurturance, and experience to whom the members of the extended family often turn (Jackson 1980; Martin and Martin 1978). Frazier (1939:120) referred to her as a "warm, compassionate, but resolute person who inspired her children and grandchildren to achieve." Moreover he described her role in the family as nurse, midwife, mother, educator, minister, disciplinarian, and transmitter of the family heritage—the ideal dominant family figure (Frazier 1939, 1966).

FAMILIAL INTERACTION AND SUPPORT

The African American extended family is characterized by a familial interaction network and a kinship system of help and support. A consistent finding in the research on social networks is the frequent socializing among African American family members (Aoyagi 1978; Hale 1982; McLanahan, Wedemeyer, and Adelbery 1981) and the high degree of residential propinquity among related households (Aschenbrenner 1978; Martin and Martin 1978; Stack 1974; Wilson 1984). There is also an emphasis on participation in family occasions, especially funerals, holiday celebrations, and birthdays (Aschenbrenner 1978; Martin and Martin 1978; McAdoo 1978; Stack 1974). For example, African American women often list relatives as friendship contacts (Hale 1982; Martin and Martin 1978; Stack 1974). Moreover, the nature of familial interaction expands the extended-family relationship into the African American community (Aschenbrenner 1978).

The African American family's major component for survival, the "kinship help system" (McAdoo 1978), is a network of relatives, friends, and neighbors providing each other with emotional and economic support and acting as supplements and protection for the African American family (Martin and Martin 1978; McAdoo 1978). This "kin-help survival insurance policy" (H. P McAdoo 1981) serves as a buffer against negative environmental forces and provides a pattern of responses for coping with external stress by supplementing nuclear family units (Gutman 1976; Martin and Martin 1978; H. P. McAdoo 1981; Stack 1974); for example, nurturance, material assistance, and aid are provided by a network of kin and friends to dependent loved ones (Martin and Martin 1978).

Two kinds of assistance offered by the kinship help system are expressive and instrumental aids. Expressive aid is the emotional, nontangible support given to family members, while instrumental aid is tangible, material support (Billingsley 1968). According to Martin and Martin (1978), money, which is the primary instrumental commodity, is generally contributed in three ways: on an emergency basis; on a periodic basis as it is available; and on a regular basis by certain family members. Most of the money goes to "Momma," or the dominant family figure. Often financial help is given on an individual basis, without pressure to pay it back.

Other examples of instrumental aid include donating clothing, food, and babysitting services. An instance described by Stack (1974) involved a bartering system developed by a network of friends and relatives in a small town. The system allowed one woman, for example, to trade babysitting for transportation and beautician services. The system was fueled in part by economic necessity and in part by a sense of obligation.

Expressive aid is often given by the elderly members of the African American family network who share many survival techniques (Cohen 1984; Darden and Darden 1978; Hale 1982; Martin and Martin 1978). Home remedies, ways to prepare food cheaply, ways to get by with less, and ways to make more with less are just a short list of such techniques (Darden and Darden 1978; Hale 1982).

Generally, research on the kinship help system focuses on support for single-parent family units. This body of literature suggests that single-parent families have more contact with extended-family members than dual-parent families do (Field et al. 1980; Hetherington, Cox, and Cox 1978; Kellam, Ensminger, and Turner 1977; McLanahan, Wedemeyer, and Adelbery 1981). Divorced and single adolescent mothers can cope with the stress of single parenting within familial networks (Colletta 1979, 1981). The quality of care for children for single parents increases when the extended family is involved (Hetherington, Cox, and Cox 1978; Kellam, Ensminger, and Turner 1977). Single mothers have reported that family networks are more popular than friendship or conjugal networks (McLanahan, Wedemeyer, and Adelbery 1981). Field et al. (1980) found that although preterm infants of adolescent mothers had more problems than preterm infants of adult mothers, adolescent mothers were more likely to live with their family of origin than adult mothers, which could offset the negative outcomes of adolescent extramarital pregnancy (Field et al. 1980).

Another aspect of the kinship help system is the informal adoption procedures of the African American extended family. These procedures indicate the reluctance of and lack of access afforded single African American mothers to place their children in adoption agencies; the difficulties the formal structure has in placing an African American child in an adoptive home; and the attitudes that African American families have toward their children and the value they place on them (Billingsley and Giovannoni 1972; Hale 1982). Hill and Shackleford (1977) found that 66 percent of the white babies born out of wedlock in 1968 were adopted or placed in foster homes, but only 7 percent of African American out-of-wedlock babies were formally adopted or placed.

Martin and Martin (1978) indicate that children are absorbed into extended families for a variety of personal or situational reasons, such as economic necessity; being the first, last, or only child of a subextended unit, who is absorbed because of family troubles; being a child who may present special problems for the subextended family unit; being a child living in an abusive family situation; and being a child who was unwanted. Hill and Shackleford (1977) provide additional reasons for informal adoption: death or illness of the child's parents; separation or divorce of the parents; immaturity of an unwed mother; and proximity of a relative to a particular school. Also, informal adoption may occur as a result of the personal needs of the adopter. For example, the adopter may gain status within the extended family; may feel obligated to adopt; or may want a second chance to rear children. Finally, informal adoption is an expression of a basic African American attitude regarding dependent children. Because African American families are reluctant to turn their dependent children over to nonrelatives (such as foster homes) (Billingsley and Giovannoni 1972), they are willing to absorb related children to prevent legal adoption outside the extended family (Aschenbrenner 1978; Hill and Shackleford 1977; Martin and Martin 1978; Shimkin, Louis, and Frate 1978; Shimkin and Uchendu 1978).

Most often, informal adoption involves the children of single, indigent, adolescent mothers. The adoption occurs without any formal agreement as to the length of time the child will live with relatives. Although they begin as temporary arrangements, they often become permanent.

Most informally adopted children are aware that their "parents" are not their biological ones, and often they have contact with their "real" parents, especially their mothers (Martin and Martin 1978). Informally adopted children are treated no differently from the other children in the extended family. They seldom grow up feeling stigmatized by other family members. They often are close to grandmothers, referring to them as "Momma" (Martin and Martin 1978; Stack 1974).

Impact on Children

In general, most empirical research on the extended family has examined the effect of the grandmother's presence on outcomes for the child and child rearing within populations at risk. For example, Egeland and Srofe (1981) observed that twelve-month-old infants who were first classified as avoidant and anxious but as securely attached six months later were likely to be living in three-generational households composed of their mothers, their grandmothers, and their mother's siblings. Crockenberg (1981) found that the presence of a responsive, sensitive grandmother seemed to buffer the infant against the deleterious influence of an insensitive mother.

Kellam and his associates (Kellam, Ensminger, and Turner 1977; Kellam et al. 1982) found different long-term effects of living arrangements involving variations of extended-family structure on the child's achievement and social adjustments. Children from two-parent, mother/grandmother, mother/aunt, and mother/other families were found to be achieving and adjusting at adequate rates. However, children from mother only and mother/stepfather families were functioning below the rates of other children. Although these studies indicate that the long-term effects for children are negative in a one-parent or stepfather situation, it is not clear how any of the various family structures affect outcomes for the child.

Several studies indicate that the extended family's involvement with childcare indirectly benefits the child of an adolescent mother by allowing the mother the opportunity to improve her situation. For example, in Furstenberg and Crawford's (1978) study, adolescent mothers who remained in their mother's household were more likely to complete school and were less likely to continue to receive public assistance than girls who set up separate households. Colletta and Lee (1983) found that the amount, source, and impact of social support available to the adolescent mother was dependent on the mother's needs. Adolescent mothers who attended school or worked received more assistance with childcare, living arrangements, and housework, and reported more peer group and individual support than did adolescents who neither worked nor attended school. The working and school-attending adolescent mothers more often reported feeling in control of their lives than did the other mothers.

It appears that those adolescent mothers who are involved in some form of self-improvement are not doing less mothering. Field and Ignatoff (1981) compared adolescent mothers' interactions with infants aged twelve to twenty-four months when alone and when in the presence of the infants' grandmothers. Whereas the overall amount of stimulation the infant received was not affected by the grandmother's presence or absence, mothers were slightly less active in playing with talking to, and teaching the infant during the grandmother's presence. Grandmothers, however, spent more time watching the mother/infant interaction than involving themselves in a triadic interaction or participating in a grandmother/infant interaction. Although all the grandmothers were primary caregivers for their grandchildren, both the grandmothers and their self-improving daughters appeared by their actions to be acknowledging the adolescents' maternal role. Furthermore, although grandmothers reported more responsive and less punitive interactions with their infant grandchild than did their daughters, Stevens (1984) suggests that the presence of an infant seemed to provide the context in which the grandmother helped the young mother acquire accurate information about her baby's normative development. In general, the young mothers reported feeling their mothers' support for their role as parent.

Overall, the literature appears to suggest that the extended family may have more indirect than direct effects on the child (Tinsley and Parke 1984). However, additional research is needed on the impact of family structures and interactions on outcomes for the child.

Impact on Parents and Other Adult Family Members

Several researchers have examined the normal, functional African American family (Hale 1982; Jackson 1980; Staples and Smith 1954; Wilson 1984, 1986). These studies have focused on the differential impact of family roles on perceived (Staples and Smith 1954; Wilson 1984, 1986) and actual (Wilson and Tolson 1986) child-rearing experiences. In general, the results indicated differences in perceptions of grandmothers' and fathers' behavior. Grandmothers perceived themselves and were perceived as being actively involved in child-rearing activities (Wilson 1984) and affecting the attitudes of their daughters (Staples and Smith 1954) when they lived with the family as opposed to living in the community. Fathers of sons were perceived as participating more actively in rearing their children than fathers of daughters (Wilson 1986). Whereas grandmother's presence in the family did not affect the perception of the father's role, her absence did affect her involvement with the children of her single adult daughter (Wilson 1986). To study actual experiences, Wilson and Tolson (1986) examined the relative influences of family structure and grandmother's residence on family members' frequency of interaction. Comparing the single-adult and multiple-adult situations, they found that additional adults acted more as relievers for the primary caregiver than as participants in adult/child interactions.

Because of the potential of familial and social-network involvement as a source of child-rearing assistance and a way of reducing the stress levels of single parents, several researchers have looked for differences in the patterns of such involvement of African American one-parent families. However, Lindblad-Goldberg and Dukes (1985), comparing mothers who were receiving mental-health services with those who were not receiving such services, found no differences between the two groups in the number, composition, length, and emotional importance of relationships.

In a study that examined the assistance given to primary caregivers of children experiencing chronic pain from sickle cell anemia, Slaughter and Dilworth-Anderson (1988) found that primary caregivers, who were in all cases the mother, depended most often on the child's father for emotional aid and encouragement, independent of whether the father was present in or absent from the home. The assistance donated by the extended family was a function of the child's father's status in the home. More instrumental assistance was donated when the father was absent than when he was present. In addition, the assistance usually took the form of relieving the mother of daily chores, like cleaning, meal preparation, and transportation. The extended family was never reported as donating direct assistance to the care of the sick child. The child's father was reported as sharing equally in the care responsibilities of the sick child when he was present in the home. Moreover, the maternal kin were reported as donating assistance more often than paternal kin. Specifically, the mother's mother and sister were often the providers of assistance. The mother's mother more often donated instrumental services, whereas the mother's sisters donated emotional support.

Impact on Elderly Family Members

Studies comparing elderly individuals' involvement in extended-family activities report mixed results. For example, Mindel (1980), comparing African American, Anglo, and Hispanic elderly populations, found that elderly African Americans and Hispanics had higher levels of interaction and exchange. In addition, he found the African American elderly were more involved and had a more functional extended-family system than their counterparts. Mindel's findings are supported by others who found that, when controlling for age and sex, African American elderly parents give and receive more help (Mutran 1985) and have larger and more active familial networks than white elderly parents (Cantor 1979; Jackson 1970, 1971). Mutran (1985) suggests that the greater amount of help received by elderly parents was due largely to socioeconomic factors. However, aid given to the middle and younger generations appears to be a function of both racial and socioeconomic factors (Mutran 1985).

Other studies have found the differences between African American and white elderly involvement in extended-family activities to be relatively small (Allen 1979; Cantor 1979; Hofferth 1984; Rubenstein 1971). Specifically, there were few differences once marital status (Hofferth 1984) and socioeconomic status (Allen 1979) of the middle generation were controlled. Poor and single mothers elicit more assistance from their mothers than do their counterparts. These apparent contradictions suggest either that there may have been little difference between African American and white samples or that the differences are becoming increasingly smaller.

Mindel and Wright (1982) clarified these discrepant results by examining the nature of elderly involvement in extended-family activities. Overall, African American elderly both participated more formally in childcare and other household maintenance task and participated more informally in telephoning and other socioemotional contacts than whites. However, when social class was controlled, differences between the two groups were substantially reduced. The African American and white samples reported different kinds of involvement in formal and informal extended-family activities. For example, white elderly were involved in more informal activities—telephoning and entertaining relatives—whereas African American elderly were involved in more formal activities—attending or hosting family celebrations or movable feasts. Overall, group-specific effects appeared to account for those differences that were significant between African American and white samples (Mindel and Wright 1982).

Implications and Conclusions

Several implications for social policies, clinical interventions, and family research are suggested by this review of the context of African American family life. Given the changing structure and composition of the American family, the African American extended family may become a model of resilience and survival. Family demographers note that increasing rates of divorce and extramarital births have led to a higher incidence of one-parent families among all groups (Martin and Tolson 1983; H. P. McAdoo 1981; Pearce 1978). During the 1970s, the rate of marriages dissolving as a result of divorce, separation, or desertion reached 50 percent. Although the current rate is believed to range between 35 and 45 percent, the forecasters are not predicting substantial declines in marital dissolution. Likewise the rate of extramarital pregnancy and births has substantially increased, particularly for adolescents (Furstenberg 1980). Furthermore, an increasing number of mothers are keeping their children rather than giving them up for adoption (Martin and Tolson 1983; Pearce 1978).

The high rates of marital dissolution and extramarital births correspond to the increasing trend of one-parent families living below poverty levels. Commonly referred to as "the femininization of poverty" (H. P. McAdoo 1981; Pearce 1978), the increasing number of single mothers has resulted in large proportions of these families living below the poverty line. This trend has alarmed officials (H. P. McAdoo 1981), who worry about the aversive effects on future generations of Americans.

Although these trends have intensified for all families, the high rates of marital dissolution, extramarital births, and poverty have been part of African American family life for a long time. During the 1950s the rate of marital dissolution for African American families was 35 percent, while the rate of extramarital births was 25 percent. Currently these rates have reached 58 percent and 35 percent, respectively (U.S. Bureau of the Census 1989). Investigations of African American families have shown that the negative effects associated with one-parent family units are mitigated by the extended-family network (Field et al. 1980; Kellam et al. 1982; McLanahan et al. 1981; Wilson 1984; Wilson and Tolson 1986). In addition, role sharing and role flexibility involving older children reportedly relieve some of the pressure of rearing young children alone (Hill 1972; Minuchin 1974).

Clearly, if rising divorce rates and extramarital births are indicators of a changing American standard, then sex and childbirth are no longer the exclusive province of marriage. Because demographers do not foresee families returning to the situation of the 1950s and 1960s, it is important that public policy reflect the reality of American family life. Public policy on family life should support and enhance those familial structures that have been found successful in rearing children in the past. Especially with regard to African Americans, public and social policies should be designed to protect the integrity of the extended family. One-parent and extended families should be seen as healthy alternatives to two-parent family units. One specific example of a positive change can be seen in the Bureau of Labor and Statistics policy that eliminated the term "female-headed families" for the more descriptive and neutral category "single-parent families" (Scanzoni 1971; Straus 1977).

Several investigators (Aponte and Van Deusen 1981; Boyd 1982; Hines and Boyd-Franklin 1982; Minuchin 1974) have discussed the implications for clinical interventions with the African American extended family. They consistently point out that given the complex African American familial embeddedness, the therapist must be willing to expand the definition of family to include extended-family members (Hines and Boyd-Franklin 1982). One family-systems approach has used a procedure referred to as family genograms, which help to determine the roles played by family members (Hines and Boyd-Franklin 1982). This procedure acts as a screening device by allowing the therapist to assess generational patterns and extended-family influences. Also, the genogram permits the therapist to outline the objectives of family therapy and solicit family members' assistance in resolving issues. This approach to the African American family may help preserve the cultural and societal context in which the family exists. In addition, Mitchell-Jackson (1983) has suggested that psychotherapy and personality models advanced by African American theoreticians should receive increasing use because they incorporate African and African American value systems to understand behavior and to effect behavior change.

One of the most important implications is the need for systematic research on extended families. As the extended family becomes increasingly common, it becomes increasingly important that we understand the impact of this familial form on child and family development. Several areas in need of research are grandparent/grandchild interaction patterns and influences, the impact of informal adoption and foster care on child development, the impact of multiple-adult situations on family and child development, the interaction pattern of siblings (both natural and adopted), and the influence of extended family on other social systems.

However, in order to carry out such research, theories and methodologies must be developed that can address these concerns (Petersen 1969; Rodman 1980). As Peterson (1969) and Slesinger (1980) point out, the complex set of variables that affect socioeconomic level and familial structure and composition makes empirical comparison extremely difficult if not impossible in certain circumstances. For example, Peterson's (1969) attempt to compare cross-cultural samples failed not only because of familial inclusion problems across the two samples but also because of major variations within each cultural sample. Current research methodologies are not easily generalizable across studies because the extended family involves many dyadic combinations and endless interaction. In addition, researchers have persistently defined the family unit as mother, father, and children. However, it has become increasingly clear that the nuclear family form is only one of several. It is important that family researchers take this reality into account so that the phenomenon of family is not idealized but understood.

The African American family is an alternative family system. The extended-family organization is a coping mechanism activated by the high incidence of poverty, unemployment, extramarital births, and marital dissolutions in the African American community. The general influence of the extended family is reflected in the continued viability and preservation of the African American populace. Interestingly, the specific influences of the extended family are probably more indirect than direct. For example, extended-family involvement takes the form of relieving the single mother of some household tasks but not primary childcare tasks (Slaughter and Dilworth-Anderson 1988), participating in adult/adult exchanges rather than in adult/child exchanges (Wilson and Tolson 1986), and providing emotional support to the mother (Hale 1982; Lindblad-Goldberg and Dukes 1985; Slaughter and Dilworth-Anderson 1988). Also, it appears that single mothers, elderly family members, and children of single-parent families are more involved in extended-family activities than are their white counterparts.

The literature, as reflected to some extent in this chapter, centers on determining the impact of the extended family on the coping mechanisms of high-risk groups such as teenage mothers, unemployed African American men, and the elderly. Although it is documented that African American two-parent families participate in extended-family activities significantly more than their white counterparts (Hays and Mindel 1973; Hofferth 1984; McAdoo 1978; Tienda and Angel 1982), other questions regarding the nature of their participation, as either donors or recipients, the conditions under which such participation occurs, and the consequences for family life have not been sufficiently addressed. Another aspect of the African American extended family about which there is a paucity of information is the factors involved in its formation. Studies might address not only the advantages of participating in extended-family activities—for example, additional sources of income and adult help—but also the disadvantages—restrictions on adult decision-making opportunities and interpersonal relationships. Future research on the African American familial network should address its specific function as an alternative child welfare system and its implications for clinical intervention as a coping mechanism. In order to empirically investigate the African American family network, theories and methodologies must be developed that can address the complex structural and interactional variations that are possible in it (Lewis 1984; Peterson 1969; Rodman 1980). Because the rates of divorce and the subsequent formation of single-parent families are increasing, it is critical that we understand how the African American family might serve as a viable alternative for other American communities.

The African American community, not unlike other communities, has acted as an advocate for the welfare of its children. However, as Billingsley and Giovannoni (1972) have noted, the African American community has for a long time performed those services without the recognition of the larger society. More importantly, the child welfare community has not involved, consulted with, or cooperated with the African American community. With open communication, understanding, and involvement on the part of the majority American community, the African American community can serve as a resource to the society's child welfare services and systems and, in return, can obtain improved services from those larger systems.

Acknowledgments

The preparation of this chapter was supported by grants from the National Science Foundation (PRM-8210411), the Spencer Foundation, the Rockefeller Foundation, and the Carter G. Woodson Institute of Afro-American and African Studies.

References

Adams, B. N. 1970. "Isolation, Function and Beyond: American Kinship in the 60's." *Journal of Marriage and the Family* 32:575–597.
Agresti, B. F. 1978. "The First Decades of Freedom: Black Families in a Southern County, 1870–1885." *Journal of Marriage and the Family* 46: 697–706.
Ainsworth, M. D. S. 1979. "Attachment as Related to Mother-Infant Interaction." *Advances in the Study of Behavior* 9:1–51.

Akbar, N. 1976. *The Community of Self.* Chicago: Nation of Islam Office of Human Development.

Allen, W. R. 1979. "Class, Culture, and Family Organization: The Effects of Class and Race on Family Structure in Urban America." *Journal of Comparative Family Studies* 10:301–313.

Angel, R., and M. Tienda. 1982. "Headship and Household Composition among Blacks, Hispanics and Other Whites." *Social Forces* 61:508–531.

Aoyagi, K. 1978. "Kinship and Friendship in Black Los Angeles: A Study of Migrants from Texas." In *The Extended Family in Black Societies,* edited by D. B. Shimkin, E. M. Shimkin, and D. A. Frate, 277–355. The Hague: Mouton.

Aponte, H., and J. Van Deusen. 1981. "Structural Family Therapy." In *Handbook of Family Therapy,* edited by A. Gurman and D. Kniskern, 310–360. New York: Brunner/Mazel.

Aschenbrenner, J. 1978. "Continuities and Variations in Black Family Structure." In *The Extended Family in Black Societies,* edited by D. B. Shimkin, E. M. Shimkin, and D. A. Frate, 181–200. The Hague: Mouton.

Baumrind, D. 1971. "Current Patterns of Parental Authority." *Developmental Psychology Monographs* 4(1):99–102.

Beck, R. W., and S. H. Beck. 1984. "Formation of Extended Household during Middle Age." *Journal of Marriage and the Family* 46:277–287.

Beck, S. H., and R. W. Beck. 1989. "The Incidence of Extended Households among Middle-Aged Black and White Women." *Journal of Family Issues* 10(2):147–168.

Belsky, J., E. Robins, and W. Gamble. 1984. "The Determinants of Parental Competence." In *Beyond the Dyad,* edited by M. Lewis, 257–280. New York: Plenum.

Billingsley, A. 1968. *Black Families in White America.* Englewood Cliffs, N.J.: Prentice-Hall.

Billingsley, A., and J. M. Giovannoni. 1972. *Children of the Storm: Black Children and American Child Welfare.* New York: Harcourt Brace Jovanovich.

Blassingame, J. W. 1979. *The Slave Community: Plantation Life in the Antebellum South.* New York: Oxford University Press.

Boyd, N. 1982. "Family Therapy with Black Families." In *Minority Mental Health,* edited by E. E. Jones and S. J. Korchin, 227–250. New York: Praeger.

Cantor, M. A. 1979. "Neighbors and Friends: An Overlooked Resource in the Informal Support System." *Research on Aging* 1:434:463.

Cazenave, N. A. 1979. "Middle-Income Black Families: An Analysis of the Provider Role." *Family Coordinator* 28:583–593.

Cohen, M. 1984. "The Ethnomedicine of Garfina (Black Caribs) of Rio Tinto Honduras." *Anthropological Quarterly* 57:16–27.

Colletta, N. D. 1979. "Support Systems after Divorce: Incidence and Impact." *Journal of Marriage and the Family* 41:837–846.

———. 1981. "Social Support and Risk of Maternal Rejection by Adolescent
    Mothers." *Journal of Psychology* 109(2):191–197.
Colletta, N., and D. Lee. 1983. "The Impact of Support for Black Adolescent
    Mothers." *Journal of Family Issues* 4:127–143.
Crockenberg, S. B. 1981. "Infant Irritability, Mother Responsiveness and So-
    cial Support Influences on the Security of Infant-Mother Attachment."
    Child Development 52:857–865.
Cutright, P. 1971. "Income and Family Events: Family Income, Family Size
    and Consumption." *Journal of Marriage and the Family* 33:161–173.
Daly, M., M. Wilson, and S. J. Weghorst. 1982. "Male Sexual Jealousy."
    Ethology and Sociobiology 3(1):11–28.
Darden, N. J., and C. Darden. 1978. *Spoonbread and Strawberry Wine*. New
    York: Doubleday, Anchor Books.
Duncan, O. D. 1969. "Inheritance of Poverty of Inheritance of Race?" In *On
    Understanding Poverty,* edited by D. P. Moynihan, 85–110. New York: Ba-
    sic Books.
Egeland, B., and L. A. Srofe. 1981. "Attachment and Early Maltreatment."
    Child Development 52:44–52.
Field, T. M., and E. Ignatoff. 1981. "Videotaping Effects on Play and Inter-
    action Behaviors of Low Income Mothers and Their Infants." *Journal of
    Applied Developmental Psychology* 2:227–236.
Field, T. M., S. M. Widmayer, S. Stringer, and E. Ignatoff. 1980. "Teenage,
    Lower Class, Black Mothers and Their Preterm Infants: An Intervention
    and Developmental Follow-up." *Child Development* 51:426–436.
Flanagan, W. G. 1978. "The Extended Family as an Agent of Social Change."
    Paper presented at 9th World Congress of the International Sociological
    Association, Uppsala University, Uppsala, Sweden, August.
Fogel, R., and S. Engelman. 1974. *Time on the Cross*. 2 vols. Boston: Little,
    Brown.
Foster, H. J. 1983. "African Patterns in the Afro-American Family." *Journal
    of Black Studies* 14:201–232.
Franklin, J. H. 1967. *From Slavery to Freedom*. New York: Knopf.
Frazier, E. F. 1939. *The Negro Family in the United States*. Chicago: University
    of Chicago Press.
———.1966. *The Negro Family in the United States*. Rev. ed. Chicago: Uni-
    versity of Chicago Press.
Furstenberg, F. 1980. "Burdens and Benefits: The Impact of Early Childbear-
    ing on the Family." *Journal of Social Issues* 36:64–87.
Furstenberg, F., and D. B. Crawford. 1978. "Family Support: Helping Teen-
    agers to Cope." *Family Planning Perspectives* 10:322–333.
Gecas, J. 1976. "The Socialization and Childcare Roles." In *Role Structure and
    Analysis of the Family,* edited by F. I. Nye, 33–59. Beverly Hills, Calif.:
    Sage.

Genovese, E. D. 1976. *Roll, Jordan, Roll.* New York: Random House.

Glick, P. C. 1976. "Living Arrangements of Children and Young Adults." *Journal of Comparative Family Studies* 7:321–333.

———. 1981. "A Demographic Picture of Black Families." In *Black Families,* edited by H. P. McAdoo, 106–126. Beverly Hills, Calif.: Sage.

Glick, P. C., and H. J. Norton. 1979. "Marrying, Divorcing and Living Together in the U.S. Today." *Population Bulletin* 32(5):3–33.

Guthrie, P. 1979. "Black Families on St. Helena Island: The Mother/Daughter-in-Law Relationship." Paper presented at conference, Black Women: A Historical Perspective, National Council of Negro Women, Washington, D.C., November.

Gutman, H. G. 1976. *The Black Family in Slavery and Freedom. 1750–1925.* New York: Vintage.

Hale, J. E. 1982. *Black Children: Their Roots, Culture, and Learning Styles.* Provo, Utah: Brigham Young University Press.

Hays, W. C., and C. H. Mindel. 1973. "Extended Kinship Relations in Black and White Families." *Journal of Marriage and the Family* 25:51–57.

Heiss, J. 1977. *The Case of the Black Family: A Sociological Inquiry.* New York: Columbia University Press.

Herskovits, M. J. [1941] 1958. *The Myth of the Negro Past.* Boston: Beachon Press.

Hetherington, E. M., M. Cox, and R. Cox. 1978. "The Aftermath of Divorce." In *Mother-Child, Father-Child Relations,* edited by J. H. Stevens, Jr., and M. Matthew, 149–176. Washington, D.C.: National Association for the Education of Young Children.

Hill, R. B. 1972. *The Strengths of Black Families.* New York; Emerson Hall.

Hill, R. B., and L. Shackleford. 1977. "The Black Extended Family Revisited." *Urban League Review* 1:18–24.

Hines, P. M., and N. Boyd-Franklin. 1982. "Black Families." In *Ethnicity and Family Therapy,* edited by M. McGoldrick, J. K. Pearce, and J. Gaurdano, 84–107. New York: Guilford Press.

Hofferth, S. L. 1984. "Kin Network, Race, and Family Structure." *Journal of Marriage and the Family* 46:791–806.

Holloman, R. E., and F. E. Lewis. 1978. "The 'Clan': Case Study of a Black Extended Family in Chicago." In *The Extended Family in Black Societies,* edited by D. B. Shimkin, E. M. Shimkin, and D. A. Frate, 201–239. The Hague: Mouton.

Hughes, A. L. 1982. "Confidence of Paternity and Wife Sharing in Polygynous and Polyandrous Systems." *Ethology and Sociobiology* 3(3):125–137.

———.1984. "Analyzing Human Kin Groups." *Ethology and Sociobiology* 5(3):179–192.

Jackson, J. J. 1970. "Kinship Relations among Urban Blacks." *Journal of Social Behavioral Sciences* 16:1–13.

———. "Sex and Social Class Variations in Black and White Parent-Adult Child Relationships." *International Journal of Aging and Human Development* 2:96–106.

———. 1974. "Ordinary Black Husbands-Fathers: The Truly Hidden Men." *Journal of Social and Behavioral Sciences* 20:19–27.

———. 1980. *Minorities and Aging.* Belmont, Calif.: Wadsworth.

Johnson, D. M., and R. R. Campbell. 1981. *Black Migration in America.* Durham, N. C.: Duke University Press.

Kamin, I. J. 1974. *The Science and Politics of I.Q.* Potomac, Md.: Erlbaum.

Kellam, S. G., R. G. Adams, C. H. Brown, and M. E. Ensminger. 1982. "The Long-Term Evolution of the Family Structure of Teenage and Older Mothers." *Journal of Marriage and the Family* 46:539–554.

Kellam, S. G., M. A. Ensminger, and J. T. Turner. 1977. "Family Structure and the Mental Health of Children." *Archives of General Psychiatry* 34: 1012–1022.

Ladner, J. A. 1971. *Tomorrow's Tomorrow: The Black Woman.* New York: Doubleday, Anchor Books.

Lamb, M. E., and A. B. Elster. 1985. "Adolescent Mother-Infant-Father Relationship." *Developmental Psychology* 21:768–773.

Lammermeire, P. J. 1973. "Urban Black Family of the Nineteenth Century: A Study of Black Family Structure in Ohio Valley: 1850–1880." *Journal of Marriage and the Family* 35(3):440–456.

Landry, B., and M. P. Jendrek. 1978. "The Employment of Wives in Middle-Class Black Families." *Journal of Marriage and the Family* 40(4):787–798.

Langston, E. J. 1980. "Kith and Kin: Natural Support Systems: Their Implications for Policies and Programs for the Black Aged." In *Minority Aging Policy Issues for the '80s,* edited by E. P. Stanford, 125–145. San Diego, Calif.: University Center on Aging, College of Human Services, San Diego State University.

Lee, G. R. 1977. *Family Structure and Interaction.* Philadelphia: Lippincott.

Lewis, M. 1984. "Social Influences on Child Development." In *Beyond the Dyad,* edited by M. Lewis, 1–13. New York: Plenum.

Lieberson, S. 1980. *A Piece of Pie.* Berkeley: University of California Press.

Lieberson, S., and D. K. Carter. 1979. "Making It in America: Differences between Black and White Ethnic Groups." *American Sociological Review* 44:347–366.

Lindblad-Goldberg, M., and J. L. Dukes. 1985. "Social Support in Black, Low-Income, Single-Parent Families; Normative and Dysfunctional Patterns." *American Journal of Orthopsychiatry* 55:42–58.

McAdoo, H. P. 1978. "Factors Related to Stability in Upwardly Mobile Black Families." *Journal of Marriage and the Family* 40:761–776.

———. ed. 1981. *Black Families.* Beverly Hills, Calif.: Sage.

McAdoo, J. 1981. "Black Father and Child Interactions." In *Black Men,* edited by L. E. Gary, 115–130. Beverly Hills, Calif.: Sage.

McCombs, H. G. 1985. "Black Self-Concept: An Individual Collective Analysis." *Journal of Intercultural Relations* 9:1–18.
McLanahan, S. S., N. V. Wedemeyer, and J. Adelbery. 1981. "Network Structure, Social Support and Psychological Well-Being in the Single-Parent Family." *Journal of Marriage and the Family* 43:601–611.
Martin, E. P. and J. M. Martin. 1978. *The Black Extended Family.* Chicago: University of Chicago Press.
Martin, J. H. and D. J. Tolson. 1983. "Family Composition in Virginia: Female-Headed Families, 1970–1980." *Newsletter of the University of Virginia Institute of Government* 59:53–57.
Meacham, M. 1983. "The Myth of the Black Matriarchy under Slavery." *Mid-American Review of Sociology* 8:23–41.
Mindel, C. H. 1980. "Extended Familism among Urban Mexican American, Anglos, and Blacks." *Hispanic Journal of Behavior Science* 2:21–34.
Mindel, C. H., and R. Wright. 1982. "Assessing the Role of Support Systems among Black and White Elderly." Paper presented at 35th annual meeting of the Gerontological Society of America, Boston, November.
Minuchin, S. 1974. *Families and Family Therapy.* Cambridge: Harvard University Press.
Mitchell-Jackson, A. 1983. "The Black Patient and Traditional Psychotherapy: Implications and Possible Extensions." *Journal of Community Psychology* 11:303–307.
Monthly Labor Review. 1984. "The Black Population: A Statistical View, 1970–82." *Monthly Labor Review* 107(4):44–51.
Mutran, E. 1985. "Intergenerational Family Support among Blacks and Whites: Responses to Culture or to Socioeconomic Differences?" *Journal of Gerontology* 40:382–389.
Meyers, H. F. 1982. "Research on the Afro-American Family: A Critical Review." In *The Afro-American Family: Assessment, Treatment and Research Issues,* edited by B. A. Bass, G. E. Wyatt, and G. J. Powell, 35–68. New York: Grune & Stratton.
Nobles, W. W. 1974. "African Root and American Fruit: The Black Family." *Journal of Social and Behavioral Sciences* 20:52–64.
———.1978. "Toward an Empirical and Theoretical Framework for Defining Black Families." *Journal of Marriage and the Family* 40:679–688.
———. 1980. "African Philosophy: Foundations for Black Psychology." In *Black Psychology,* 2d ed., edited by R. Jones, 41–57. New York: Harper & Row.
Nye, F. I. 1976. "Role Constructs: Measurement." In *Role Structure and Analysis of the Family,* edited by F. I. Nye, 15–31. Beverly Hills, Calif.: Sage.
Otto, J. J., and A. M. Burns III. 1983. "Black Folks and Poor Buckras: Archeological Evidence of Slave and Overseer Living Conditions on an Antebellum Plantation." *Journal of Black Studies* 14:185–200.

Pearce, D. 1978. "The Feminization of Poverty: Women, Work, and Welfare." *Urban and Social Change Review* 11:28–36.

Peters, M., and C. deFord, 1978. "The Solo Mother." In *The Black Family: Essays and Studies,* edited by R. Staples, 192–201. Belmont, Calif.: Wadsworth.

Peterson, K. K. 1969. "Kin Network Research: A Plan for Comparability." *Journal of Marriage and the Family* 31:271–280.

Power, T. G. 1985. "Mother- and Father-Infant Play: A Developmental Analysis." *Child Development* 56:1514-1524.

Reid, J. 1982. "Black America in the 1980s." *Population Bulletin* 37(4): 3–37.

Rodgers-Rose, L. F. 1980. "Some Demographic Characteristics of the Black Woman: 1940 to 1975." In *The Black Woman,* edited by L. F. Rodgers-Rose, 29–42. Beverly Hills, Calif.: Sage.

Rodman, H. 1980. "Are Conceptual Frameworks Necessary for Theory Building? The Case of Family Sociology." *Sociological Quarterly* 21: 429–441.

Rubenstein, D. 1971. "An Examination of Social Participation of Black and White Elderly." *Aging and Human Development* 2:172–188.

Rubin, R. H. 1974. "Adult Male Absence and the Self-Attitudes of Black Children." *Child Study Journal* 4:33–45.

Savage, J. E., A. W. Adair, and P. Friedman. 1978. "Community-Social Variables Related to Black Parent Absent Families." *Journal of Marriage and Families* 40(4):779–786.

Scanzoni, J. H. 1971. *The Black Family in Modern Society.* Boston: Allyn & Bacon.

Scanzoni, L. D., and J. H. Scanzoni. 1981. *Men, Women and Change: A Sociology of Marriage.* New York: McGraw-Hill.

Shimkin, D. B., G. J. Louis, and D. A. Frate. 1978. "The Black Extended Family: A Basic Rural Institution and a Mechanism of Urban Adaptation." In *The Extended Family in Black Societies,* edited by D. B. Shimkin, E. M. Shimkin, and D. A. Frate, 25–149. The Hague: Mouton.

Shimkin, D. B., E. M. Shimkin, and D. A. Frate, eds. 1978. *The Extended Family in Black Societies.* The Hague: Mouton.

Shimkin, D. B., and V. Uchendu. 1978. "Persistence, Borrowing, and Adaptive Changes in Black Kinship Systems: Some Issues and Their Significance." In *The Extended Family in Black Societies,* edited by D. B. Shimkin, E. M. Shimkin, and D. A. Frate, 391–406. The Hague: Mouton.

Slaughter, D. T., and P. Dilworth-Anderson. 1988. "Care of Black Children with Sickle Cell Disease: Fathers, Maternal Support and Esteem." *Family Relations* 37:281–287.

Slesinger, D. P. 1980. "Rapid Changes in Household Composition among Low Income Mothers." *Family Relations* 29:221–228.

Smith, M. J. 1980. "The Social Consequences of Single Parenthood: A Longitudinal Perspective." *Family Relations* 29:75–81.

Soldo, B., and P. Lauriat. 1976. "Living Arrangements among the Elderly in the United States: A Log-Linear Approach." *Journal of Comparative Family Studies* 7:351–366.

Stack, C. B. 1974. *All Our Kin: Strategies for Survival in a Black Community.* New York: Harper & Row.

Staples, R. 1978. "Race, Liberalism-Conservatism and Premarital Sexual Permissiveness: A Bi-racial Comparison." *Journal of Marriage and the Family* 40(4):733–742.

Staples, R., and J. W. Smith. 1954. "Attitudes of Grandmothers and Mothers toward Child Rearing Practices." *Child Development* 25:91–97.

Stevens, J. H. 1984. "Black Grandmothers' and Black Adolescent Mothers' Knowledge about Parenting." *Development Psychology* 20(6):1017–1025.

Straus, M. A. 1977. "A Sociological Perspective on the Prevention and Treatment of Wife Beating." In *Battered Women*, edited by M. Roy, 194–238. New York: Van Nostrand Reinhold.

Sweet, J. A. 1977. "Further Indicators of Family Structure and Process for Racial and Ethnic Minorities." Paper presented at the Conference on the Demography of Racial and Ethnic Groups, Austin, Tex., October.

Tienda, M., and R. Angel. 1982. "Determinants of Extended Household Structure: Cultural Pattern or Economic Need?" *American Journal of Sociology* 87:1360-1383.

Tinsley, B. R., and R. D. Parke. 1984. "Grandparents as Support and Socialization Agents." In *Beyond the Dyad*, edited by M. Lewis, 161–195. New York: Plenum.

Tolson, T. J. F., and M. N. Wilson, 1990. "The Impact of Two- and Three-Generational Black Family Structure on Perceived Family Climate." *Child Development* 61:416–428.

U.S. Bureau of the Census. 1989. *Household and Family Characteristics: March 1988.* Current Population Reports, Series P-20, no. 437. Washington, D.C.: Government Printing Office.

Ventura, J. N., and M. B. Stevenson. 1986. "Relations of Mothers' and Fathers' Reports on Infant Temperament, Parents' Psychological Functioning and Family Characteristics." *Merill-Palmer Quarterly* 32:275–289.

Wilson, M. N. 1984. "Mothers' and Grandmothers' Perception of Parental Behavior in Three-Generational Black Families." *Child Development* 55(4): 1333–1339.

———. 1986. "Mothers', Fathers', and Grandmothers' Perception of Parental Activity in Three-Generational Black Families." Paper presented at the national convention of the Association of Black Psychologists, Washington, D.C.

Wilson, M. N., and T. F. J. Tolson, 1986. "A Social Interaction Analysis of

Two- and Three-Generational Black Families." In *In Praise of Fifty Years: Groves Conference on the Conservation of Marriage and the Family,* edited by P. Dail and R. Jewson, 43–53. Lake Mills, Iowa: Graphic Publishing.

Wilson, M. N., T. F. Tolson, I. Hinton and M. Kiernan. 1989. "Flexibility and Sharing of Childcare Duties in Black Families." *Sex Roles* 22(7/8):409–425.

Young, V. H. 1970. "Family and Childhood in a Southern Negro Community." *American Anthropologist* 72:269–288.

———. 1974. "A Black American Socialization Pattern." *American Ethnologist* 1:405–412.

5

RONALD L. TAYLOR

Child Rearing in African American Families

Well, son, I'll tell you: Life for me ain't been no crystal stair.
—LANGSTON HUGHES,
"Mother to Son"

Although research on African American child socialization has been conspicuous in the psychological and sociological literature since the late 1940s, the preponderance of this work is marked by multiple interpretative and methodological problems (Harrison, Serafica, and McAdoo 1984; Spencer, Brookins, and Allen 1985), faulty conceptualizations (Ogbu 1982; Young 1974), and the intrusion of ethnocentric values on the analysis of data (Allen 1978; Myers 1982; Staples 1971). A perusal of the literature presents a confusing and contradictory image of African American children. They are simultaneously presented as "both hero and villain, as both superior and inferior, as both the normal product of an organized social response to oppression and a pathological deviation from the normal social order" (Myers and King 1983:289).

These contradictory images reflect, among other things, a failure to grasp the considerable complexity associated with the processes of socialization and psychosocial development among African American children and youth in American society (Boykin and Toms 1985; Taylor 1976a), and the persistence of a conceptual apparatus ill-suited to this purpose. However, revisionist perspectives, incorporating a multidimensional, multicausal orientation and sophisticated methodologies, have begun to generate new insights into the characteristics, dynamics, and developmental outcomes of socialization in African American families.

This chapter reviews some of the research on child rearing in African American families. It is divided into four sɛctions. The first identifies some of the major shortcomings of previous investigations of African American child socialization and the apparent shifts in theoretical and problem orientations that such limitations have inspired in the literature. The second section considers the general socialization matrix of African American children and some of the critical issues to be addressed in empirical investigations of socialization processes in these families. Selected findings from the research of African American child socialization are reported in the third section, and the implications of these finding for future research and current practice are considered in the concluding section.

Race, Socialization Theory, and Research

Socialization, both as a concept and as a field of study in the social and behavioral sciences, encompasses an exceedingly broad range of phenomena (Inkeles 1969; Zigler and Child 1973). At the most general level, socialization refers to the process by which individuals acquire the knowledge, perceptions, values, attitudes, and behaviors that enable them to become competent members of groups and of the society to which they belong (Hartup 1978). It embraces childcare and training, the acquisition of language and self-concept, and the learning and enactment of social roles. The term simultaneously describes "a process or input, external to the person, the individual's experience of the process, and the end product or output" (Inkeles 1969:615). As society's basic institution, the family assumes major, if not exclusive, responsibility for early socialization, furnishing the child with an initial milieu and shaping a view of the social world.

The various aspects of socialization are approached from divergent perspectives and levels of analysis by social and behavioral scientists. Whereas psychologists have focused on the nature of the parent/child relationship and its effects on cognitive development, motivation, competence, and other personality variables in children (Baldwin 1980; Hartup 1978), sociologists, less concerned with personality development, have concentrated their efforts on delineating the broad sociohistorical context and the institutional apparatuses that influence individual learning and development. They emphasize, among other things, differential patterns of family interaction and the role of class-associated differences in child-rearing techniques, goals, and parental value systems in determining socialization outcomes in children and youth (Lerner and Spanier 1978).

Although the study of childhood socialization has produce a voluminous literature, relatively few studies have focused on African American children and the nature of socialization in their families (Bartz and Levine 1978; Harrison, Serafica, and McAdoo 1984). Moreover, as a number of literature reviews (Boykin and Toms 1985; Myers, Harris, and Rana 1979; Taylor 1976a) have shown, much of the empirical work in this area is of questionable validity and of limited import for understanding some of the critical dimensions of psychosocial development among African American children and youth, based as it is on theoretical constructs and assumptions that fail to take adequately into account their experiences in American society.

In assessing previous and contemporary studies devoted to socialization and the psychosocial development of African American children and youth, critics cite the ethnocentric bias implicit in much of this work (Bartz and Bartz 1970; Boykin 1986; Young 1970); the tendency to rely on a social-pathology, or "social-deficit," model in interpreting aspects of African American social life and behavior (Myers 1982; Valentine 1971); the treatment of African American families as homogeneous units and the ignoring of contextual and other sources of variability among such families (Allen 1978; Clark 1983); and the tendency to ignore or misinterpret evidence of distinctive cultural values and social norms among African American families that inform socialization practices and outcomes (Lewis 1975; Peters 1985; Young 1970). As a result, a distorted and pejorative view of these families has been perpetuated in the literature.

Although far less apparent in recent literature, the tendency to evaluate African American child-rearing practices from an idealized norm of white middle-class behavior has, nonetheless, been a prominent feature of research and other works in these areas since the 1940s (Howard and Scott 1981; Staples 1971). This ethnocentric bias, while acknowledging the existence of distinctively African American social organizations (for example, churches and civic, business, and political organizations), denies the existence of an indigenous African American culture that informs the social life and behavior of this group (Bartz and Bartz 1970; Boykin 1986).

The denial of African American culture as a vital force in the life of African American communities and families is consonant with the liberal ideological commitment to the principle of equality—that is, the belief that all people are equal under the law and are entitled to be treated as such—as well as the prevailing mythology of American society as a cultural melting pot. However, as Bartz and Bartz (1970:32) observe, this liberal ideology has often mistakenly equated equality with sameness: "The application of this misinterpreted egalitarian principle to social science data has often left the investigator with the unwelcome task of describing [black] behavior not as it is, but rather as it deviates from the normative system defined by the white middle-class."

It is but a short distance from the ethnocentric view that African Americans are "100 percent American" and nothing else, with "no values and culture to guard and protect" (Glazer and Moynihan 1963:53), to the conclusion that these families are "an impoverished version of the American white family, in which deprivation has induced pathologenic and dysfunctional features" (Young 1970:269). This view, dominant in the social science literature of the 1960s and the intellectual rationale for the social-intervention programs of the Great Society era (Zigler and Valentine 1979), saw African American children as products of unhealthy or "pathological" environments, seriously handicapped not only by the material deprivations associated with poverty but by negative experiences in their families and communities that induced a range of social and psychological deficits (Deutsch 1963; Hunt 1971; Young 1974). The deficit model was particularly influential in the literature on the language development, cognitive style, and emotional development of African American children. Other deficiencies were found in the areas of need achievement (Katz 1969), feelings of control over one's fate (Gurin 1969), and ability to defer gratification (Deutsch 1963; Lessing 1969).

Although variants are still found in the literature on African American child development, the deficit model has been sharply criticized and rejected by researchers who argue that this approach too readily interprets differences in the behavior and attitudes of these children as deficits (Baumrind 1971; Myers 1982; Ogbu 1979); is founded on data derived from studies of African American families at a distance (Bartz and Levine 1978; Hannerz 1969; Harrison, Serafica, and McAdoo 1984); and too frequently ignores the considerable heterogeneity among children from so-called culturally deprived backgrounds in language abilities, cognitive styles, and instrumental competence (Myers and King 1983; Ogbu 1985; Spencer 1985). Without denying the actual or potential debilitating effects of poverty and family disorganization on African American children, critics argue that there is no one-to-one relationship between economically deprived social circumstances and psychosocial outcomes for children (Bronfenbrenner 1979, 1958; Ogbu 1986; Silverstein and Krate 1975) and that, in the absence of an ethnohistorical perspective and ethnographically based research on the cultural and environmental contexts of African American child development, deficit-oriented comparative studies amount to little more than speculation (Phinney and Rotheram 1987).

The tendency to treat African American families as an "undifferentiated categorical mass of sameness" (Blackwell 1975:xi), ignoring the diversity and heterogeneity in their value orientations, attitudes, and life-styles, has been another major source of distortion and ill-founded conclusions about child-rearing practices and child development in these families. Findings derived from low-income African American families have frequently been generalized and accepted as descriptive of the family life of all African American families, thereby nourishing popular but unwarranted stereotypes (Nobles 1978; Peters 1981). Indeed, even among low-income African American families, as Lewis (1967) so forcefully demonstrated in his detailed investigation of child-rearing practices among such families in Washington, D.C., there are wide variations in family organization and life-styles. Thus, one of the principal effects, Lewis observes, of treating low-income African American families as though they are a homogeneous category is the tendency "to impute to a total category, such as the lower class, the depreciated, and probably more dramatic and threatening, characteristics of a segment of that category" (p. 154). In short, the confounding of race and class has been a characteristic weakness of many studies devoted to child-rearing and socialization processes in African American families (Allen 1985; Staples and Mirande 1980; Walters and Walters 1980), as has the tendency to ignore regional variations as well as other demographic factors in research designs (Bell-Scott and Taylor 1989; Boykin 1986; Young 1970).

The assumption of universal norms of behavior, the denial of African American culture, and the tendency to treat these families as a homogeneous category have all contributed to what Nobles (1978) and King (1978) have called transubstantive errors—that is, errors "wherein one defines or interprets the behavior and/or medium of one culture with 'meanings' appropriate to and consistent with another culture" (Nobles 1978:683). A similar view has been expressed by the anthropologist Young (1970), whose study of family organization and child-rearing practices in a southern African American community revealed the existence of a coherent, structured, and highly distinctive culture. She writes: "Where a historically and culturally distinct social group is studied, cultural differences should be assumed and the direct application of [social science] theory derived from other cultures should not" (p. 275). In short, the failure of social and behavioral scientists to go beyond the surface similarities to examine the behavior and life-styles of African Americans in their own right—that is, in their proper ecological and cultural contexts—has resulted in inaccurate assessments of the realities of African American family life, including the distinct socialization agenda for children.

These and other criticisms of the research literature on African American families and socialization helped to inspire significant revisions in theory and research in these areas during the 1970s. In fact, that decade saw the production of more research on African American family life than did any other period in the history of African American family studies (Staples and Mirande 1980). Emphasis shifted from a social-pathology perspective to an appreciation of the resilience and adaptiveness of these families under a variety of environmental conditions. Allen (1978) calls this new emphasis the cultural-variant perspective, which treats African American families as different but legitimate functional family forms. The differences result, in large measure, from differences in the cultural origins (African versus European) of African American and white families, which are reinforced by differences in historical experiences and socioeconomic positions in American society. From this perspective, "black language, cognitive styles, behavior patterns, and value preferences are socialized by-products adaptive to the black world" (Myers and King 1983:288). Similarly, African American children are seen as neither superior nor inferior to white children but simply as different. Although proponents of the cultural-difference model disagree as to the sources and content of cultural expressions in the social life of African-Americans (Banks 1976; Gutman 1976; Nobles 1978; Staples and Mirande 1980), they agree that evidence points to distinctive cultural patterns and behavioral practices indigenous to the United States (Hannerz 1969; Myers 1982; Young 1970) as well as to modes of conduct and orientation consistent with West African traditions (Boykin 1986; Lewis 1975; Nobles 1978).

Although the cultural-variant, or cultural-difference, model is generally credited with having provided an alternative to social-deficit perspectives long dominant in the literature on African American families, nonetheless the model has remained on an abstract level of conceptualization, untested by systematic research (Staples and Mirande 1980). In fact, some proponents of this perspective have been criticized for the tendency to exaggerate the adaptive strength and resilience of African American families, and for confusing adaptations to material deprivation and racial oppression with social health or well-being (Myers and King 1983; Ogbu 1985). In addition, the failure of proponents to acknowledge the strong and abiding commitment of these families to mainstream American values and practices has also been noted (Boykin and Toms 1985), as has their neglect of a number of critical issues associated with the socialization of African American children in a variety of institutional contexts (Allen 1978; Myers and King 1983).

Such criticisms notwithstanding, the cultural-variant and other revisionist perspectives on African American family life have provided a much-needed corrective to the ethnocentric and historically pejorative tradition of scholarship in this area by highlighting the limitations of conventional perspectives and assessments; focusing on the diversity, strengths, and assets of African American families; and illuminating many of the cultural features distinctive to their social organization (Boykin 1986). At the same time, the apparent limitations of revisionist perspectives have, in turn, inspired efforts to refine the theoretical and conceptual apparatus for the empirical study of African American families and child socialization (Ogbu 1985; Spencer, Brookins, and Allen 1985).

The Socialization Matrix for African American Children

In emphasizing the resilience and adaptiveness of African American families under conditions of structured inequality, revisionist scholars drew attention to the "missing context" (Bronfenbrenner 1979), or ecological milieu (its macrocosmic as well as its microcosmic elements), within which child socialization occurs, and the implications of this gap in knowledge for assessing development in terms of environmentally relevant outcomes. This new emphasis coincided with inchoate intellectual transformations already underway in the broad field of family studies (though notably absent from African American family studies), where research on families and human development was increasingly based on a life-span, or life-course, perspective, with its emphasis on time, process, and context (Elder 1984; Lerner and Spanier 1978). From this perspective, the study of families and socialization processes centers on social adaptation to multiple environments, which requires developmental, ecological, and historical analysis. Increasingly, as Hartup (1978:35) notes, "social scientists have learned, as their ethological colleagues learned long ago, that the adaptive significance of social activity can only be appreciated in systemic (polyadic) terms and with reference to survival in a particular social and cultural context."

Thus contextual analyses of child socialization involve much more than analysis of the microenvironment of parent/child interactions or intrafamilial processes; they must take account of macrocosmic forces (social, economic, and political) that determine the structural parameters, cultural imperatives, and thus the socialization agendas of parents and other child-rearing agents (Hartup 1978; Inkeles 1968). To assess the impact of such forces on the nature of child-rearing practices in African American families, Ogbu (1982, 1985) proposes a cultural-ecological approach, which he defines as "the study of institutionalized and socially transmitted patterns of behavior that are interdependent with features of the environment" (1982:262). More specifically, this approach focuses on the adaptive behaviors and strategies devised by identifiable cultural groups in a society for dealing with resources and new and recurrent problems. It conceives of child-rearing practices as "culturally organized formulae" for developing in children the instrumental competence appropriate for negotiating their sociocultural environment and for exploiting the opportunities available to them. In short, the cultural-ecological model, Ogbu contends, enables the investigator to "study the linkage between adult adaptations to ecological pressures, personality characteristics, and behavior resulting from such adaptations, and their relationship to childrearing practices" (1982:262).

It is generally acknowledged that the economic or subsistence system of a society tends to exert the most powerful influence on the nature of those instrumental competences or skills to be inculcated in children during socialization (Barry, Child, and Bacon 1959; Inkeles 1968). But as Ogbu (1985) points out, the strategies that people employ in responding to their subsistence or economic needs vary with the nature of their "effective environment"—technoeconomic resources and knowledge—and with the degree of access to the economic system. Thus, different populations "have evolved different strategies appropriate to the respective environments, and these strategies determine to a large degree, the repertoire of instrumental competences—physical skills, cognitive skills, communicative skills, social-emotional skills, etc.—characteristic of members of each population" (Ogbu 1985:51). In other words, in a stratified society, which provides differential access to economic opportunities and different resource environments for its members, different cultural imperatives are likely to require the acquisition of different instrumental competences appropriate to each particular environment.

Ogbu contends that marked differences in the historical and economic realities of African American and white American families have induced African Americans to "inculcate in their children language, cognitive, motivational, and social competences that differ from those of their white counterparts" (1982:255). These differences, he notes, are most pronounced among low-income African American families in the inner cities, where opportunities for adult participation in conventional economic activities are severely limited and where alternative subsistence economies, survival strategies, and folk theories of achievement and success have evolved that dictate the choice of child-rearing techniques or practices and the instrumental competences to be acquired.

Ogbu's analysis highlights a feature of child socialization documented in the work of a number of other scholars—namely, the necessity for African American children to adapt to two cultures simultaneously (Bronfenbrenner 1979; Valentine 1971; Young 1969). To be sure, the need to develop bicultural competence is by no means peculiar to African American children (Phinney and Rotheram 1987), but the cultivation of this capacity in their children present African American parents with a special and complex dilemma in view of their historical experiences and contemporary status in this society. Despite their manifest commitment to mainstream American values in the socialization of their children, these families are typically confronted with the realities of negotiating a historically racist and hostile environment, and with the imperatives that arise from a cultural tradition that is sharply at odds with prevailing mainstream ideology (Praeger 1982).

Boykin (1986) suggests that the socialization experience of African American children is best characterized as a "triple quandary"—as the need to negotiate three realms of experience: the mainstream, the minority, and the African American. Each of these experiential domains has its own psychological and behavioral repertoires, which frequently operate at cross-purposes. Unlike the experience of their white counterparts, for whom these three realms are largely isomorphic and easily integrated, the experiences of African American children and their families are fraught with discontinuities and contradictions. Consequently, these families may approach the socialization task in a variety of ways. As Boykin and Toms (1985:47) correctly observe:

> There is no monolithic Black experience. There is no singular socialization pathway. Indeed, there is a tapestry of variegated socialization possibilities. The particular socialization experiences in any one Black family would be represented by 1) the extent to which mainstream goals and values are promoted or embraced; 2) the particular domains in which these goals and values have been promoted or adopted; 3) the extent to which Black cultural socialization goals have been overtly articulated and promoted; 4) the orientation pattern and display of responses utilized to cope with oppressed minority status; and 5) the extent of Black cultural conditioning of children.

In short, how African American families perceive their life chances and those of their children will determine, in part, the relative emphasis given to the three domains of experience in dispatching their socialization functions.

The context of African American child socialization is powerfully influenced by myriad structural, cultural, and ecological forces, and by a diversity of demands for instrumental competences specific to these children. However, the interaction of these forces and their relative contributions to developmental outcomes among African American children have yet to receive systematic attention, although efforts have been made to synthesize and order the diverse factors and relationships that past research has shown to be influential in determining developmentally relevant outcomes for African American children (Blau 1981; Spencer, Brookins, and Allen 1985).

Emerging frameworks for empirical investigations of African American child socialization are beginning to incorporate a dynamic-interactional model of this process, emphasizing "the consequences of differing material circumstances, family characteristics, cultural patterns, and institutional settings for black child development" (Spencer, Brookins, and Allen 1985:301). The following section reviews some of the major findings accumulated from these empirical investigations, noting current gaps and limitations in scientific knowledge in this area.

African American Child Socialization: Characteristics, Dynamics, and Outcomes

In accounting for the outcomes of child socialization, researchers have typically focused on the following antecedent conditions: parental and family background characteristics; child-rearing orientations or goals; and parental child-rearing practices, including the quality of parent/child interactions (Allen 1985; Walters and Walters 1980). These conditions serve as the organizing framework for the following review and evaluation of the empirical literature on African American child socialization and developmental outcomes.

PARENTAL AND FAMILY BACKGROUND CHARACTERISTICS

Among those parental or family characteristics most often cited as having a substantial or significant influence on socialization outcomes for children are socioeconomic status and its correlates, family structure (single-parent versus two-parent), ethnicity or race, and such parental characteristics as age and sex (Allen 1985; Bronfenbrenner 1979; Phinney and Rotheram 1987; Staples and Mirande 1980; Walters and Walters 1980). Because of its presumed consequences for family structure, parental roles, and other features of the immediate sociocultural context of child development, the socioeconomic status of the family has received by far the most intensive investigation in the general literature on child socialization, if not in the research literature on African American children (Deutsch 1973; Hess 1970; H. P. McAdoo 1988). Although much of the research on class-associated differences in child-rearing goals, practices, and parental value systems has been sharply criticized on both methodological (Deutsch 1973; Johnson and Leslie 1965) and substantive (Harrison, Serafica, and McAdoo 1984; Zigler and Child 1973) grounds, there is considerable agreement concerning the influence of socioeconomic status on such broad dimensions of behavior as family roles and relationships, parental conceptions of parenthood, parental expectations for children, and general expressive styles and modal reactions to stress (Bartz and Levine 1978; Myers and King 1983; Zigler and Child 1973).

However, the extent to which the general findings regarding the effects of socioeconomic status (SES) on parental child-rearing orientations and behavior can be generalized to African American families remains unclear, given the limitations of standard measures of SES (occupational status and education) when applied to African American populations (Blau 1981; Deutsch 1973) and the failure of most research designs to control for the interactive effects of race and class (Allen 1978; Staples and Mirande 1980). In her study of socialization processes in middle- and working-class African American and white families, Blau (1981:18) observed that "greater consistency is found among the components of social status in the case of white than black families" and that "the use of occupational status and/or educational attainment does not truly serve to equalize the social environments in which children in the two races are reared." Thus, racial comparisons with respect to SES and family processes, including child-rearing practices, must be interpreted with great caution.

Family structure or composition (single-parent versus two-parent households) is likewise associated with outcomes for children in both African American and white families (Allen 1985; Scanzoni 1971). Numerous studies have shown that two-parent households are more successful in fostering high educational aspirations and achievement in their children than are single-parent households by virtue of the greater economic resources and other advantages that tend to accrue to two-parent families (Levitan and Belous 1981; Scanzoni 1985). Limited resources, together with multiple demands and responsibilities pose serious problems for single parents in discharging their child-rearing functions, resulting in social and psychological disadvantages for their children (Levitan and Belous 1981). Because the proportion of one-parent households is considerably greater among African American than white families and because a larger proportion of African American than other children live apart from either parent (Glick and Norton 1979), African American children are more likely to experience the social and psychological disadvantages associated with single-parent households than are other children (Myers and King 1983), especially the material or economic disadvantages. For instance, in 1984, more than half (54 percent) of all African American children were living in single-parent households with a median income of less than one-third that of African American husband/wife households (U.S. Bureau of the Census 1986).

Although there is little doubt that single-parent households are generally worse off economically than two-parent households, the net effects of being reared in such households are often difficult to disentangle or separate from economic or social-status variables (or both) (Levitan and Belous 1981; Silverstein and Krate 1975). Indeed, the body of research concerning the impact on child development of single-parent households suggests that the patterns are highly complex and defy simple conclusions (Baumrind 1971; Bronfenbrenner 1979; Levitan and Belous 1981). In one of the few empirical studies that sought to go beyond the compositional properties of the family unit to identify those internal processes that account for competence and achievement in children, Clark (1983:1) found in his intensive investigation of one- and two-parent households of low-achieving and high-achieving African American children that "it is the overall *quality* of the family's life style, not the composition, or status, or some subset of family process dynamics, that determines whether children are prepared for . . . competent performance." If Clark's analysis is correct, then much more attention must be given to the internal structure and cultural patterns of African American households and how these factors affect children's psychosocial development.

Yet, the increasingly younger ages at which single women are having to assume the responsibilities of motherhood present them and their children with a special set of problems (Ladner 1988). The incidence of out-of-wedlock childbearing among African American females ages fifteen to nineteen, for example, rose from 57 percent to 83 percent in 1981, and approached unity in 1985, when 90 percent of births to these teenagers were out of wedlock (Taylor 1987). Being an unmarried teenage mother is associated with many negative social, economic, and psychological consequences for the young female as well as the child. Compared with youth who postpone childbearing, teenage mothers have lower educational attainment, less income, higher unemployment (Card and Wise 1978) are more dependent on welfare (Moore and Burt 1982), are more likely to experience psychological problems associated with pregnancy (McLaughlin and Micklin 1983), are more likely to abuse or neglect their children (Furstenberg, Lincoln, and Menken 1981), and are more likely to have daughters who also become unwed teenage mothers (Chilman 1983). Moreover, babies of teenage mothers are more likely to be premature, to have low birth weight, and to die within the first months or year (National Center for Health Statistics 1980). Should they survive, these children are more likely to experience long-term problems such as mental retardation, cerebral palsy, and other birth injuries or neurological defects that require lifelong care (Alan Guttmacher Institute 1981). In short, the problems posed for teen mothers in discharging their socialization functions in this context are frequently overwhelming given their age and immaturity. Although the impact of premature fatherhood on adolescent males is less well documented, most teenage fathers are generally unprepared psychologically to assume the role of parent and provider for a family, and frequently experience depression and emotional conflict over their new status and responsibilities (Robinson and Barret 1987; Taylor 1989).

Although family structure, SES, age, and other variables are undoubtedly important in shaping the socialization of African American child rearing, these factors alone hardly account for the specific aspects of family organization, interaction, and cohesiveness that contribute to successful or unsuccessful socialization outcomes. "It is the family members' beliefs, activities, and *overall* cultural style" (Clark 1983:2) that must be the focus of attention in accounting for differential developmental outcomes in African American children.

PARENTAL GOALS IN CHILD-REARING

It is generally acknowledged that the most encompassing socialization goal of African American parents of all socioeconomic backgrounds is the preparation of their children to function in both the African American and mainstream cultures (Harrison, Serafica, and McAdoo 1984; Lewis 1975; Peters 1981; Spencer 1987). This overarching goal is reflected in the emphasis given to behavioral flexibility, control of emotions, early independence, and resiliency in the socialization of children (Clark 1983; Cross 1987; Ogbu 1985; Scanzoni 1985; Young 1984).

Differences in child-rearing beliefs and emphases, if not in techniques or practices, have been reported in a number of comparative studies of African American and other ethnic families (Bartz and Levine 1978; Durrett, O'Bryant, and Pennebaker 1975; Geismar 1973). For example, in their study of African American, Anglo, and Chicano mothers and fathers in a working-class neighborhood in the Midwest, Bartz and Levine (1978) found significant variations among these families with respect to their emphasis on the orientation toward parental control, support, permissiveness, strictness, egalitarianism, accelerated development, and the child's utilization of time. In contrast to white and Chicano parents, African American parents were typified by their strong belief "in the value of strictness, expecting early assumption of responsibility by a child for his or her own body functions and personal feelings, expecting that child's time will be used wisely and not wasted, encouraging a child's involvement in decision making, and exhibiting loving concern and care while also desiring to closely monitor a child's behavior to assure certain goals, i.e., obedience, achievement" (pp. 717–718). The researchers note, however, that observed ethnic differences in beliefs were largely matters of degree rather than reflections of opposing viewpoints. Similar results are reported by Durrett, O'Bryant and Pennebaker (1975) in their study of African American, Mexican American, and white low-income families, and by Geismar (1973) in his investigation of African American and white parents.

Beyond the overriding goal of preparing children for a bicultural existence and the desire to inculcate attitudes and behaviors designed to protect them from the dangers of racism (Powell 1983; Rainwater 1974), the goals and values associated with child rearing in African American families are strongly conditioned by their environments—the physical and socioeconomic contexts in which they are embedded—and by the nature of their experiences in their family of origin, as modified by subsequent experiences and influences such as friends and associates (Blau 1981; Clark 1983; Spencer 1985).

Given the myriad stress-inducing factors and exigencies of daily living associated with low-income ethnic status, it may be anticipated that low- and middle-income African American parents differ with respect to the emphasis given to certain qualities or virtues to be achieved in child socialization: low-income parents emphasizing the value of characteristics or qualities perceived to be necessary for survival in a context of severely restricted parental and communal resources (for example, the importance of mother-wit, early independence); middle-income parents aspiring to inculcate attributes (for example, perseverance, self-control) consistent with success and mobility in the larger society (Allen 1985; Blau 1981; Hess 1970; Silverstein and Krate 1975; Spencer 1985; Zegiob and Forehand 1975).

One of the major problems encountered in drawing valid conclusions about the child-rearing values and goals of African American parents is the paucity of systematic data currently available in this area. Many of the studies that do exist involve relatively small, unrepresentative samples, utilize inadequate indices of child-rearing values and practices, and focus on a limited range of value-relevant phenomena. The uneven, and often contradictory, results of studies that attempt to relate parental values or practices (or both) to developmental outcomes in African American children underscore the need for a sophisticated theoretical formulation of these links.

CHILD-REARING PRACTICES

Studies of child rearing in African American families have been available since the 1940s, when a series of publications sponsored by the American Council on Education focused on these families and child development in the context of a rigid system of racial segregation (Sutherland, 1942). These studies were consistent in the finding that the color/caste system exerted a powerful influence on the child-rearing practices of African American parents and on the development and behavior of their children. Thus, African American mothers were shown to be more rigid, punitive, and demanding in their child-rearing practices than white mothers. However, in their study of race and class differences in child rearing, Davis and Havighurst (1946) concluded that African American mothers and lower-class mothers in general were more permissive in their child-rearing practices than were white middle-class mothers. Moreover, they argued that class was more important in accounting for observed differences in child-rearing practices than race. However, Sears, Maccoby, and Levin (1957) drew opposite conclusions from their Boston study: that middle-class mothers were more permissive than lower-class mothers in their child-rearing practices and that such class differences occurred independently of race or ethnic differences.

In an effort to reconcile these and other contradictory findings on the relationship between social class and maternal reports of child-rearing practices in American families, Bronfenbrenner (1958) undertook a detailed review of the studies on child rearing published between 1928 and 1957, and concluded that the results of both studies were valid because of changes in child-rearing practices that had occurred over time in middle- and lower-class families. On the whole, middle-class parents were reported to be "developmental" in their approach to child rearing, attuned to the inner states of the child, and encouraging of a "democratic" relationship with their children. In contrast, lower-class parents were reported to be "traditional" in their child-rearing practices, preferring that children conform to external standards of conduct and community norms of respectability, and emphasizing obedience and respect for authority. A number of studies and reviews published subsequently to Bronfenbrenner's review reaffirm, in many respects, these general features of middle- and lower-class parental styles (Bartz and Levine 1978; Blau 1981; Deutsch 1973; Hess 1970; Zegiob and Forehand 1975).

In a series of studies involving African American mothers from four socioeconomic levels and their four-year-old children, Hess and associates (Hess and Shipman 1965; Hess et al. 1968) found SES differences on a range of observed and reported maternal behaviors, preferred teaching styles, and control strategies. In interacting with their children, middle-class mothers were observed to employ a "personal-subjective" teaching style, characterized by attentiveness to the child's feelings, interests, and preferences, the employment of explicit verbal instructions to the child about specific tasks and expectations, and the use of motivational and influence techniques involving explicit or implicit rewards. Working- and lower-class mothers were shown to favor a "status-normative" teaching style, involving an emphasis on physical compliance with imperative commands and instructions, less sensitivity to the moods and perspectives of the child, a more "restricted" communicative style, and the use of more coercive forms of punishment control. Baumrind (1968, 1971) observed similar differences in parental styles among African American families, and she identified them as "authoritative" and "authoritarian."

Likewise, Clark (1983) identifies two communicative styles preferred by low-income African American families in child rearing, both of which are shown to influence school achievement and competence in their children. The first he refers to as the "sponsored independence" style, in which parents exert their influence on the child in an "authoritative"—firm but responsive—manner. This style is characterized by active parental involvement in the child's home and school activities; consistent monitoring of the child's use of time and space; explicit achievement-centered rules and norms for behavior; regular praiseworthy sentiments expressed for the child's talents, abilities, and achievements; and liberal nurturing and support. A second style, referred to as "unsponsored independence," is associated with an "authoritarian"—arbitrary and unresponsive—mode of conduct toward the child, and is characterized by limited involvement and interest in the child's activities, inconsistent or nonexistent parental expectations and standards for responsible child behavior in the home or neighborhood, frequent criticism and expressions of dissatisfaction regarding the child's ability and worth, and infrequent engagement in achievement-training activities with the child. Among other things, Clark's study is important in demonstrating that parenting styles are as much a function of the context, resources, and network of social relationships of these parents as they are of socioeconomic or compositional properties of the family unit.

In her analysis of socialization and sex roles in African American families, Lewis (1975:232) concluded: "While sex is relatively unimportant and few patterned differences of behavior are seen between little boys and little girls, age and relative birth order are crucial determinants of differential treatment and behavioral expectations in black families." Lewis's conclusion is supported by a number of other studies (Ladner 1971; Rainwater 1974; Young 1970). Schutz (1977) found no differential socialization by sex during infancy and early childhood among the low-income African American families he studied in St. Louis. He concluded that gender-role socialization for males occurred largely outside the home and under the tutelage of peers. However, Lewis attributes the relative absence of emphasis on differential socialization by gender during early childhood to elements of African American culture that tend to synthesize rather than dichotomize traditional behavioral traits ascribed to males and females. She contends that African American child-rearing practices "instill in both male and female infants similar traits of assertiveness, willfulness, and independence" (1975:236). Indeed, both mothers and fathers are observed to display similar styles of interacting with children: Both are nurturing, affectionate, and have close physical contact with babies (J. McAdoo 1988; Young 1970, 1974).

By school age, however, as the research conducted by Blau (1981) shows, differential treatment and parental expectations by sex are apparent. Summarizing the findings from her study of middle- and working-class African American and white mothers of fifth- and sixth- graders drawn from three communities in Chicago, Blau (1981:161) reports:

In both races, maternal ambition is conditioned most by the child's sex at the low-SES level: among whites, mothers exhibit higher ambition for sons, and among blacks, ambitions are higher for daughters. In both races, mothers invest [time and other resources] more in daughters than in sons, but among blacks such sex differences are most pronounced at the middle-SES level and least pronounced at the high-SES level. Among whites such sex differentiation is most pronounced at the middle and high SES levels. In both races, aversive discipline is more frequently employed toward sons than daughters. These differences are most pronounced among blacks and most pronounced among whites at the high-SES level.

Lewis (1975) suggests one explanation for differential treatment and expectations for African American male and female children as they grow older: Early patterns of child socialization reflect the imperatives of African American culture, while later patterns reflect "more closely the structure of expectations and opportunities provided for black men and women by the dominant society . . . . At this later stage black socialization is adaptive to macrostructural constraints" (p. 237), as they operate differentially for African American males and females.

From the foregoing discussion it is apparent that African American parental goals and values are transmitted through a complex process involving indigenous cultural elements, social experiences, and education (Bartz and Levine 1978). However, the dynamic interplay of these factors—their combined and separate influence on developmental outcomes—is not clearly understood, and important gaps in knowledge remain. For example, data are scarce with respect to the process by which African American parents prepare their children to function in the mainstream, minority, and African American cultural realms, and to cope with the inevitable stresses evoked by these multiple experiences. In sum, a good deal more needs to be known about the "multiple ecologies" of African American child development and how these contexts are "manipulated by parents, families and other adults to produce functional human beings" (Spencer 1985:306).

OUTCOMES

Parental values and child-rearing practices have been associated with a range of critical developmental and social outcomes, including language, cognitive, motivational, and interpersonal competences in children (Baldwin 1980; Deutsch 1973; Zigler and Child 1973). But, as previously noted, results from studies attempting to relate parental values and child-rearing outcomes are conflicting and contradictory, particularly in cases involving African Americans (Bartz and Levine 1978; Myers 1982). Taking a comparative perspective on African American family life, with an emphasis on "social deficits," many studies have concluded that the nature of African American socialization is an important source of poor academic motivation, low achievement, poor self-esteem, and antisocial behavior among children and youth (Deutsch and Deutsch 1968; Hunt 1971; Silverstein and Krate 1975). However, a number of investigations refute the conclusion that African American children experience largely negative outcomes from the socialization process (Allen 1985; Hare 1980; Powell 1983; Spencer, Brookins, and Allen 1985). Because a review of the extensive body of literature on the variety of developmental outcomes among these children is beyond the scope of this chapter, only results from empirical investigations of self-concept (and self-esteem) and intellectual competence or performance among African American children are addressed.

Self-Concept and Self-Esteem

Although it is widely acknowledged that self-concept and self-esteem are the products of multiple experiences of children and youth, the central role of parents and other significant others in the development of such self-attitudes has been consistently documented (Porter and Washington 1979; Rosenberg and Simmons 1971; Taylor 1976a, 1976b). For African American children, especially those from low-income families, the paucity of positive role models in the home and in the immediate environment, combined with an awareness of minority status, has been assumed to explain, in part, their relatively low aspirations and self-esteem, and the observed tendency to select and identify with whites as significant others. Moreover, family conflict and disorganization are alleged to result in ambivalence toward the child and thus in inadequate socialization and in the failure of children to establish strong identifications with their parents (see Porter and Washington 1979 for a review of this literature). Thus, from the findings of his study of low-income African American families, Rainwater (1966, 1974) concluded that it is within such families that negative self-concepts are fostered and sustained: "In lower-class culture human nature is conceived as essentially bad, destructive and immoral, [and consequently] in the identity of development of the child he is consistently exposed to identity labeling by parents as a bad person" (1966:204). Hence the family becomes, in Rainwater's analysis, the primary mediator of negative self-images and low self-esteem for children, the conduit through which their negative psychosocial development is most thoroughly accomplished.

These and other often-cited conclusions about the nature, source, and characteristics of African American self-attitudes have been challenged on methodological (Ballard and Keller 1976), analytical (Banks 1976; Cross 1985), and interpretive (Taylor 1976a) grounds. Many studies in this area suffer from basic weaknesses in both design and methods of data analysis: the use of techniques for measuring self-referent constructs lacking in construct validity; inadequate controls for age, class, race, and sex; and the use of small, unrepresentative samples. In addition, many studies fail to distinguish between racial and personal self-esteem (Cross 1985), or global and specific self-esteem (Hare and Castenell 1985; Rosenberg 1979), which are shown to be distinct, although interrelated, concepts. Moreover, the presumption that African American self-concept and self-esteem are the results, in part, of reflected white attitudes toward African Americans is open to question because it has been demonstrated that the primary sources of reference for African American children on the personal level are significant others in their community, in interaction with whom their self-regard is sustained or changed (Rosenberg 1979; Taylor 1976a).

An exceptionally well-designed study conducted by Rosenberg and Simmons (1971) provides some of the most important results on self-esteem among African American children. Their study of a large, representative sample ($n = 1,988$) of African American and white pupils in grades three through twelve in Baltimore focused on relevant aspects of the social environments of these children in order to learn how "their respective social environments would bear upon their self-attitudes and how children of each race would respond to these environmental influences" (p. 3). The African American children did not have lower self-esteem than the white children; rather, their self-esteem appeared higher: "This fact remains unchanged even when socio-economic status is controlled, indeed, it remains unchanged when SES and age are controlled simultaneously" (p. 5). The influence of family structure, school performance, and skin color on self-esteem was also assessed with similar results. On the question of skin color, for example, the researchers found that although some preference for lighter skin among African American children in the sample was observed, as a group these children were "at least as likely as whites to consider themselves good-looking and to be happy with their looks" (p. 56). Thus, many of the factors widely assumed to reduce the level of self-esteem among African American children and youth—low racial status, poverty, single-parent family structure, and poor school performance—on close examination did not have the anticipated consequences for their self-regard.

The social context within which most of these children grow up is predominantly African American, a fact that has important implications for self-concept and self-esteem. Indeed, Rosenberg and Simmons (1971) found that racial insulation and the protective effects of a consonant environment were important conditions contributing to high self-esteem among African American children: "Broader social forces have operated to place the great bulk of black children in a relatively insulated environment and this environment establishes certain barriers to assaults upon their feelings of personal worth, such as direct expressions of prejudice" (p. 30).

On the basis of such evidence and their assessment of the data from some twelve other studies, Rosenberg and Simmons concluded that although these data probably do not justify the conclusion that the self-esteem of African Americans is higher than that of whites, neither do the data support the conclusion that their self-esteem is lower. Rather, African American and white children may reach high levels of self-esteem by different routes because of their different experiences.

A number of studies support the general conclusions on African American self-esteem reached by Rosenberg and Simmons (for example, Calhoun, Kurfiss, and Warren 1976; Hare 1980; Taylor 1976a). Such findings, however, should not be interpreted to imply that these children are relatively free of negative self-concepts or feelings of inadequacy. On the contrary, some studies report that African American children have higher levels of self-regard but lower feelings of personal efficacy (Hare 1980) and lower achievement orientations than their white counterparts (Blau 1981). What these and other results suggest is that race, like self-esteem, is one of several important components of the individual's self-concept, and that other phenomena are important in molding the child's feelings of self-worth (Rosenberg 1985).

In their review of studies on African American identify and self-esteem for the period 1968–1978, Porter and Washington (1979) concluded that new studies of general differences in self-esteem among African American and white populations were unnecessary in view of the empirical evidence now in hand. Instead, they recommended that future work in this area focus on the relationship among racial self-esteem, personal self-image, and social structure: "Variations in racial and personal self-esteem should be investigated with careful attention both to the effect of macrostructural factors and the specific situational and personal contexts in which these factors operate" (p. 70). In short, African American self-esteem and the context in which it emerges should be studied in its own right, free of normative interpretations and "transubstantive" errors.

Intellectual Competence and Scholastic Performance

Racial differences in children's measured intellectual ability and scholastic performance have been documented repeatedly in the literature. However, the sources and magnitude of such differences are a matter of continuing debate. Although some investigators have proffered a genetic interpretation of these differences (for example, Jensen 1969), others have advanced a structural or environmental explanation, pointing to the effects of SES, family structure, patterns of parent/child interaction, and other social processes on the development of intellectual competence and scholastic achievement in children (Bartz and Bartz 1970; Blau 1981; Silverstein and Krate 1975). Those who subscribe to a genetic interpretation assume that I.Q. scores and similar measures are a true index of cognitive skills as well as strong predictors of scholastic achievement, while proponents of an environmental view dispute the validity and reliability of such measures, particularly for African American children and youth. They note, for example, the cultural bias inherent in standard I.Q. tests, the narrow range of abilities assessed by such measures, the tendency to confuse competence with performance, and the variability of performance among children under differing conditions.

As presently constructed, most standard I.Q. tests are culturally biased in that they reflect a single frame of reference that favors individuals familiar with this perspective and the material information being requested (Silverstein and Krate 1975). Yet, acknowledging cultural bias does not explain why many African American children score as high or higher on such tests as their white counterparts (Blau

1981). It is also the case that I.Q. tests assess only one form of intellectual ability—namely, scholastic competence—while ignoring other abilities such as creativity and sustained problem solving. Hence, it is not surprising that I.Q. test scores are moderately good predictors of scholastic achievement among children as schools are currently organized. Moreover, as a number of investigators have shown, the poor performance of minority and low-income children on conventional I.Q. tests has often been interpreted as a "true" measure of the level of their intellectual competence, when in fact such poor performance is frequently the result of contextual factors (unfamiliar and impersonal testing settings, race and skills of test administrators) or a function of differences in behavioral reactions of African American and white children to aspects of a test situation (Ogbu 1986; Zigler, Abelson, and Seitz 1973). Similarly, sharp increases in I.Q. scores of African American children when contextual factors are manipulated to reduce anxiety and increase test-taking confidence suggest that observed differences between them and white children are, in large measure, a function of motivation rather than competence (Boykin 1986; Silverstein and Krate 1975).

In view of the shortcomings of I.Q. tests, including the tendency on the part of school personnel and other professionals to misuse them, some critics advise abolishing such tests as measures of cognitive processes or abilities. Although the elimination of mass testing in schools would diminish the widespread practice of sorting children on the basis of supposedly objective standardized test scores, it would not cause the observed differences in school performance between African American and white children to disappear. Indeed, as Blau (1981:xvii) observes: "The important issue is not tests or their abolition but rather the identification of the properties of social structures and the social processes that promote differential intellectual and scholastic competence among children being reared in families that are very differently situated in American society." In sum, it is now clearer than ever that the context of child development is a critical determinant of cognitive processes and overt performance, and that a better understanding of differential levels of competence and achievement among children must be sought in the properties of the social environment rather than in the characteristics of children themselves (Bronfenbrenner 1979).

Such variables as race, SES, sex, and religious or denominational affiliation have all been shown to exert some independent influence on the intellectual ability and school performance of children (Blau 1981;

Deutsch 1973; Hess 1970). Moreover, the effects of these variables are mediated by social processes within families. Blau's (1981) study is exceptional in the thoroughness with which it assesses the contributions of structural (race, SES, sex, and religious affiliation) and socialization (parental child-rearing values and behavior) variables to the intellectual and scholastic competence of African American and white children. Blau interviewed middle- and working-class mothers of 579 African American and 523 white fifth and sixth graders enrolled in integrated and segregated schools in three communities in Chicago. Extensive data were obtained on parental background and present status, family structure, parental child-rearing values and practices, and other social factors that have been found to influence the development of intellectual competence in children "in order to account for their differences in measured ability in the early years of schooling" (p. xv). As a measure of intellectual competence and scholastic achievement, the most recent I.Q. and achievement test scores were obtained from school records for each child involved in the study.

Blau employed two alternative models in identifying the sources of observed variations in intellectual and scholastic competence within and between the two races: a "structural model," including such variables as the SES origins and current status of parents, religious and denominational affiliation and religiosity of mothers, family structure, and sex of the study child; and a "socialization model," including mother's membership in organizations, family size, mothers' valuation of education, investment in the child, and belief in and use of aversive discipline.

Assessing the effects of the several components of the structural model on children's intellectual and scholastic achievement, Blau found that although the SES of the family was a significant predictor of children's I.Q. and achievement-test scores, a decomposition of SES into four constituent variables—parents' social-class origins, parents' educational attainment, occupational status of higher-ranking parent, and mother's social milieu (her network of family, friends, and associates)—revealed that mother's social milieu, followed by parents' social-class origins, were better predictors of African American children's I.Q. scores (though not of achievement-test scores) than white children's, where parents' educational attainment was the strongest predictor. In addition, religious and denominational affiliation was also found to exert some influence on children's I.Q. scores and scholastic achievement, with its having a more negative effect on African

American than on white children. A Baptist or other fundamentalist affiliation, for instance, was shown to depress I.Q. scores, while a nondenominational or nonreligious background had a weak but significant positive effect on African American children's scores. Blau concluded that "differences in the religious constituency and involvement of the two races are a significant source of the disparity in black and white children's I.Q. scores independently of socioeconomic differences" (1981:190).

Among family variables, the mother's years in the labor force since birth of the child and mother's organizational memberships were positive predictors of African American I.Q. scores (but negative predictors for white children), whereas family size exerted the strongest negative effect. Interestingly, the presence of the father in the home had no significant effect on these children's I.Q. scores but did exert a small positive effect on their achievement-test scores. Sex of the child was found to be a significant predictor of white children's I.Q. scores (with girls scoring higher than boys), but not of African American children's scores. For girls of both races, SES was a stronger predictor of I.Q scores than it was for boys, as was family size; and presence of father in the home was found to benefit girls but had no independent effect on boys' scores.

However, Blau found that the effects of structural variables on children's I.Q. scores and scholastic achievement were mediated by three dimensions of socialization within families—namely, mother's valuation of education, investment of resources in the child (time, effort, knowledge, and money), and the belief in and use of aversive discipline. These three dimensions of socialization were found to be interrelated for both races. In general, African American mothers exceeded their white counterparts in their ambitions for their children's future attainment and were not found to invest fewer of the resources at their disposal than white mothers. However, sex of the child conditioned maternal values and socialization strategies in both groups. African American mothers were found to hold higher ambitions for their daughters than for their sons, and to invest more time and resources in them.

Moreover, a major difference between parents was found in the use of aversive forms of control in socializing children. Reliance on aversive forms of control was not only more prevalent among African American parents of all socioeconomic levels, but they were used more frequently in disciplining sons than daughters. As Blau (1981:

204) noted, "Next to SES, sex of the child is the strongest single predictor of how extensively black mothers rely on aversive forms of control as a means of socializing their children." The greater use of aversive forms of control among African American mothers is explained in part by the influence of their religious beliefs and affiliations—that is, by the prevalence of fundamentalist values, which stress obedience and conformity in child rearing, while discouraging curiosity and flexibility.

Thus, although maternal valuation of education and investment in the study child were predictors of test performance among children of both races, the weight exerted by each dimension was slightly stronger on white than on African American scores "because discipline, a predictor only of black children's scores, serve[d] to weaken the effects of higher maternal ambition and investment in children" (p. 204). In short, Blau concluded that the complex effects of race, sex of child, and social-structural and religious variables tended to exaggerate the observed differences in the test performance of African American and white children and that, when taken systematically into account, they fully explain racial disparities.

The results of Blau's study highlight the multiple sources of variability in the intellectual competence and scholastic achievement of African American children, as well as the complexities involved in drawing valid conclusions about the measured intelligence of these children relative to their white counterparts. As this and other studies (for example, Clark 1983; MacKenzie 1984) make clear, the poor intellectual skills and school performance of many African American children result not from any intrinsic intellectual incompetence on their part but from the circumstances of their existence, which often sap their energies, dampen their spirit, and diminish their strivings for competence and mastery.

Implications and Conclusions

Reviewing the vast literature on African American families makes one keenly aware of the diversity in values, life-styles, family structure, and religious beliefs and practices among such families, and the highly complex ways in which these variables interact to influence the process and outcomes of child socialization. Yet, African American families share in common the task of preparing their children to function competently in both the mainstream and African American cultures, each of which requires the cultivation of distinctive psychological and behavioral repertoires.

How these families approach and discharge this task is not clearly understood, but there is some evidence (for example, Young 1974) that, insofar as African American cultural values are concerned, they tend to be transmitted largely through a "tacit" socialization process-that is, "a process through which children pick up modes, sequences, and styles of behavior through their day-to-day encounters with parents and other family members" (Boykin and Toms 1985:42)—rather than through formal and systematic instruction. Thus, rather than being socialized to an articulated set of conventions or rules for behavior, African American children tend to be socialized to cultural styles and motifs. This tacit socialization process may explain, as the anthropologist Young (1974:412) observes, "why Black Americans' behavior has often been analyzed as pragmatic rather than culturally conditioned . . . . Culture is more easily recognized when it takes the form of specific rule-based and value-based behavior than when it consists of modes, sequences and styles of behavior." Indeed, such a tacit cultural-conditioning process is congruent with verbal and nonverbal modes of communication encompassed by the Africentric perspective, and with such components of this perspective as affectivity, spirituality, expressive individualism, and communalism (Boykin 1986). Nonetheless, additional systematic research in this area could provide useful insights into the process by which African American children are prepared to negotiate the majority and minority realms of experience, and could help to account for the cultural and adaptive styles these children display.

Except for a few investigations, the preponderance of extant research on African American child socialization still lacks a developmental perspective—a life-course view of human development that attempts to integrate psychological and sociocultural factors within a dynamic-interactional and historical frame of reference (Lerner and Spanier 1978). A life-course developmental perspective is essential to a comprehensive understanding of those factors that promote stability as well as change in the personalities and behavior of African American children over time. Indeed, the need for such a perspective seems critical for adequate assessments of the consequences for African American children of recent and dramatic changes in the environments of African American families residing in the inner cities, where, as a consequence of perverse demographic trends, deteriorating local economies, and intractably high levels of urban poverty, they are experiencing increasing difficulties discharging their socialization responsibilities (Taylor 1989).

Their difficulties are exacerbated by the growing disharmony and disequilibrium of community institutions that traditionally facilitate the socialization process. As Ianni (1983:71) has observed: "Not only are the institutions in the inner city often in competition with each other and so unable to provide a coordinated structure of socialization to protect the growing child and adolescent against the vicissitudes of urban living, [but] the size and complexity of such areas provide an opportunity structure for spontaneous structures of socialization to develop which are detrimental to the [child]." These developments are bound to have long-term consequences for African American development and require immediate and systematic attention.

Indeed, both common sense and research tell us that sustained family stress, whether occasioned by chronic unemployment, inadequate income, the need for health care, family discord, or continuing exposure to a life-threatening environment, increases the risk for children of impaired psychosocial development. As one study concludes: "Children surrounded by chaos, defeat, unpredictability, and despair are less likely to learn the rules of an orderly universe, to develop logical reasoning skills, or to believe in their own efficacy. In homes where economic and social stresses are high and parental education low, children are less likely to have conversations with adults of a kind and frequency that stimulate the development of language and logical reasoning" (Schorr 1988:181).

To be sure, many African American children can and do make it in such socially impoverished environments but usually as a result of supportive relationships within or outside the family, or because of their own personal ego strength. Lacking such supports or personal resources, other children succumb to feelings of frustration, impotence, worthlessness, and despair. In the absence of intervention, such attitudes are likely to become chronic and debilitating.

How policymakers and social service professionals can effectively contribute to a reduction in the actual or potential risks to such children has been outlined by Schorr (1988). Assessing the wide range of social programs targeted for poor families and children since the 1950s, Schorr concludes that the most successful interventions are those that "see the child in the context of family and the family in the context of its surroundings" (p. 257).

The implication of this conclusion, as well as the conclusion to be drawn from much of the research cited, is that child welfare policies and practices are likely to be effective in enhancing the well-being of African American and other minority children when they are attuned to and are respectful of the bicultural context within which these children and their families are embedded. For African American children, this requirement implies increased awareness of the ways in which cultural values inform their cognitive and behavioral styles, and the potential for cultural conflict inherent in their attempts to deal simultaneously with their own ethnicity and the majority culture. Failure to appreciate this conflict has often resulted in misinterpretations of the cognitive, motivational, or behavioral characteristics of African American children and the perpetuation of myths and stereotypes about the qualities of their families.

Although medical, mental health, and social service professionals are beginning to recognize the importance of minority values and beliefs for optimal service delivery, such insights have yet to be incorporated into child welfare policies and practices and are unlikely to be so in the near future as long as such policies and practices aspire to uniformity in addressing the special needs of minority children and their families. What is essential, therefore, is the inclusion of transcultural perspectives in the formulation and implementation of social welfare policy.

Just as awareness of the cultural context is vital in understanding the nature of African American child development and the socialization agendas of these families, so too is awareness of the broad social context within which such families are situated. In a word, African American families, like all families, do not exist in a historical or cultural vacuum but are profoundly influenced by the nature of their relationship to the larger society. It is in grasping the dynamics of this complex relationship that one can understand changes in African American parental values and child-rearing practices, and the implications of these changes not only for developmental outcomes among their children but for social policy and practice.

References

Alan Guttmacher Institute. 1981. *Teenage Pregnancy: The Problem That Hasn't Gone Away.* New York.
Allen, W. R. 1978. "The Search for Applicable Theories of Black Family Life." *Journal of Marriage and the Family* 40:117–129.

————. 1985. "Race, Income, and Family Dynamics: A Study of Adolescent Male Socialization Processes and Outcomes." In *Beginnings: The Social and Affective Development of Black Children,* edited by M. Spencer, G. Brookins, and W. Allen, 273–292. Hillsdale, N. J. Erlbaum.

Baldwin, A. 1980. *Theories of Child Development.* New York: Wiley.

Ballard, B., and H. Keller. 1976. "Development of Racial Awareness: Task Consistency, Reliability, Validity." *Journal of General Psychology* 129:3–11.

Banks, W. 1976. "White Preference in Blacks: A Paradigm in Search of a Phenomenon." *Psychological Bulletin* 3:1179-1186.

Barry, H., I. L. Child, and M. I. Bacon. 1959. "Relations of Childtraining to Subsistence Economy." *American Anthropologist* 61:51–63.

Bartz, K., and E. Levine. 1978. "Childrearing by Black Parents: A Description and Comparison to Anglo and Chicano Parents." *Journal of Marriage and the Family* 40:709–720.

Bartz, S., and J. Bartz. 1970. "Early Childhood Intervention: The Social Science Base of Institutional Racism." *Harvard Educational Review* 40:29–50.

Baumrind, D. 1968. "Authoritarian vs. Authoritative Control." *Adolescence* 3:255–272.

————. 1971. "Current Patterns of Parental Authority." *Developmental Psychology Monograph:* 99–102.

Bell-Scott, P., and R. L. Taylor, 1989. "The Multiple Ecologies of Black Child Development." *Journal of Adolescent Research* 4:119–124.

Blackwell, J. E. 1975. *The Black Community: Diversity and Unity.* New York: Dodd, Mead.

Blau, Z. S. 1981. *Black Children/White Children: Competence, Socialization and Social Structure.* New York: Free Press.

Boykin, A. W. 1986. "The Triple Quandary and the Schooling of Afro-American Children." In *The School Achievement of Minority Children,* edited by U. Neisser, 57–92. Hillsdale, N. J.: Erlbaum.

Boykin, A. W., and F. D. Toms. 1985. "Black Child Socialization: A Conceptual Framework." In *Black Children,* edited by H. P. McAdoo and J. L. McAdoo, 33–54. Beverly Hills, Calif.: Sage.

Bronfenbrenner, U. 1958. "Socialization and Social Class through Time and Space." In *Readings in Social Psychology,* 3d ed., edited by E. E. Maccoby, T. M. Newcomb, and E. L. Hartley, 400–424. New York: Holt.

————. 1979. "Contexts of Childrearing: Problems and Prospects," *American Psychologist* 34:844–850.

Calhoun, G., J. Kurfiss, and P. Warren. 1976. "A Comparison of Self-Concept and Self-Esteem of Black and White Boys." *Clearinghouse* 50:131–133.

Card, J. J., and L. L. Wise. 1978. "Teenage Mothers and Teenage Fathers: The Impact of Early Childbearing on the Parents' Personal and Professional Lives." *Family Planning Perspectives* 10:199–205.

Chilman, D. 1983. *Adolescent Sexuality in a Changing American Society.* New York: Wiley.

150   R. L. TAYLOR

Clark, R. M. 1983. *Family Life and School Achievement: Why Poor Black Children Succeed or Fail.* Chicago: University of Chicago Press.

Cross, W. E. 1985. "Black Identity: Rediscovering the Distinction between Personal Identity and Reference Group Orientation." In *Beginnings: The Social and Affective Development of Black Children,* edited by M. B. Spencer, G. K. Brookings, and W. R. Allen, 155–172, Hillsdale, N.J.: Erlbaum.

———. 1987. "A Two-Factor Theory of Black Identity: Implications for the Study of Identity Development in Minority Children." In *Children's Ethnic Socialization,* edited by J. S. Phinney and M. J. Rotheram, 117–133. Beverly Hills, Calif.: Sage.

Davis, A., and R. Havighurst. 1946. "Social Class and Color Differences in Childrearing." *American Sociological Review* 2:698–710.

Deutsch, C. P. 1973. "Social Class and Child Development." In *Review of Child Development Research,* edited by B. M. Caldwell and H. N. Ricciuti, vol. 3, 233–282. Chicago: University of Chicago Press.

Deutsch, C. P., and M. Deutsch. 1968 "Brief Reflections on the Theory of Early Childhood Enrichment Programs." In *Early Education,* edited by R. D. Hess and R. M. Bear, 83–90. Chicago: Aldine.

Deutsch, M. 1963. "The Disadvantaged Child and the Learning Process." In *Education in Depressed Areas,* edited by A. H. Passow, 163–179. New York: Columbia University Press.

Durrett, M. E., S. O'Bryant, and J. W. Pennebaker. 1975. "Childrearing Reports of White, Black, and Mexican-American Families." *Developmental Psychology* 11:871.

Elder, G. H. 1984. "Families, Kin and the Life Course: A Sociological Perspective." In *Review of Child Development Research: The Family,* edited by R. Parke, 80–136. Chicago: University of Chicago Press.

Furstenberg, F., R. Lincoln, and J. Menken. 1981. *Teenage Sexuality, Pregnancy and Childbearing.* Philadelphia: University of Pennsylvania Press.

Geismar, L. L. 1973. *555 Families.* New Brunswick, N.J.: Transaction Books.

Glazer, N., and D. P. Moynihan. 1963. *Beyond the Melting Pot.* Cambridge: MIT Press.

Glick, P. C., and H. J. Norton. 1979. "Marrying, Divorcing and Living Together in the U. S. Today." *Population Bulletin,* 32(5): 3–33.

Gurin, P. 1969. "Internal-External Control in the Motivational Dynamics of Negro Youth." *Journal of Social Issues* 25:29–53.

Gutman, H. G. 1976. *The Black Family in Slavery and Freedom, 1750–1925.* New York: Pantheon.

Hannerz, U. 1969. *Soulside: Inquiries into Ghetto Culture and Community.* New York: Columbia University Press.

Hare, B. R. 1980. "Self-Perception and Academic Achievement Variations in a Desegregated Setting." *American Journal of Psychiatry* 137:683–689.

Hare, B. R., and L. A. Castenell. 1985. "No Place to Run, No Place to Hide: Comparative Status and Future Prospects of Black Boys." In *Beginnings:*

The Social and Affective Development of Black Children, edited by M. B. Spencer, G. K. Brookins, and W. R. Allen, 201–214. Hillsdale, N.J.: Erlbaum.

Harrison, A., F. Serafica, and H. P. McAdoo. 1984. "Ethnic Families of Color." In *Review of Child Development Research,* edited by R. D. Parke, 329–367. Chicago: University of Chicago Press.

Hartup, W. 1978. "Perspectives on Child and Family Interaction: Past, Present and Future." In *Child Influences on Marital and Family Interaction: A Life Span Perspective,* edited by R. Lerner and G. Spanier, 23–42. New York: Academic Press.

Hess, R. D. 1970. "Social Class and Ethnic Influences upon Socialization." In *Carmichael's Manual of Child Psychology,* edited by P. H. Mussen, vol. 2, 457–557. New York: Wiley.

Hess, R. D., and V. C. Shipman. 1965. "Early Experiences and the Socialization of Cognitive Modes in Children." *Child Development* 34:869–886.

Hess, R. D., V. C. Shipman, J. Brophy, and R. Bear. 1968. "Cognitive Environments of Urban Preschool Negro Children." In *Report to the Children's Bureau.* Washington, D. C. : Social Security Administration, U. S. Department of Health, Education and Welfare.

Howard, H., and R. Scott. 1981. "The Study of Minority Groups in Complex Societies." In *Handbook of Cross-Cultural Human Development,* edited by R. Munroe, R. Munroe, and B. Whiting, 113–152. New York: Garland.

Hunt, J. 1971. "Parent and Child Centers: Their Basis in the Behavioral and Educational Sciences." *American Journal of Orthopsychiatry* 41:13–38.

Ianni, F. A. J. 1983. *Home, School, and Community in Adolescent Education.* ERIC Document Reproduction Service no. ED 336 300. New York: Institute for Urban and Minority Education, Columbia University.

Inkeles, A. 1968. "Society, Social Structure, and Child Socialization." In *Socialization and Society,* edited by J. A. Clausen, 73–129. Boston: Little, Brown.

———. 1969. "Social Structure and Socialization." In *Handbook of Socialization Theory and Research,* edited by D. A. Goslin, 615–632. Chicago: Rand McNally.

Jensen, A. R. 1969. "How Much Can We Boost I.Q. and Scholastic Achievement?" *Harvard Educational Review* 39(1):1–123.

Johnson, K. P., and G. R. Leslie. 1965. "Methodological Notes on Research in Childrearing and Social Class." *Merrill-Palmer Quarterly* 11:345–358.

Katz, I. 1969. "A Critique of Personality Approaches to Negro Children with Research Suggestions." *Journal of Social Issues* 25(3):13–27.

King, L. M. 1978. "Social and Cultural Influences on Psychopathology." *Annual Review of Psychology* 29:405–433.

Ladner, J. A. 1971. *Tomorrow's Tomorrow: The Black Woman.* New York: Doubleday, Anchor Books.

———. 1988. "The Impact of Teenage Pregnancy on the Black Family: Policy

Directions." In *Black Families*, 2d ed., edited by H. P. McAdoo, 296–305. Beverly Hills, Calif.: Sage.

Lerner, R., and G. Spanier. 1978. *Child Influences on Family and Marital Interaction: A Life-Span Perspective*. New York: Academic Press.

Lessing, E. E. 1969. "Racial Differences in Indices of Ego Functioning Relevant to Academic Achievement." *Journal of Genetic Psychology* 115: 153–167.

Levitan, S. A., and R. S. Belous. 1981. *What's Happening to the American Family?* Baltimore: Johns Hopkins University Press.

Lewis, D. 1975. "The Black Family: Socialization and Sex Roles." *Phylon* 36:221–237.

Lewis, H. 1967. "Culture, Class, and Family Life among Low-Income Urban Negroes." In *Employment, Race, and Poverty*, edited by A. M. Ross and H. Hill, 149–174. New York: Harcourt, Brace & World.

McAdoo, H. P., ed. 1988. *Black Families*. 2d ed. Beverly Hills, Calif.: Sage.

McAdoo, J. 1988. "The Role of Black Fathers in the Socialization of Black Children." In *Black Families*, 2d ed., edited by H. P. McAdoo, 257–269. Beverly Hills, Calif.: Sage.

McLaughlin, S. C., and M. Micklin. 1983. "The Timing of the Birth and Changes in Personal Efficacy." *Journal of Marriage and the Family* 45:47.

Moore, K. A., and M. R. Burt. 1982. *Private Crisis, Public Cost: Political Perspectives on Teenage Childbearing*. Washington, D.C.: Urban Institute.

Myers, H. F. 1982. "Research on the Afro-American Family: A Critical Review." In *The Afro-American Family: Assessment, Treatment and Research Issues*, edited by B. A. Bass, G. E. Wyatt, and G. J. Powell, 35–68. New York: Grune & Stratton.

Myers, H. F., M. Harris, and P. E. Rana. 1979. *The Black Child in America, 1927–1977: An Annotated Bibliography*. Westport, Conn.: Greenwood Press.

Myers, H. F., and L. M. King. 1983. "Mental Health Issues in the Development of the Black American Child." In *The Psychosocial Development of Minority Group Children*, edited by G. J. Powell, 275–306. New York: Brunner/Mazel.

National Center for Health Statistics. 1980. "Final Natality, 1978." *Monthly Vital Statistics Report* 29:1–27.

Nobles, W. W. 1978. "Toward an Empirical and Theoretical Framework for Defining Black Families." *Journal of Marriage and the Family* 40:679–688.

Ogbu, J. U. 1979. "Social Stratification and Socialization of Competence." *Anthropology and Education Quarterly* 10(1):3–20.

———. 1982. "Socialization: A Cultural Ecological Perspective." In *The Social Life of Children in a Changing Society*, edited by K. Borman, 253–267. Hillsdale, N.J.: Erlbaum.

———. 1985. "A Cultural Ecology of Competence among Inner-City Blacks." In *Beginnings: The Social and Affective Development of Black Chil-*

dren, edited by M. B. Spencer, G. K. Brookins, and W. R. Allen, 44–66. Hillsdale, N.J. : Erlbaum.

———. 1986. "The Consequences of the American Caste System." In *The School Achievement of Minority Children: New Perspectives*, edited by U. Neisser, 19–56. Hillsdale, N.J.: Erlbaum.

Peters, M. F. 1981. "Parenting in Black Families with Young Children: A Historical Perspective." In *Black Families*, edited by H. P. McAdoo, 211–224. Beverly Hills, Calif.: Sage.

———. 1985. "Racial Socialization of Young Black Children." In *Black Children*, edited by H. P. McAdoo and J. L. McAdoo, 159–173. Beverly Hills, Calif.: Sage.

Phinney, J. S., and M. J. Rotheram, eds. 1987. *Children's Ethnic Socialization: Pluralism and Development*. Beverly Hills, Calif.: Sage.

Porter, J. R., and R. E. Washington. 1979. "Black Identity and Self-Esteem: A Review of Studies of Black Self-Concept, 1968–1978." In *Annual Review of Sociology*, edited by A. Inkeles, 5, 53–74. Palo Alto, Calif.: Annual Reviews.

Powell, G. J. 1983. "Coping with Adversity: The Psychosocial Development of Afro-American Children." In *The Psychosocial Development of Minority Children*, edited by G. J. Powell, 49–76. New York: Brunner/Mazel.

Praeger, J. 1982. "American Racial Ideology as Collective Representation." *Ethnic and Racial Studies* 5:119.

Rainwater, L. 1966. "Crucible of Identity: The Negro Lower-Class Family." *Daedalus* 95(1):172–216.

———. 1974. *Behind Ghetto Walls: Black Family Life in a Federal Slum*. Chicago: Aldine.

Robinson, B., and R. L. Barrett. 1987. "Self-Concepts and Anxiety of Adolescent and Adult Fathers." *Adolescence* 22:611–616.

Rosenberg, M. 1979. *Conceiving the Self*. New York: Basic Books.

———. 1985. "Summary." In *Beginnings: The Social and Affective Development of Black Children*, edited by M. B. Spencer, G. K. Brookins, and W. R. Allen, 231–234. Hillsdale, N.J.: Erlbaum.

Rosenberg, M., and R. Simmons. 1971. *Black and White Self-Esteem: The Urban School Child*. Washington, D. C.: American Sociological Association.

Scanzoni, J. H. 1971. *The Black Family in Modern Society*. Boston: Allyn & Bacon.

———. 1985. "Black Parental Values and Expectations of Children's Occupational and Educational Success: Theoretical Implications." In *Black Children*, edited by H. P. McAdoo and J. L. McAdoo, 113–122. Beverly Hills, Calif.: Sage.

Schorr, L. 1988. *Within Our Reach: Breaking the Cycle of Disadvantage*. New York: Doubleday, Anchor Books.

Schutz, D. A. 1977. *Coming up Black: Patterns of Ghetto Socialization*. Englewood Cliffs, N.J.: Prentice-Hall.

Sears, R. R.,. E. E. Maccoby, and H. Levin. 1957. *Patterns of Childrearing*. Evanston, Ill.: Row & Peterson.

Silverstein, B., and R. Krate. 1975. *Children of the Dark Ghetto: A Developmental Psychology*. New York: Praeger.

Spencer, M. B. 1985. "Cultural Cognition and Social Cognition as Identity Correlates of Black Children's Personal-Social Development." In *Beginnings: The Social and Affective Development of Black Children*, edited by M. B. Spencer, G. K. Brookins, and W. R. Allen, 215–230. Hillsdale, N.J.:Erlbaum.

———. 1987. "Black Children's Ethnic Identity Formation: Risk and Resilience of Castelike Minorities." In *Children's Ethnic Socialization: Pluralism and Development*, edited by J. S. Phinney and M. J. Rotheram, 103–116. Beverly Hills, Calif.: Sage.

Spencer, M. B., G. K. Brookins, and W. R. Allen, eds. 1985. *Beginnings: The Social and Affective Development of Black Children*. Hillsdale, N.J.: Erlbaum.

Staples, R. 1971. "Toward a Sociology of the Black Family: A Theoretical and Methodological Assessment." *Journal of Marriage and the Family* 33: 119–138.

Staples, R., and A. Mirande. 1980. "Racial and Cultural Variations among American Families: A Decennial Review of the Literature on Minority Families." *Journal of Marriage and the Family* 42:887–904.

Sutherland, R. 1942. *Color, Class and Personality*. Washington, D.C.: American Council on Education.

Taylor, R. L. 1976a. "Black Youth and Psychosocial Development: A Conceptual Framework." *Journal of Black Studies* 6:353–372.

———. 1976b. "Psychosocial Development among Black Children and Youth: A Reexamination." *American Journal of Orthopsychiatry* 64:4–19.

———. 1987. "Black Youth in Crisis." *Humboldt Journal of Social Relations* 14:106–133.

———. 1989. "African-American Inner-City Youth and the Subculture of Disengagement." *Urban League Review* 12:15–24.

U.S. Bureau of the Census. 1986. *Household and Family Characteristics: March 1985*. Current Population Reports, Series P-20, no. 411. Washington, D.C.: Government Printing Office.

Valentine, C. A. 1971. "Deficit, Difference and Bicultural Models of Afro-American Behavior." *Harvard Educational Review* 41(2):137–157.

Walters, J. M., and L. H. Walters. 1980. "Parent-Child Relationships: A Review, 1970–1979." *Journal of Marriage and the Family* 42:807–822.

Young, D. R. 1969. "The Socialization of American Minority Peoples." In *Handbook of Socialization Theory and Research*, edited by D. A. Goslin, 1103–1140. Chicago: Rand McNally.

Young, V. H. 1970. "Family and Childhood in a Southern Negro Community." *American Anthropologist* 72:269–288.

————. 1974. "A Black American Socialization Pattern." *American Ethnologist* 1:405–412.

Zegiob, L., and R. Forehand. 1975. "Maternal Interactive Behavior as a Function of Race, Socioeconomic Status and Sex of the Child." *Child Development* 46:564–568.

Zigler, E., W. Abelson, and V. Seitz. 1973. "Motivational Factors in the Performance of Economically Disadvantaged Children on the Peabody Picture Vocabulary Test." *Child Development* 44:294–303.

Zigler, E., and I. L. Child. 1973. *Socialization and Personality Development.* Reading, Mass.: Addison-Wesley.

Zigler, E., and J. Valentine, eds. 1979. *Project Head Start: A Legacy of the War on Poverty.* New York: Free Press.

6

PAULA G. GOMES
and
C. ALDRENA MABRY

Negotiating the World: The Developmental Journey of African American Children

Childhood remembrances are always a drag.
—N. GIOVANNI,
"Black Judgements"

The African American child makes a unique journey to both master normal developmental tasks and meet the environmental challenges of racism, discrimination, oppression, and poverty. Despite these barriers, many children of African American families manage to reach high levels of achievement and excellence. Retaining their African heritage has been a past and continuous struggle for African Americans in a society with Eurocentric values and traditions that are psychologically and culturally incompatible. A review of developmental tasks in the context of an Africentric perspective provides one structural framework for examining the complexities faced by the African American child.

The Africentric paradigm rejects the historical notion that African Americans were stripped of their African heritage through the institution of slavery. It proposes that commonalities in language, dialect, spirituality, religion, and philosophical orientation exist between African Americans and their African ancestors. Africentrism rejects the deficit model of child development, which bases normalcy on white, middle-class behavior patterns. The Africentric paradigm supports

156

competence-based, theoretical models of normal child development, which address the values, customs, attitudes, societal goals, and behavioral orientations of African people. As an underlying conceptual framework, this perspective can stimulate new ways of thinking about, understanding, and investigating African American child development.

This chapter reviews theoretical and research approaches to child development, provides an overview of the stages of child development, analyzes the socialization role of the African American family, examines the impact of education during the developmental process, and suggests intervention strategies to enhance the maturational processes of the African American child. The goal is to provide information to and enhance the awareness of those dedicated to fostering the optimal growth and development of African American children.

Theoretical Approaches and Research Challenges

Ways of studying child development have been examined, challenged, and reformulated during the past two centuries. The theoretical and research approaches that emerged in response to the growth and development of African American family patterns during and subsequent to slavery were descriptive. By examining slave narratives written during the late 1800s, these studies provided information about child-rearing and socialization practices of early African American families (Du Bois 1908; Herskovitz [1941] 1958; Woodson 1936).

This descriptive approach to examining African American family patterns was replaced by deficit-oriented research models. Deficit-oriented approaches have been used by social and behavioral scientists to determine the innate or constitutional factors that contribute to the discrepancy between the functioning of African American and white children. The underlying premise of the deficit approach is that the behaviors and skills of white middle-class children represent normal patterns of development, while variations observed among children of color are aberrations that produce deficits. The biogenetic-hereditarian model proposes that the genetic inferiority of African Americans has contributed to differences in overall functioning between the races. Emerging in the 1930s, the cultural-deprivation model paralleled the biogenetic-hereditarian model, offering an alternative explanation of differences in racial and cultural life-styles. Most researchers focused on what was described as social pathology and inadequate life experiences in the African American community (Baratz and Baratz 1970). African Americans were depicted as pathological and deviant; and the differences observed between them and white Americans were attributed to the inadequacies of African American families and children.

This emphasis on the deficits of African American culture developed because traditional theories of personality and human development fail to provide a comprehensive understanding of African Americans. Therefore, most of the research and theory used to assess African American children's levels of cognitive, emotional, and physiological development and their models of communication, level of play, relationships with parents, and family functioning is based on a Eurocentric paradigm. Theories and research, formulated with insufficient information, result in a focus on the deficiencies rather than the strengths of African American culture.

To change the direction of research and theories, ecological approaches have been applied to the study of African American child development. Ecologically oriented research provides a framework that promotes a sociological and psychological understanding of relationships within and outside the family system (Billingsley 1968). As summarized by Peters (1981:216): "Ecological research examines Black families and parent-child interaction from a culture-specific or functional perspective, and the Black family's socialization of its children [is] considered in terms of the values and realities of its Afro-American culture."

Ecological models incorporate competence-based approaches to the study of African American children, which expand the understanding of family practices (parent/child interactions, child rearing, socialization). Competence-based models acknowledge the unique coping and cognitive problem-solving skills that African American children must incorporate into their behavioral repertoire in order to survive the effects of racism and discrimination. The cultural-difference, comparative-relevant, and Africentric models are ecological approaches that have been applied to the study of African Americans.

The cultural-difference and comparative-relevant models promote cultural pluralism and the exploration of social, linguistic, familial, and behavioral practices of culturally different people (Allen 1978; Baratz and Baratz 1970; Labov 1970). Most of the published research focuses primarily on low-income African American children, consists of race-comparative and interracial studies, and omits race-homogeneous studies (L. Grant 1988; McLloyd and Randolph 1984). According to McLloyd and Randolph (1984), these works impede the development of a rich knowledge base about African American children and limit the understanding of intragroup variability and functioning. The Africentric model, in contrast, promotes the examination of family structure and life-style, cultural practices and adaptations, intragroup differences, interdependent relationships to other racial and ethnic groups, and the biculturation process.

Examination of the theoretical and research approaches used to investigate the process of African American child development points to the conceptual gaps and failures of traditional Eurocentric models. The significant decrease in research articles published by mainstream journals about African American children has generated great concern (L. Grant 1988; McLloyd and Randolph 1984). Rogoff and Morelli (1989) report that researchers are beginning to respond to this concern. They indicate that "pioneering researchers of minorities are beginning to look at the contexts in which children from different cultures develop; and these efforts provide a basis for a greater understanding of how culture channels development. Some of the most interesting efforts involve combining approaches from anthropology and education with those of psychology" (p. 347). Research conducted from a multicultural, multidisciplinary perspective is deemed necessary to generate reliable information about cultural differences and human functioning. The challenges for researchers in the social sciences studying African American children and culture are to synthesize observational data gathered in qualitative research studies; to develop theoretical constructs, propositions, and hypotheses; and to proceed with quantitative research. Acquisition of reliable data is crucial for validating theories about the growth and development of African American children.

Maturational Processes and Socialization

As with other children, the African American child's introduction to the world is through the eyes of parents and family members. Family beliefs and experiences determine, for example, the racial views and perspectives the family presents to the child. Family beliefs, attitudes, and behavior contribute to the child's political and spiritual beliefs and the child's attitudes toward race. Socioeconomic status, race, religion, and geographic location are variables that influence the family's socialization practices. This socialization process dictates the child's initial response to education and school, which is the second major socialization experience for children. Educational settings also affect the maturational process of the child by promoting cognitive, affective, and social development. School experiences may support or challenge the lessons learned in the home. The integration of these experiences contribute to the child's self-esteem, achievement, motivation, and sense of identity, and determines how the child interacts, adapts, and attains personal goals in the environment.

This section provides an overview of the socialization experiences of African American children in nuclear and extended families, school, and the community. The roles of race, gender, and class in these various settings are examined, and peer relations and identity issues are explored to determine how they influence the African American child's ability to negotiate and function in the American environment.

PRENATAL PERIOD

Healthy child development involves the interaction of genetic and environmental factors (Hetherington and Parke 1975). The biological process begins with conception and progresses as the zygote subdivides into millions of other cells by the process of mitosis (Biehler 1976). This tiny cell subdivision begins the process of development of the organs, systems, and functions of the human body. Within two to eight weeks, the zygote becomes an embryo, which is about one inch in length. Although development is primitive at this level, all major organs and body systems are developing. Development follows the orthogenetic principle of progression through stages, from undifferentiated to differentiated to integrated. For example, during the fetal period, although there is rapid muscular development, the nervous system is also becoming mature, and differentiation leads to the emergence of a system with increasingly refined and circumscribed reflexes, responses, and movements (Hetherington and Parke 1975). Massive gross development occurs prior to fine, integrated functioning.

As the human fetus emerges during the developmental process, expectant mothers report that by the end of the fourth or fifth month the fetus at least occasionally moves, kicks, and hiccups. By the sixth month, the eyes of the human fetus have developed, and the opening and closing of the eyes may occur. By twenty-eight weeks, the fetus enters the age of viability, where the physical systems are sufficiently advanced so that if birth occurs, the infant may survive outside the womb (Hetherington and Parke 1975). Although normal development occurs in a fixed, invariable sequence, with body parts and systems developing at approximately the same time in all fetuses, females have been found to be more developmentally advanced at birth than males. The exact cause of this gender differentiation is unknown.

The human fetus is most susceptible to extraneous stimuli during the first trimester of the prenatal period. Pregnancy risk factors, which include the mother's dietary habits, preexisting health conditions, as well as the ingestion of nicotine, alcohol, drugs, and other nonnutritive substances, have been found to significantly threaten or alter normal health and development of the fetus (Biehler 1976).

Sickle cell anemia is a hereditary birth defect that seems to be carried through the genetic structure of about 8 percent of African Americans. In most, the tendency of the blood to sickle is not associated with deleterious symptoms. About one in forty, however, is afflicted with the severe, chronic, and sometimes fatal form of sickle cell anemia (Hetherington and Parke 1975). Adverse symptoms tend to occur most often either when both parents of the child are carriers of the sickling gene or at very high altitudes, where oxygen deprivation causes the blood vessels to clog, causing severe pain, tissue damage, and death when critical vessels are blocked in the brains and lungs.

INFANCY

The normal human baby emerges from the warm, secure environment of the mother's womb after approximately forty weeks. At birth, the infant's behavior is innate and instinctual. Sucking, grasping, crying, and rooting reflexes are present. The newborn infant is motivated primarily toward pleasure and survival. In the early months, infants sleep, eat, and visually explore bright colors, patterns, and light in their environment. The human face, particularly that of the mother or primary caretaker, is also a major orienting visual stimulus (Hetherington and Parke 1975). The infant quickly learns that the caretaker's presence signals the beginning of feeding, touching, and other caretaking activities. The special relationship or bonding between infant and caretaker that occurs during the early phase of life determines how the child explores and responds to the environment. The nature of this relationship affects later psychomotor, cognitive, and psychological development (Bettelheim 1967; Bowlby 1958; Ribble 1944).

Erik Erikson (1963) postulated that each individual goes through eight stages or crises in order to achieve mastery of the environment. How successfully the child negotiates each of these stages or crises determines, according to Erikson, his or her subsequent ability to cope with each of the succeeding crises in child development. Erikson's first stage—basic trust versus mistrust—corresponds to birth through the first year of life. The development of trust depends on the parents' success in meeting the child's needs during that first year. For Erikson, when the child can confidently expect need reduction and love, this expectation is generalized to the world at large. However, when care and need reduction are inconsistent, inadequate, and filled with continual rejection, the child's world view becomes one of suspicion and mistrust (Elkind 1970).

Studies of effective child-rearing techniques during infancy demonstrate that good mothers or good caretakers use physical contact and soothe their children with contact, have a heightened sensitivity to the infant's signals of discomfort and insecurities, establish feelings of mutual delight between themselves and their children, and encourage the children to feel that they have the capabilities to affect and change their environment (Biehler 1976).

During the first two years of life, the human infant experiences rapid growth and adjustment to the new environment. The innate, instinctual orienting reflexes progress into large, complex movements that are coordinated and voluntary. Psychomotor development in childhood has been studied over the years to examine the specific ages at which children achieve certain milestones. Bayley (1965) examined the development of African American children and found a general trend toward psychomotor superiority in development, which he suggested was genetically determined. In addition, Smart and Smart (1972) reported that African American children's teeth erupt early and permanent teeth are more mature and larger in size than those of white American children.

Although the sequence of psychomotor development is the same among children, the exact ages of skill acquisition vary within a wide range. The average child, for example, starts walking at twelve to thirteen months of age, although others may start at nine months and for some children walking may be delayed until eighteen months. The current child-development literature deemphasizes exact timetables for various psychomotor stages and, instead, encourages appreciation of individual differences. When overall development is delayed, physicians and other professionals recommend various tests to assess the child's development.

Cognitive development is the process whereby the infant organizes, stores, and memorizes information, and otherwise makes intellectual sense of the environment. The infant is born with some cognitive processes, while others evolve from interactions with and experiences in the environment. Jean Piaget's (1926) theory of cognitive development has been widely accepted as universal. According to this theory the infant and child actively explore and manipulate the environment in order to understand, and, therefore, adapt to it. For Piaget, the process of adaptation begins at birth with universal, innate reflexes and continues into various other stages as the infant discovers increasingly sophisticated modes of operation. The infant is born with a schema, a basic pattern of organized behavior. Adaptation includes two processes: assimilation and accommodation. In assimilation the infant utilizes and interprets new information and incorporates it into the already existing schema. In accommodation the infant changes responses to environmental demands. When the new experiences do not fit into the existing schema, the infant changes to accommodate the new information.

Piaget identified four crucial stages of cognitive development: sensorimotor, preoperational, concrete operations, and formal operations. Although it is widely accepted that all children pass through the stages in the same order, Piaget (1970) also posited that all children go through the stages at about the same ages. The stages build on each other, and the attainments in later stages depend on the mastery of developmental tasks in previous stages. The sensorimotor stage exists from birth to about two years of age. It is categorized by progress in the development of reflexes and habits, and by the imitation and initiation of language. Object permanence is established, whereby the child is able to understand that objects in the environment are permanent and exist in cognitive awareness even when out of visual sight. The child's attention is oriented primarily toward things that move in the environment.

Language development in children appears to be a universal phenomenon; all children, regardless of race, are born with a genetic endowment to learn the complex system of rules needed for communication with a society (Hetherington and Parke 1975). During the first few weeks of life, the infant learns to distinguish the human voice from nonhuman sounds. The mother or primary caretaker's voice is distinguishable from that of other humans. The infant is also capable within the first few weeks of modulating cooing and babbling in response to other sounds. Papolia and Olds (1925) reported that all children, regardless of culture or background, make the same initial sounds (phonemes) and follow the same basic rate, sequence, and rules in language acquisition. All children are believed to acquire language through the processes of imitation, repetition, and reinforcement (Piaget 1926). First words are usually spoken near the end of the first year. One- and two-word phrases occur on the average between eighteen and twenty-four months of age. Language at this stage reflects the child's incomplete cognitive organization. For example, "car" may be used to refer to trucks, cars, and other types of transportation. Although the child may understand that a truck and a car are different, "car" is the only word the child has for vehicles at this stage.

Lenneberg (1967) found that human language-learning capacity is a correlate or result of the maturational process. Houston (1970) postulated that the development of language may be innate or biologically determined. Chomsky (1968) found that children learn language as a result of being placed in an environment where the language is spoken. Osser (1970) agreed that the child learns the unique structural rules and linguistic codes of the language within a specific environment. Language development thus appears to be the natural result of the child's innate ability, the child's readiness to learn as a result of maturational and growth processes, and the impact of the spoken language in the particular cultural environment.

EARLY CHILDHOOD

Early childhood refers to ages two to six. Piaget's preoperational stage (two to seven years) corresponds to this stage of development, which is characterized by language acquisition (discussed later in this section). Symbolic and fantasy play activities are also present. The preoperational child is egocentric and unable to take another person's point of view. The child cannot fully comprehend the nature of relationships or the idea of reciprocity. Although capable of understanding that he or she has a brother, the child is unable to comprehend that the brother has a sister. The child centers on one unique feature of an object (for example, color or shape) and is unable to integrate other features.

Erikson's second stage—autonomy versus shame and doubt—occurs in the second year of life, and the third stage—initiative versus guilt—occurs from the third through fifth year; combined, these stages correspond to early childhood. Erikson (1963) argued that in the second stage, the child begins to demonstrate new motor and mental abilities, and is proud of the initiation and development of these skills. According to Erikson, if the child's ability to manipulate is not supported and encouraged, or if the parents or caretakers do for the child what he or she is capable of doing for himself or herself, feelings of shame and doubt are reinforced. These feelings will later interfere with autonomy strivings in adolescence (Elkind 1970). In the third stage—initiative versus guilt—parents and caretakers must give children the freedom to initiate their own motor responses and not restrict their self-motivated behaviors, play, or questions.

Play is a universal activity among children; it contributes to and influences the developmental process. Many psychologists and researchers in child development (Comer and Poussaint 1976; Erikson 1963; Piaget and Inhelder 1969; Wilson 1978) view play as crucial "child's work," necessary for healthy cognitive, social, and emotional growth. The type of play varies according to the age of the developing child. The child begins by engaging in solitary play. Parallel play, or playing alongside another child, is later established. Cooperative play, where the child is able to interact with another in play (for example, by throwing a ball), is achieved during the first and second years.

Through play, the child expresses and develops an understanding of the world by mastering and manipulating the environment through fantasy and imagination. Children imitate and practice what they see, hear, and experience in the environment. Piaget (1926) indicated that play facilitates cognitive development. Themes in play can represent perceptions of the social and emotional experiences in children's lives. Toys serve as their bridge to reality. When toys are specific replicas of objects in the environment, children can use them to understand the adult world.

Applying Erikson's theory to the African American child, DiAngi (1976) suggests that cultural factors, child-rearing practices, and racial and skin-color prejudices within the family and society may help or hinder the progression of the child through these stages. For example, if parents favor one child over another because of skin color or discourage the child's autonomy and initiative because of racism in the society, the child does not develop a positive self-image or world view because natural strivings for trust, autonomy, and initiative are frustrated. Subsequently, the child develops a negative self-image, becomes distrustful of others, and feels guilty about suppressing the drive to achieve and master the environment.

Most researchers have found that ethnoracial awareness starts in early childhood, between the ages of three and five (Clark and Clark 1939; McAdoo 1985; Powell-Hopson and Hopson 1988; Semaj 1980). According to Semaj (1980:76–77):

> By age 4 or 5, children understand that people are categorized into various ethno-racial groups and have some understanding of the group to which they belong, but do not understand the permanence of this classification. Between the ages of 6 and 9, the child's cognitive abilities mature resulting in the acquisition of conservation abilities and the development of racial constancy. By the ages of 8 [to] 11, impersonal and social cognitive development increases, revealing qualitative and quantitative changes in social affect to race.

Semaj stresses that in response to increased experiences with prejudice, the child may lose some of the positive identification with being African American that had been achieved at an early age. He suggests that "Black children in America do not hate themselves, but many do achieve what can be considered a bicultural identity by age 11" (p. 77). This process requires balancing two cultures, which results in the loss or devaluation of personal and cultural perspectives in order to integrate the views of the majority culture.

Language acquisition takes place at a rapid pace between the ages of twenty and thirty-six months. The child's vocabulary expands greatly to incorporate reality. Some stuttering and disfluencies in the child's speech are common during this period but usually disappear by the age of four. By then, most children comprehend basic rules of grammar and syntax. They can make meaningful sentences within their limited linguistic repertoire.

Hunt (1969) found that until the age of two, the cognitive developmental processes of the African American child do not differ significantly from those of children in other cultures. After the age of two, however, when children learn to label the events and objects around them with language, the labels used by the African American child and the linguistic models by which the African American child communicates are different because the environment is culturally different although the process of labeling is not different. The African American child is not deficient in communication skills but merely uses different labels to define the experiential and environmental milieu.

Although there are commonalities in the language of African Americans and white Americans because of interaction and imitation between the cultures, Wilson (1978) reports that about 80 percent of African Americans speak a "radical, nonstandard" English called "Black English." Black English reflects history, a vast cultural background, and the blending of the diverse languages of different African tribes with the language of the Europeans.

LATE CHILDHOOD

Late childhood, ages six to twelve, corresponds to Piaget's stage of concrete operations (ages seven to eleven). It is characterized by the child's awareness of immediate reality, or the "here and now." The child has an organized system by which objects are manipulated in the environment. Although less egocentric, the child has difficulty understanding the hypothetical and is unable to go far beyond concrete experience. Erikson's fourth stage—industry versus inferiority—occurs in late childhood, from the age of six to the onset of puberty. According to Erikson, the child in this stage develops a sense of "industry" and starts to receive some systematic instruction in school. The role and influence of parents, teachers, and peers are important to help the child master industry. Parents and teachers must encourage the child to ask questions, to make things, and to finish incomplete projects. If the efforts of the child are ridiculed instead of rewarded, the child develops feelings of inferiority and may not try to perform at his or her best. Once feelings of inferiority exist, the child's desire for work may diminish (Elkind 1970).

DiAngi (1976) notes that to negotiate this stage successfully an African American child must be placed in an environment where he or she is continually challenged, stimulated, and encouraged to learn and achieve. If the child is in an atmosphere that is not conducive to learning, frustration may lead to the internalization of negative feelings. The African American child may then develop a negative attitude toward the academic experience and may seek success among peers who share these frustrations.

During Piaget's concrete-and-formal-operations stage, age seven and above, the child is capable of daydreaming and fantasy, which are forms of mental play. Role playing and imitation of adults (mother, father, teacher) are other aspects of this type of play; with them the child learns to experience another's point of reference. McLloyd (1985) described this type of play as pretend play and views it as valuable in cognitive development. Shade and Edwards (1987), observing African American children at play, posit that pretend play is oriented toward mimicry of people and situations observed within the African American community. Pelligrini (1980) found a strong positive correlation between high frequency of sociodrama and pretend play and skills in reading, spoken language, and writing.

Huizinga (1950) examines play as a social and cultural construction and suggests that it involves the various archetypal activities of different cultures. White (1980) suggests that most African American children are likely to be involved in creative play in which they use cast-off furniture and other objects found in their environment. Individual play—where the children interact with toys and objects such as crayons, paper, pencils, and blocks—occurs less often. As the maturational process proceeds in late childhood, play becomes increasingly social. Through sports and games the child explores relationships, rules, roles, and expectations, and learns as well how to get along with others in an adaptive fashion. The child learns to cope with losing and fighting, and how to manage conflicts during cooperative play. Through reading, storytelling, listening to the radio, and watching television, the developing child attempts to understand and conceptualize reality further.

Shade and Edwards (1987) present the possibility that the kind of play encouraged in the African American family reinforces the values and goals of the culture. It provides the children with the opportunity to negotiate hierarchical relationships, accurately perceive emotions, and empathize with others, all of which are important traits of children with high social intelligence.

Gender-role identification also occurs in late childhood. The socialization experiences of the child in the home, school, and community significantly influence this developmental process. When children are exposed to traditional and nontraditional role models and experiences, they may develop a broad repertoire of gender-role behaviors. The presence of parents, teachers, and other role models has a significant effect on the identity of boys and girls. For African American boys, in particular, a positive relationship with a consistent male role model enhances gender-role development. In the absence of this relationship, other males, including peers, may become the primary socializing agents and have a strong influence on a boy's self-discipline, sex-role development, morality, academic achievement, and interpersonal relationships (Hare 1987; Kunjufu 1984, 1986a, 1986b; Wilson 1978).

PREADOLESCENCE AND ADOLESCENCE

Preadolescence lasts from twelve to fourteen. According to Piaget, from the age of twelve the child is in the stage of formal operations. With abstract reasoning skills established, the child can now engage in higher-level thought processes. The child is capable of problem solving and deductive reasoning. The child also becomes interested in and preoccupied with rules. People who disobey rules, as perceived by the formal-operations child, should be severely punished.

Erikson's fifth stage—identity versus role confusion—is one of the most critical, occurring during the period of adolescence. Adolescents seek some semblance of harmony and order within themselves and the world. If this harmony is not achieved, the result is role confusion. During adolescence peer relations are a major influence in psychological functioning. The youth peer group has been identified as an established entity in the African American community; in it adolescents seek approval, esteem, opportunities for achievement, and positive recognition (Hare 1987; Kunjufu 1984). For many African American youth, these peer experiences are critical because they encourage the achievement of competence, personal growth, and independence by creating a sense of belonging and connectedness for the adolescent.

As African American children enter late adolescence, they begin to solidify their racial identity. Researchers have developed various models to illustrate the stages of race consciousness and identity development that move African Americans from feelings of pain to a sense of pride (Cross 1971; Milliones 1980; Jackson 1976; Thomas 1971). Successful acquisition of a positive African American identity requires synthesis of internal and external experiences. This process is influenced by cultural, familial, societal, and historical factors. African American families and communities can assist adolescents in developing a positive racial identity by celebrating the unique aspects of African American culture.

Grier and Cobbs (1968) maintain that if the African American adolescent fails to establish a place in the societal group, a negative individual or group identity may develop. For economically and emotionally deprived African American youth, severe frustration and negative self-images may cause identification with peers who reject societal norms. Juvenile delinquency, criminal and violent activity, gang membership, and other acts of rebellion may result. Increases in economic distress, single parenting, and negative views about education have left many adolescents vulnerable to the short-term gratification of delinquent activities.

Sexual-identity development is influenced by physical and emotional maturation during preadolescence and adolescence. This period of sexual exploration is marked by confusion because of physiological changes, social pressures, awareness of moral issues, and identification of sexual feelings and preferences. Adolescent sexual behavior is a major concern because of high rates of teen pregnancy, early sexual experimentation, sexually transmitted diseases, and the acquired-immune-deficiency (AIDS) epidemic. Despite sex education, media campaigns, AIDS-prevention efforts, and high mortality rates, adolescents continue to engage in unprotected sexual activity (Brooks-Gunn, Boyer, and Hern 1988; Brooks-Gunn and Furstenberg 1989; Jenkins 1988). For many adolescents, engaging in risky sexual activities is the result of a combination of factors. Mastery of the developmental task of long-term planning and anticipation of consequences is achieved during this stage of maturation. Therefore, an adolescent's failure to employ mature decision-making and reasoning skills regarding sexual activities may be due to developmental immaturity.

According to Erikson, if the tasks of this stage are not successfully completed, the adolescent is not adequately prepared for adulthood and the later stages of development, which are characterized by intimacy, generativity, integrity. Therefore, an environment that provides support and creative solutions is needed to assist adolescents through this confusing and challenging developmental stage.

Families: Sources of Hope, Strength, and Survival Skills

The African American family plays an important and crucial role in the developmental process of the child by creating the surroundings for the initial socialization experiences. The family meets the basic physical and emotional needs of the child, supplies guidance in the mastery of intrapsychic and developmental tasks, and prepares the child to survive and cope in an oppressive society. The goal for many parents is to assist the child with the development of survival skills that will aid in the attainment of self-actualization. African American nuclear and extended families meet these various challenges during the developmental years through cultural, traditional, and historical channels.

The African American family has been described in various ways. Billingsley (1968) sees it as a unit embedded in a network of interdependent relationships within the African American community and the wider (white) society. Shimkin and Uchendu (1978) highlight the unique cultural resources within families. Nobles (1981) describes the African American family as emphasizing strong family ties, unconditional love, and respect for self and others. The family facilitates acceptance, validation, and the transmission of knowledge and information critical to the survival of the members. Besides these qualities, Hill (1972) delineates five strengths of African American families: a strong work orientation; extended family bonds; egalitarian role functioning; strong religious orientation; and educational aspirations.

Recent economic changes in the United States have affected African American families by increasing the rates of unemployment, poverty, and crime. Wilson (1989:381) reports that "most Black families are not poor, however, 31% in recent decades lived in poverty and 52% of Black one-parent families were classified as poor." African American children are more likely than white American children to be raised in a poor, single-parent household and to be confronted with the stressors of lack of time, money, and energy that contribute to emotional distress and frustration (Hare 1987; Kunjufu 1984). These children are usually more vulnerable than others to child abuse, inadequate nutrition and health care, suicide, crime, and emotional deprivation.

Demographic shifts, changes in family structure, and the movement from overt to subtle forms of racism in the United States pose further difficult challenges for African American children today. In most two-parent families, both parents are working, and they are living away from extended-family members. The number of single-parent families has risen as a result of increases in the divorce rate, increases in teenage motherhood, and the personal choices of women and men. These societal changes have led to increased demands for day care and after-school activities and have decreased the time parents have available for their children.

Nevertheless, the extended family continues to be a major source of support for single- and two-parent families. In the African American community, this family pattern provides direct and indirect support for children and others (Tatum 1987; Wilson 1989). Wilson (1989:380) indicates that "the extended family's central feature, the familial support network," is manifested in the family members' "propinquity, communication, and cooperation."

African American parents in predominantly white communities face the challenge of providing cultural and community activities that promote children's exposure to and familiarity with African American culture. Tatum (1987) studied middle-class African American families residing in predominantly white communities and their process of survival. She highlighted the complexities of biculturation and specific strategies to manage the social difficulties their children faced. She found that the retention of traditional African American values—promotion of education, religious affiliation and involvement, mutual support and cooperation of family members, and close relationships with extended family—contributed to the survival and success of these families. Parents can also use the resources of the African American community, through religious and volunteer groups, social and public-service organizations, athletic and educational networks, and mental health and prevention services, to meet the needs of their children.

The African American child must integrate African American and Euro-American cultural values in order to achieve and to succeed in school, employment, and social interactions. This socialization process may create feelings of ambivalence and frustration because of the inherent racism that exists in American society. For example, when African American children enter school they are often expected to communicate, interact, and learn according to styles that are distinctly different from their styles at home (Ogbu 1985; Vogt, Jordan, and Thorp 1987). The preferred or accepted styles of communication are based on Euro-American norms and must be utilized or adhered to in school and work settings. The implicit message is that African American styles of talking, walking, dressing, thinking, and interacting are not acceptable (Ogbu 1985). African American families, therefore, must counteract these messages by providing educational experiences that are rich in culture and tradition.

The Impact of Education

Children spend most of their time once they are school age in educational settings. They move from the major influence of family members to that of teachers, curriculum, and classmates. Schooling fosters "cognitive, affective and social development; and influences the development of a stable self image, acquisition of interaction skills with classmates and peers, learning of social customs and mores, coming to like or dislike school and many other things" (Entwisle and Alexander 1988:450).

The child's initial response to school and the academic process is greatly influenced by parental views on education. Family and community perspectives may vary from identifying education as the primary strategy for surviving, or "making it," in an oppressive society, to viewing it as a major contributor to oppression.

In the classroom, the teacher's responses, comfort level with students of color, views, and expectations influence the child's academic success. Many teachers are confused about how to treat and instruct students of color in their classes. Teaching approaches vary from ignoring to becoming too involved in the student's life. C. Grant (1988) indicates that some teachers take the color-blind approach; some involve students of color when a yearly cultural event happens; and some become "missionaries" in order to help the student. Grant stresses that these efforts usually result in negative responses to education and the academic experience.

Holliday (1985) reports that African American children are socialized to employ a persistent, assertive problem-solving style. However, teachers often reject these traits and label them as inappropriate, which contributes to the child's sense of helplessness. Kunjufu (1984) identifies the fourth grade as a pivotal year for African American boys in academic and personal achievement. Kunjufu attributes the decline in their performance during this year to "less-than-deserved teacher competency in the primary grades, few male teachers, parental apathy, increased peer pressure, and greater emphasis on mass media" (p. 15). These stressors influence the process of adjustment and future academic success of the African American child.

For some minority children, adjustment difficulties in the classroom have been attributed to their cultural backgrounds and exposure to interactional learning styles that are different from those of the mainstream public school (Ogbu 1987). As we have seen, African

American children in predominantly white schools are required to master white learning styles and behavior patterns, to cope with being different and the external responses to these differences, and to manage resistance to their presence by finding ways to integrate into the environment. Predominantly African American schools may foster a cultural milieu that conflicts with the larger society's beliefs and expectations of the educational process. Therefore, in many of these academic institutions, traditional Euro-American values are incorporated into the curriculum to instruct students about these differences. The Eurocentric focus of the American educational system has denied all students the opportunity to learn about the racially diverse Americans who have made major contributions to the development and success of the United States. Requirements for school systems include the integration of a multicultural educational model, modifications in curricula and textbooks, attention to diverse learning styles, the use of teaching styles that empower all students, and the promotion of social change (C. Grant 1988; Royal 1988).

Ogbu (1987) observes that beyond cultural differences in the learning process, academic adjustment problems, especially for African American children, are related to distrust of educational institutions because of perceptions of past and current maltreatment and discrimination. If children see individuals in their community who have been given an inadequate education, who have been discriminated against in finding jobs, and who have otherwise been the victims of institutionalized racism, their motivation to achieve academically is diminished. Many African American communities have established programs and cultural experiences for children to compensate for the educational and socialization gaps that exist in most school systems and in some African American family networks.

Many researchers have attempted to identify the factors contributing to the poor school achievement of low-income African American children, the disproportionate number of minority children in educable mentally retarded classes, and motivation difficulties of African American children. Many studies in this area have focused on intelligence testing. The I.Q.-testing debate has primarily highlighted the consistent fifteen-point difference in scores between African Americans and white Americans. Some researchers have attributed the discrepancies in functioning between African American and white children to cultural deprivation, low self-esteem, and genetic inferiority of African American children (Eysenck 1971; Jensen 1969;

Shockley 1972). Educators, researchers, and other professionals have challenged these claims and proposed that the cultural bias of assessment techniques, examiner and teacher variables, and substandard educational opportunities are responsible for the difficulties faced by African American children on I.Q. test (Kaufman 1979; Kunjufu 1984; *Larry P. v. Wilson Riles;* C-71-2270 (N.D. Cal.) 1979; Manni, Winikur, and Keller 1984; Mercer and Ysseldyke 1979). Factors affecting I.Q.-test performance continue to be a prominent focus also in the psychological literature.

Moore (1987) found that significant differences between African American and white children occur because of the cultural milieus in which they are socialized. Parental education, income, and child-rearing practices were also found to be major factors that influenced ethnic-group differences in children's skill and performance levels (Moore 1985, 1987). Unfortunately, many studies have focused on the deficits of African American children instead of examining the limitations of the educational environment, the curriculum, assessment techniques, and the intelligence paradigm.

Limited attention has been given to the study of learning potential and learning styles. Learning potential, according to Feurstein (1979), is the individual's ability to become "modified" by a learning experience. "Modifiability" is an individual's capacity for "acting on and responding to sources of information" (Manni, Winikur, and Keller 1984:104). In their use of assessment techniques, many examiners fail to assess what children can learn and focus primarily on what they have already learned. Learning style has been defined by certain cognitive, affective, and psychological behaviors that serve as relatively stable indicators of how learners perceive, interact with, and respond to the learning environment. Emichovich and Miller (1988) reviewed studies on the matching of teaching and learning styles and found significant increases in academic achievement and positive attitudes toward learning when students were taught according to their learning style. Many African American children employ a relational learning style (Akbar 1981; Hale 1982; Kunjufu 1984), which is characterized as one that emphasizes the unique and specific qualities of a phenomenon, notions of difference rather than variations or commonalities of things, fluent spoken language, and affective responses. Further research is needed to investigate teaching and learning styles in order to enhance the educational process for African American children.

Curriculum development and educational reform continue to be a major focus of early childhood education research. C. Grant (1988) proposed the implementation of an education program based on an integrated analysis of class, race, and gender. The goal is for students to understand the effects of power, economics, and culture in society so that they become able to serve the interests of all citizens, especially people of color, the poor, women, and individuals with handicapping conditions. In other words, changes in programming, curriculum, and teaching styles must parallel actual changes in the educational and employment opportunities available to African Americans and others. Teachers and other professionals have an ultimate responsibility to provide quality education for all students. An important feature of education should be to empower students to achieve, and to confront social and cultural barriers to success.

Enhancing Developmental Experiences

The many factors that contribute to the developmental experiences of African American children continue to be explored, challenged, and investigated by social scientists. The conceptual gaps of traditional theoretical and research models are illustrated by the omission of race-homogeneous studies in the literature, which can provide valuable insights about the diversity of African Americans. Research conducted from a multicultural, multidisciplinary perspective is necessary for the acquisition of reliable information pertaining to cultural differences and human functioning. The challenge for researchers interested in the development of African American children is to determine how culture influences the developmental process. Synthesis of observational data gathered in qualitative research studies that examine all aspects (familial, social, educational, cultural) of the African American child's life is critical.

The African American family assumes an important role in the developmental process by molding and shaping the infant's experiences with the environment. Parents or caretakers should provide consistent physical contact and stimulation for the infant. In early childhood, caretakers should encourage the inherent drive for mastery and support the strivings for independence demonstrated by the toddler. During the stages of early childhood, late childhood, and adolescence, children should be exposed to traditional and nontraditional gender-role models and experiences, and to the rich traditions and practices of African American culture. These experiences foster positive racial and gender-role identity and increase self-esteem. Nuclear and extended families can assist the African American child to develop survival skills that promote self-actualization. Families can provide a secure environment of support, acceptance, and validation in which the child can experiment and can practice skills necessary for achievement. The family, through the transmission of knowledge, information, and past experiences of family members, can help the child understand the biculturation process and internalize the valuable lessons needed to overcome societal barriers to success.

Because children spend most of their time in educational settings, school systems must examine the impact of the educational process on all children. Most studies that investigate education and African American children focus on the deficiencies of the children instead of the limitations of educational programming, assessment techniques, and classroom structure. School systems must integrate a multicultural educational model, modify curricula and textbooks, acknowledge diversity in learning styles, and utilize teaching styles that empower all students.

The African American community has a strong tradition of emphasizing the importance of history, education, and achievement. This community must continue to provide complementary educational opportunities that focus on cultural awareness, social advancement, and historical events to enhance the racial and ethnic pride of African American children. In order to respond to the increased and growing national crises of poverty, crime, drugs, homelessness, teen pregnancy, AIDS, homicide, and suicide, the African American community must generate the strength and energy to combat these social tragedies. Religious and volunteer groups (African American churches and Big Brothers and Big Sisters of America), social and public-service organizations (fraternities, sororities, civil rights organizations, leadership-skills groups), athletic and educational networks (mentor and tutorial programs), and mental health and prevention services (Head Start, teen support groups) must respond to the special needs of children in the African American community. African American families must utilize community mental health services that provide comprehensive support to children, adults, couples, families, and special groups facing stressful life circumstances. Family and community networking is needed to give African American children the necessary problem-solving, mediation, and negotiation skills for surviving the challenges of their developmental journey.

References

Akbar, N. 1981. "Cultural Expressions of the African American Child." *Black Child Journal* 2:10.
Allen, W. R. 1978. "The Search for Applicable Theories in Black Family Life." *Journal of Marriage and the Family* 40:117–129.
Baratz, S., and J. Baratz. 1970. "Early Childhood Interventions: The Social Science Base for Institutional Racism." *Harvard Educational Review* 40(1): 29–47.
Bayley, N. 1965. "Comparison of Mental and Motor Test Scores for Age 1–15 Months by Sex, Birth Order, Race, Geographic Location and Parents." *Child Development* 36:379–412.
Biehler, R. F. 1976. *Child Development: An Introduction*. Boston: Houghton Mifflin.
Bettelheim, B. 1967. "Where Self Begins." *New York Times Magazine,* February 12.
Billingsley, A., 1968. *Black Families in White America*. Englewood Cliffs, N. J.: Prentice-Hall.
Bowlby, J. 1958. "The Nature of the Child's Tie to His Mother." *International Journal of Psychoanalysis* 39:35.
Brooks-Gunn, J., C. Boyer, and K. Hern. 1988. "Preventing HIV Infection and AIDS in Children and Adolescents." *American Psychologist* 43(11): 958–964.
Brooks-Gunn, J., and F. Furstenberg. 1989. "Adolescent Sexual Behavior." *American Psychologist* 44(2):249–257.
Chomsky, N. 1968. *Syntactic Structures*. The Hague: Mouton.
Clark, K. B., and M. P. Clark, 1939. "The Development of Consciousness of Self and the Emergence of Racial Identification in Negro Preschool Children." *Journal of Social Psychology* 10:591–599.
Comer, J. P., and A. F. Poussaint. 1976. *Black Child Care*. New York: Simon & Schuster.
Cross, W. E. 1971. "Negro-to-Black Conversion Experience: Toward a Psychology of Black Liberation." *Black World* 29(9):13–27.
DiAngi, P. 1976. "Erikson's Theory of Personality Development as Applied to the Black Child." *Perspectives in Psychiatric Care* 14(4):184–185.
Du Bois, W. E. B. 1908. *The Negro American Family*. Atlanta: Atlanta University Press.

Elkind, D. 1970. "Erik Erikson's Eight Stages of Man." *New York Times Magazine* April 5.

Emichovich, C., and G. E. Miller. 1988. "Effects of Logo and Cai on Black First Graders' Achievement. Reflectivity and Self Esteem." *Elementary School Journal* 88(5):473–487.

Entwisle, D. R., and K. L. Alexander. 1988. "Factors Affecting Achievement Test Scores and Marks of Black and White First Graders." *Elementary School Journal* 88(5): 449–471.

Erikson, E. 1963. *Childhood and Society.* New York: Norton.

Eysenck, H. J. 1971. *The IQ Argument.* New York: Library Press.

Feurstein, R. 1979. *The Dynamic Assessment of Retarded Performers: The Learning Potential Assessment Device, Theory, Instruments and Techniques.* Baltimore: University Park Press.

Grant, C. 1988. "The Persistent Significance of Race in Schooling." *Elementary School Journal* 88(5):561–569.

Grant, L. 1988. "Introduction: Regenerating and Refocusing Research on Minorities and Education." *Elementary School Journal* 88(5): 441–448.

Grier, W. H., and P. M. Cobbs, 1968. *Black Rage.* New York: Basic Books.

Hale, J. E. 1982. *Black Children: Their Roots, Cultures, and Learning Styles.* Provo, Utah: Brigham Young University Press.

Hare, B. R. 1987. "Structural Inequality and the Endangered Status of Black Youth." *Journal of Negro Education* 56(1):100–121.

Herskovits, M. J. [1941] 1958. *The Myth of the Negro Past.* Boston: Beacon Press.

Hetherington, E. M., and R. D. Parke. 1975. *Child Psychology: A Contemporary View.* New York: McGraw-Hill.

Hill, R. B. 1972. *The Strengths of Black Families.* New York: Emerson Hall.

Holliday, B. 1985. "Towards a Model of Teacher-Child Transactional Process Affecting Black Children's Academic Achievement." In *Beginnings: The Social and Affective Development of Black Children,* edited by M. Spencer, G. Brookins, and W. Allen, 117–130. Hillsdale, N. J.: Erlbaum.

Houston, S. H. 1970. "A Reexamination of Some Assumptions about the Language of the Disadvantaged Child." *Child Development* 41(4):947–963.

Huizinga, H. 1950. *Homo Ludens: A Study of the Play Element in Cultures.* Boston: Beacon Press.

Hunt, J. M. 1969. *The Challenge of Incompetence and Poverty.* Urbana: University of Illinois Press.

Jackson, B. 1976. "The Function of a Black Identity Development Theory in Achieving Relevance in Education of Black Students" (Doctoral dissertation, University of Massachusetts, 1976). *Dissertation Abstracts International* 37:5667A.

Jenkins, R. 1988. "Adolescent Sexuality." In *Black Families in Crisis: The Middle Class,* edited by A. F. Coner-Edwards and J. Spurlock, 90–98. New York: Brunner/Mazel.

Jensen, A. R. 1969. "How Much Can We Boost IQ and Scholastic Achievement?" *Harvard Educational Review* 39(1):1–123.

Kaufman, A. 1979. *Intelligence Testing with the WISC-R.* New York: Wiley.

Kunjufu, J. 1984. *Developing Positive Self Images and Discipline in Black Children.* Chicago: African American Images.

———. 1986a. *Countering the Conspiracy to Destroy Black Boys.* Vol. 2. Chicago: African American Images.

———. 1986b. *Motivating and Preparing Black Youth to Work.* Chicago: African American Images.

Labov, W. 1970. "The Logic of Nonstandard English." In *Language and Poverty,* edited by F. Williams, 153–189. Chicago: Rand McNally.

Lenneberg, E. H. 1967. *Biological Foundations of Language.* New York: Wiley.

McAdoo, H. P. 1985. "Racial Attitude and Self-Concept of Young Black Children over Time." In *Black Children,* edited by H. P. McAdoo and J. L. McAdoo, 213–242. Beverly Hills, Calif.: Sage.

McLloyd, V. C. 1985. "Are Toys Just Toys? Exploring Their Effect on Pretend Play of Low-Income Preschoolers." In *Beginnings: The Social and Affective Development of Black Children,* edited by M. Spencer, G. Brookins, and W. Allen, 81–100. Hillsdale, N. J.: Erlbaum.

McLloyd, V. C., and S. M. Randolph. 1984. "The Conduct and Publication of Research on Afro-American Children: A Content Analysis." *Human Development* 27:65–75.

Manni, J. L., D. Winikur, and M. R. Keller. 1984. *Intelligence, Mental Retardation and the Culturally Different Child: A Practitioner's Guide.* Springfield, Ill.: Charles C Thomas.

Mercer, J. R., and J. Ysseldyke. 1977. "Designing Diagnostic-Intervention Programs." In *Psychological and Educational Assessment of Minority Children,* edited by T. Oakland, 70–90. New York: Brunner/Mazel.

Milliones, J. 1980. "Construction of a Black Consciousness Measure: Psychotherapeutic Implications." *Psychotherapy: Theory, Research, and Practice* 17(2): 458–462.

Moore, E. G. J. 1985. "Ethnicity as a Variable in Child Development." In *Beginnings: The Social and Affective Development of Black Children,* edited by M. Spencer, G. Brookins, and W. Allen, 101–115. Hillsdale, N. J.: Erlbaum.

———. 1987. "Ethnic Social Milieu and Black Children's Intelligence Test Achievement." *Journal of Negro Education* 56(1):44–52.

———. 1981. "African-American Family Life: An Instrument of Culture." In *Black Families,* edited by H. P. McAdoo, 77–85. Beverly Hills, Calif.: Sage.

Ogbu, J. U. 1985. "Research Currents: Cultural-Ecological Influences on Minority School Learning." *Language Arts* 62(8):860–869.

———. 1987. "Variability in Minority School Performance: A Problem in

Search of an Explanation." *Anthropology and Education Quarterly* 18(4): 312–332.

Osser, H. 1970. "Biological and Social Factors in Language Development." In *Language and Poverty*, edited by F. Williams, 248–264. Chicago: Markham.

Papolia, E., and S. Olds. 1925. *A Child's World: Infancy through Adolescence.* New York: McGraw-Hill.

Pelligrini, A. 1980. "Relationship between Kindergarten Play and Achievement in Reading, Language and Writing." *Psychology in the Schools* 17: 530–535.

Peters, M. F. 1981. "Parenting in Black Families with Young Children: A Historical Perspective." In *Black Families*, edited by H. P. McAdoo, 211–224. Beverly Hills, Calif.: Sage.

Piaget, J. 1926. *The Language and Thought of the Child.* New York: Harcourt Brace.

———. 1970. "Piaget's Theory." In *Carmichael's Manual of Child Psychology,* vol. 1, edited by P. H. Mussen 703–732. New York: Wiley.

Piaget, J.,. and B. Inhelder. 1969. *The Psychology of the Child.* New York: Basic Books.

Powell-Hopson, D., and D. S. Hopson. 1988. "Implication of Doll Preferences among Black Children and White Preschool Children." *Journal of Black Psychology* 14(2):57–63.

Ribble, M. 1944. "Infantile Experience in Relation to Personality Development." In *Personality and the Behavior Disorders,* vol. 2, edited by J. Hunt, 621–651. New York: Ronald Press.

Rogoff, B., and G. Morelli, 1989. "Perspectives on Children's Development from Cultural Psychology." *American Psychologist* 40(2):343–348.

Royal, C. L. 1988. "Support Systems for Students of Color in Independent Schools." In *Visible Now: Blacks in Private Schools,* edited by D. T. Slaughter and D. J. Johnson, 55–69. New York: Greenwood Press.

Semaj, L. 1980. "The Development of Racial Evaluation and Preference: A Cognitive Approach." *Journal of Black Psychology* 6(2):59–79.

Shade, B. J., and P. A. Edwards. 1987. "Ecological Correlates of the Educative Style of Afro-American Children." *Journal of Negro Education* 56(1): 81–99.

Shimkin, D. B., and V. Uchendu. 1978. "Persistence, Borrowing, and Adaptive Changes in Black Kinship Systems: Some Issues and Their Significance." In *The Extended Family in Black Societies,* edited by D. B. Shimkin, E. M. Shimkin, and D. A. Frate, 391–406. The Hague: Mouton.

Shockley, W. 1972. "Dysgenics, Geneticity, Raciology: A Challenge to the Intellectual Responsibility of Educators." *Phi Delta Kappan* 53:297–307.

Smart, M., and R. Smart. 1972. *Readings in Child Development and Relationship.* 2d ed. New York: Macmillan.

Tatum, B. D. 1987. *Assimilation Blues: Black Families in a White Community.* New York: Greenwood Press.

Thomas, C. 1971. *Boys No More*. Beverly Hills, Calif.: Glencoe Press.

Vogt, L. A., C. Jordan, and R. Tharp. 1987. "Explaining School Failure, Producing School Success: Two Cases." *Anthropology and Education Quarterly* 18(4):276–286.

White, J. L. 1980. "Toward a Black Psychology." In *Black Psychology*, 2d ed., edited by R. L. Jones, 5–12. New York: Harper & Row.

Wilson, A. 1978. *The Developmental Psychology of the Black Child*. New York: Africana Research Publications.

Wilson, M. N. 1989. "Child Development in the Context of the Black Extended Family." *American Psychologist* 44(2):380–385.

Woodson, C. G. 1936. *The African Background Outlined*. New York: Negro Universities Press.

THREE
Benighted and
Enlightened Services

SAMUEL'S CASE (presented in the Introduction) illustrates one of the many ways African American children and their families enter the child welfare system. Sometimes during periods of crisis families voluntarily seek child welfare services. Sometimes the removal of a child is a long and cumbersome process involving frequently painful and intrusive encounters with child welfare officials. At still other times the removal of a child can occur within days or weeks on the basis of suspicious allegations. Child welfare agency intervention into the privacy and sanctity of the family "if children remain 'at-risk of maltreatment or poor care'" (Daro 1988:2) is governed by federal and state laws. In this part of the book we describe the complicated ways families and children become entangled with child welfare services, what types of services are offered, and how improvements in the delivery of services can assist African American children and their families.

Because those entering the fields of social work, nursing, education, medicine, and law have so little understanding of the array of services and issues that arise in the field of child abuse and neglect, we include a general overview chapter on this topic. Tatara's review of this field notes the origin of public intervention, the difficulties inherent in definitions of maltreatment, the scope and incidence of child abuse and neglect, the procedures used to substantiate reports of mal-treatment, and the problems that have emerged for professionals in the field. It is difficult to refute the statistical data presented in this chapter. These data describe rather impersonally the course children travel as they gain entry to the state's protective custody.

The reason for the disproportionate number of African American children within the child welfare system escapes public attention. It is generally assumed that some type of parental abuse was the precipitat-ing event leading to a child's placement, whereas most reports involv-ing African American children are precipitated by alleged neglect.

Child neglect, described as the most forgotten form of maltreat-ment and the most frequently reported reason for placement (Daro 1988), is ignored by this society. Its prevalence tends to be associated with low-income, large, and multiproblem families, and with families of color. Studies indicate strong correlations between the incidence of child neglect and lack of the basic elements of what is considered a minimal standard of living for all Americans and less correlation with the psychological makeup of the caretaker (American Humane Asso-ciation (1988). Descriptions of neglect differ from descriptions of child abuse. Allegations of neglect are based on types of neglectful acts (educational neglect, medical neglect), whereas allegations of abuse are based on the severity of the maltreatment or the characteristics of individual family members. Neglectful acts can be attributed to a wide range of parental and environmental factors. It is therefore difficult to predict which families are likely to be accused of neglecting their chil-dren. Although general support and in-home services have been ef-fective interventions in neglect cases, a significant reduction in the incidence of child neglect is likely to occur simultaneously with reforms in housing, medical care, employment opportunities, and education.

Child abuse also occurs in African American families. Hampton examines the incidence of such abuse and examines current conceptual knowledge of child abuse, especially as it is manifested in African American families. He reminds us that race is still an important deter-minant of life chances and indicates that because family-support pro-grams often do not reach African Americans, these families often experience stress related to economic hardship and social isolation. Although people of color who frequent public hospitals, emergency wards, and other public agencies are more likely, allegedly, to abuse their children than those who do not frequent these places, culturally relevant intervention programs have not been devised to reach them.

The Volunteers for Children in Need (VCIN) project, as described in the Leashore, McMurray, and Bailey chapter, offers a viable and culturally relevant approach for reaching African American families. Its foundation is the African American tradition of self-help, and it incorporates the Africentric values of collective effort, mutual aid, and cooperation. The success of the project—reuniting children in foster care with their families—depended on aggressive outreach efforts aimed toward building a community-focused and community-based support network of existing organizations, on public education about the needs and scope of the problem, and on advocacy and coordination of services by a caring and flexible staff. The VCIN demonstration project illustrates one approach for instituting ethnically sensitive practice.

Another approach is suggested in the Williams chapter, which critiques the quest for permanence for African American children. With the increasing numbers of children waiting for adoption, Williams argues that more is required than additional adoption resources. Specifically, there is a need to restructure service delivery and to expand permanency options. One underutilized permanency option is legal guardianship. She presents vignettes to illustrate the appropriateness of this option for some African American children. Williams demonstrates how legal guardianship coincides with and builds on the practices of family extendedness, child sharing and informal adoption, and cooperation among African American families.

The historical development of child welfare services for African Americans is examined in the Chipungu chapter with a particular emphasis on the values that underlie current child welfare policy. She shows, as did Billingsley and Giovannoni (1972), how these values were inadvertently or purposively used to justify the exclusionary treatment of children of color. To what degree do the values that underpin current services support or supplement values held by African Americans? To address this issue, she evaluates the effects of policies and practices based on the equitable distribution of services as well as the adequacy of child welfare policies and practices. Finally, she examines alternative policy options generated from a consideration of Africentric values.

References

American Humane Association. 1988. *Highlights of Official Child Neglect and Abuse Reporting: 1986.* Denver.

Billingsley, A., and J. M. Giovannoni. 1972. *Children of the Storm: Black Children and American Child Welfare.* New York: Harcourt Brace Jovanovich.

Daro, D. 1988. *Confronting Child Abuse: Research for Effective Program Design.* New York: Free Press.

7

TOSHIO TATARA

Overview of Child Abuse and Neglect

> May God deliver us from the curse of carelessness, from the thoughtless ill-considered deed. . . . If only we were rid of . . . the thoughtless careless acts in men who know and mean better.
> —W.E.B. DU BOIS,
> *Prayers for Dark People*

The problem of child maltreatment has legal, medical, emotional, social, economic, and cultural dimensions and thus involves people, expertise, and resources from many professions and many strata of society.[1] For years, however, two beliefs—that children "belong" to parents, who have considerable latitude in deciding how to treat them, and that government intervention into the lives of families and their treatment of children should be kept to a minimum—rarely went unchallenged in the United States. Therefore, only in recent years has the issue of child maltreatment wakened the conscience of people and attained a position on the public-policy agenda.

The purpose of this chapter is twofold: to provide information about the nature and extent of child maltreatment in the United States and to review current policies and practices designed to address this tragic problem. Issues pertaining to minority children, particularly African American children, are highlighted using available data. Because the problem of child abuse and neglect is too complex to discuss thoroughly in this limited space, the chapter presents only an overview of the current situation in order to bring several issues to the fore.

187

The Nature and Extent of the Problem

DEFINITION OF CHILD MALTREATMENT

The attempt to define child abuse and neglect has caused endless debates without any definitive resolutions. Child-rearing practices now considered abusive or neglectful were once accepted as normal parenting practices, as economic necessities in some instances, or as being within the domain of parental prerogatives even if they were somewhat harsh to children. Long after the Child Abuse Prevention and Treatment Act of 1974 (and its subsequent amendments in 1978, 1984, and 1988) provided the official federal definition of child abuse and neglect, there is still a great deal of dispute about how child maltreatment should be defined. Nevertheless, the current official definition of child abuse and neglect provided by federal law is as follows: "The physical or mental injury, sexual abuse or exploitation, negligent treatment, or maltreatment of a child . . . by a person . . . who is responsible for the child's welfare, under circumstances which indicate that the child's health or welfare is harmed or threatened thereby, as determined in accordance with regulations prescribed by the Secretary [of the U.S. Department of Health and Human Services]" (P.L. 100–294, Sec. 14).

The federal legislation of 1974 required that states enact child-abuse-and-neglect statutes by incorporating these definitions and that such state statutes make reporting of suspected child maltreatment to appropriate state authorities mandatory. Today, all fifty states and the District of Columbia have enacted such statutes, and, in most jurisdictions, professionals such as medical doctors and health-care personnel, law enforcement officials, social workers, schoolteachers, and child-care workers are required to report suspected cases of child abuse and neglect to appropriate authorities. In addition, many states have made it mandatory for nonprofessional people (the public) to report suspected cases of child maltreatment, but the types of mandated reporters and the exact nature and extent of maltreatment covered by the state statutes still vary considerably. This variation illustrates how difficult it is to establish definitions of child abuse and neglect that are uniform across all jurisdictions (Younes 1987).

EXTENT OF CHILD MALTREATMENT

Policymakers and researchers commonly use statistics reported to states, through their mandated reporting systems, to estimate the national incidence of various types of child abuse and neglect. Central actors in the effort to gather, analyze, and distribute national data on child maltreatment are the National Center on Child Abuse and Neglect (NCCAN), within the U.S. Children's Bureau, and the Children's Division of the American Humane Association (AHA), a private, nonprofit organization started almost one hundred years ago as an advocacy group to promote the prevention of cruelty to animals. Following the enactment of the Child Abuse Prevention and Treatment Act in 1974, NCCAN provided AHA with a grant to design and implement a national information system for child abuse and neglect, as well as to assist states in instituting a mandatory-reporting mechanism to receive reports of suspected child maltreatment. [2] Since the inception of this national information system, AHA has been collecting and analyzing annual statistical data from state child protective services (CPS) and other state agencies on reports of alleged child abuse and neglect. Using a national summary of the data, AHA publishes an annual report, *National Analysis of Official Child Neglect and Abuse Reporting*.

These AHA reports indicate dramatic increases in the number of reports of alleged child abuse and neglect. As Table 7.1 shows, AHA estimated that 669,000 reports were received nationwide in 1976, when national data first became available, but the number jumped to almost 2.18 million by 1987, an increase of 225.6 percent over the

Table 7.1. National Estimates of Reports of Child Abuse and Neglect, 1976–1987

	Estimate	*Percent change*	*Reports per 1,000 U.S. children*
1976	669,000	—	10.1
1977	838,000	+25.3	12.8
1978	836,000	−0.2	12.9
1979	988,000	+18.2	15.4
1980	1,154,000	+16.8	18.1
1981	1,225,000	+6.2	19.4
1982	1,262,000	+3.0	20.1
1983	1,477,000	+17.0	23.6
1984	1,727,000	+16.9	27.3
1985	1,928,000	+11.6	30.6
1986	2,086,000	+8.2	32.8
1987	2,178,000	+4.4	34.0

Sources: American Humane Association, *Highlights of Official Child Neglect and Abuse Reporting: 1987* (Denver, 1989), p. 5.

Table 7.2. Race/Ethnicity of Children Involved in Reports of Abuse and
Neglect, 1982–1986, in percent

	1982	1983	1984	1985	1986
White	64.9	67.5	67.0	51.9	65.5
Black	21.7	19.7	20.8	26.8	20.5
Hispanic	11.0	9.9	9.6	19.0	10.8
Other	2.4	2.9	2.6	2.2	3.2
N	Not reported	497,716	505,837	247,755	587,970

Sources: American Humane Association, *Highlights of Official Child Neglect and Abuse Reporting: 1982*
(Denver, 1984), p. 9; American Humane Association, *Highlights of Official Child Neglect and Abuse
Reporting: 1983* (Devner, 1985), p. 8; American Humane Association, *Highlights of Official Child
Neglect and Abuse Reporting: 1984* (Denver, 1986), p. 13; American Humane Association, *Highlights
of Official Child Negelct and Abuse Reporting: 1985* (Denver, 1987), p. 14; American Humane As-
sociation, *Highlights of Official Child Negelct and Abuse Reporting: 1986* (Denver, 1988), p. 20.
Note: Race/ethnicity information was available for only a small portion of the reported cases; see
Table 7.1 for the total number of cases each year. Figures may not add to 100 percent because of
rounding.

eleven-year period. The 1987 report indicates that more than thirty
out of every thousand children in the United States (eighteen years of
age and younger) were reported to authorities as suspected victims of
child abuse or neglect. The increases shown in Table 7.1 can be explained partly by enhanced public awareness of the problem of child
maltreatment, which has increased the number of reports, and broadened state reporting laws, which have expanded the definitions. Nevertheless, CPS professionals fear that the increasing number of reports
of alleged child abuse and neglect will continue to overload the CPS
system and severely strain its resources and its ability to conduct a
thorough investigation of each report, to develop case plans, and to
provide appropriate protective services.

Information about the race/ethnicity of children involved in these
national reports of abuse and neglect has also been available from
AHA, although this information is limited to only a small portion of
the reported cases. Table 7.2 presents the race/ethnicity percentage
breakdown of children for whom abuse or neglect was reported from
1982 through 1986. Given that African American children account for
about 15 percent of the total children's population in the United States,
they are greatly overrepresented in the reported cases of abuse and
neglect. However, experts appear to agree that the actual incidence of
child maltreatment among African American children is no greater
than the incidence among other racial groups (Gelles and Cornell
1985; Petit and Overcash 1983). Two national studies on the incidence
and prevalence of child abuse and neglect sponsored by the federal

government and published in 1980 and 1988 also reached essentially the same conclusion.[3] It is possible, as some experts suggest, that "Blacks are more likely to be recognized and reported [but] the link between race and abuse is probably tenuous and quite limited" (Gelles and Cornell 1985:56).

Reports involving Hispanic children have constituted about 10 percent of the total, as shown in Table 7.2, although in 1985 the figure rose to 19 percent. The representation of these children in the reported cases of child maltreatment has generally corresponded to the proportion of Hispanic children in the total population of children, which is slightly less than 10 percent.

TYPES OF CHILD MALTREATMENT REPORTED

AHA's information system for child abuse and neglect maintains statistics for the different types of suspected child maltreatment reported. The most recent and available statistics are for 1986 and are presented in Table 7.3.

Physical Abuse

For the purpose of national reporting, child physical abuse is divided into three types: major physical injury, minor physical injury, and unspecified physical injury. Altogether physical abuse accounted

Table 7.3. Types of Child Maltreatment
Reported, 1986

	Percentage of total reports
Major physical injury	2.6
Minor physical injury	13.9
Unspecified physical injury	11.1
Sexual maltreatment/abuse	15.7
Deprivation of necessities	54.9
Emotional maltreatment	8.3
Other	7.9

Sources: American Humane Association, *Highlights of Official Child Neglect and Abuse Reporting: 1986* (Denver, 1988), p. 22.
Note: This information was available for 323,016 of the 2.1 million children who were allegedly victims of abuse and neglect in 1986. Because some children were reported as victims of more than one type of maltreatment, the total is greater than 100 percent.

for 27.6 percent of the total reported cases of child maltreatment nationwide in 1986—that is, it allegedly affected nearly 576,000 children if we extrapolate to the total number of reported cases in 1986. Available data show that physical abuse has declined somewhat over the years. However, child fatality as a result of severe abuse or neglect has become a critical national issue, and many states are beginning to gather statistics on this tragic problem. In 1986 a total of 556 child deaths were reported by twenty states (American Humane Association 1988:24). Extrapolating from this statistic, we can estimate that nearly 1,000 children died of various types of serious maltreatment during 1986. A report issued by the National Committee for the Prevention of Child Abuse estimates that child fatalities totaled 2,225 for 1988 nationwide, a 4.6 percent increase from 1986 (Daro 1989:13).

Despite suggestions by some that race is not a major factor in the incidence of child maltreatment, statistics for child fatalities cause considerable concern. Of the previously mentioned 556 fatality cases from twenty states, AHA categorized 432 cases, for which information about a child's race/ethnicity was available, into the following racial/ ethnic groups: white—52.8 percent; African American—31.7 percent; Hispanic—11.8 percent; and other—3.7 percent (American Humane Association 1988:24). African American children are represented in these child-fatality statistics twice as much as they are in the U.S. child population. Also, studies of child-abuse fatalities in other parts of the country (conducted independently of one another in nine places, including states and cities) revealed that African American children were disproportionately represented among those who died as a result of abuse or neglect (Alfaro 1988). Although it cannot be determined whether these findings hold true for the entire country, researchers, program administrators, and advocates should be alerted to the significance of these statistics.

Neglect

Officially termed "deprivation of necessities," child neglect is defined as the failure by caretakers to provide shelter, nourishment, health care, education, supervision, and clothing, and as the inability of the child to thrive. In addition the 1984 amendments to the Child Abuse Prevention and Treatment Act extended this definition to include the withholding of medically indicated treatment to disabled infants in cases where a physician deems that such treatment is necessary.

Although there has been a slight decline in the number of child-neglect cases, it is still the most pervasive, and therefore costly, form of child maltreatment. On the whole, child neglect is more likely than other types of maltreatment to result in lengthy out-of-home placements and in serious injury or even death. In CPS neglecting parents account for most of the caseloads, and child welfare agencies must spend most of their staff time and other resources over an extended period of time for the treatment and rehabilitation of neglected children.

Sexual Abuse

CPS professionals agree that sexual-abuse cases are the most complex, difficult, delicate, and sensitive of all CPS cases because the problem of child sexual abuse has greater legal, medical, psychological, social, ethical/moral, and political implications than other forms of child maltreatment. Data show that sexual abuse is the fastest growing category of child maltreatment in the United States. For example, child sexual abuse accounted for only 3.0 percent of the total reports nationally in 1976 (American Humane Association 1988:22), but this percentage increased to 15.7 percent in 1986, as shown in Table 7.3. If these percentages are extrapolated, the number of suspected victims of child sexual abuse rose from about 20,000 in 1976 to more than 327,000 in 1986. However, these figures represent only the officially reported cases; the actual incidence and prevalence of child sexual abuse are believed to be much higher.

The public and the mass media respond with great emotionalism and concern to reports of sexual maltreatment of children. The excessively sensational coverage of some isolated child sexual-abuse cases by the mass media and the heightened awareness of the public because of such media attention may be largely responsible for the dramatic increases in the frequency of reporting of child sexual maltreatment. At the same time, some studies suggest the actual incidence of child sexual abuse has indeed been increasing at a rapid pace (Campagna and Poffenberger 1988; Finkelhor 1984, 1986; Goldstein 1987; Salter 1988).

Reflecting the concern of the public, Congress broadened the definition of child sexual abuse in the 1984 amendments to the Child

Abuse Prevention and Treatment Act in order to cover sexual exploitation and out-of-home abuse by caretakers. Thus, the current definition of child sexual maltreatment is more complete and clear than it was previously.

The reported cases of child sexual abuse reveal that African American children are noticeably underrepresented in the statistics of victims. For example, the 1986 AHA data on sexual abuse/exploitation cases show the following racial/ethnic breakdown: white—77.4 percent; African American—11.1 percent; Hispanic—8.9 percent; and other—2.7 percent (American Humane Association 1988:32). Data from all previous reporting periods provide similar racial/ethnic distributions. Given these findings, it can be postulated that victims of child sexual abuse/exploitation in the United States are more likely to be white children than African American children. Explanations for this tendency, however, are not available in the child-abuse literature.

Emotional Maltreatment

In contrast to sexual abuse, emotional maltreatment has received little public and professional attention. It appears that the biggest hindrance to increased recognition of this problem is the lack of a common definition. At the federal level, no explicit definition is provided in law. CPS workers witness this problem frequently as a component of other forms of maltreatment. Typically two types of emotional maltreatment are identified by CPS agencies: emotional neglect—defined as a failure on the part of the parents or caretakers to provide the child with necessary emotional and psychological support; and emotional abuse—described as the commission by adults of abusive acts that are detrimental to the emotional well-being of the child. The CPS community generally agrees that emotional maltreatment is often subtle and not readily observable, that this problem is grossly underreported, and that its incidence is much higher than what is reported for statistical purposes.

ALLEGED PERPETRATOR'S RELATIONSHIP TO THE CHILD

Because the AHA has not published detailed data in the past few years, the most recent national information available about the relationships of abused children to alleged perpetrators is for 1983.[4] As

Table 7.4. Type of Maltreatment and Alleged Perpetrator's Relationship to Child, 1983, in percent

	Major/minor physical injury	Sexual abuse	Depriva-tion of necessities	Emotional abuse	All types of abuse/ neglect
Natural parent	81.5	58.9	90.7	80.0	84.3
Adoptive or foster parents or stepparents	9.1	30.8	1.2	6.7	5.9
Both natural and other parents	4.7	4.4	4.8	10.0	5.9
Other relative	1.8	3.0	2.1	2.1	2.1
Nonrelative	1.6	2.3	0.1	0.5	0.5
Other	1.2	0.7	1.1	0.7	1.2
N	1,356	15,339	44,591	6,311	85,039

Sources: American Humane Association, *Highlights of Official Child Neglect and Abuse Reporting: 1983* (Denver, 1985), p. 13.
Note: This information was available for only a small number of children about whom abuse or neglect was alleged; the total number of reported cases for 1983 was about 1.5 million. Figures may not add to 100 percent because of rounding.

Table 7.4 indicates, most abusive and negligent acts were reported to have been committed by natural parents, stepparents, or adoptive or foster parents, regardless of the types of maltreatment. About one-third of the cases of sexual maltreatment of children are alleged to have been committed by adoptive or foster parents or stepparents, although natural parents are alleged perpetrators in the majority of the cases. Overall, nonfamily members account for only a small percentage of the alleged perpetrators of child abuse and neglect.

SUBSTANTIATION/UNSUBSTANTIATION OF REPORTS OF SUSPECTED CHILD MALTREATMENT

Reports of suspected child maltreatment received by CPS agencies vary considerably in urgency and in the complexity of the decisions needed to protect the child. CPS workers must determine the disposition of each case by assessing potential risks for the child, the family, and the agency. One of the most critical determinations may be the substantiated/unsubstantiated decision, in which the worker confirms or does not confirm the maltreatment alleged in a report. CPS professionals, including specialized CPS investigators in some jurisdictions, must make this determination objectively and fairly, based on all the evidence that they are able to gather. However, evidence does not always lend itself to making a clear-cut decision, and, therefore, many states use a category such as "indicated but not confirmed" to cover ambiguous or borderline cases.

Furthermore, from the standpoint of CPS, the fact that a report of alleged child maltreatment is unsubstantiated does not necessarily mean that the child and family involved in the report do not need services. In fact, most CPS agencies decide that these families need home-based support services such as family counseling. In many jurisdictions many families are categorized as "at-risk" even though specific reports of alleged child maltreatment are not substantiated. At the same time, CPS agencies may not always need to remove a child involved in a substantiated case from the home. In fact, provisions in the Adoption Assistance and Child Welfare Act of 1980 (P.L. 96–272) require that states make "reasonable efforts" to keep the family together before making a decision to place the child in substitute care even in a confirmed case of abuse or neglect.

The idea that children should be kept in their own homes, if at all possible, and that the decision to separate them from their families should be considered only as the last resort, has gained wide support among policymakers, advocates, and human service professionals. This idea has become the principal philosophical base for the popular family-preservation programs that have been initiated by many public child welfare agencies, frequently with funding support from private foundations (Edna McConnell Clark Foundation 1985; Hutchinson 1983; Magri 1984). Through the provision of intensive family-based services, these programs help strengthen families at risk of child abuse and neglect.

Although it varies from one year to another, the substantiation rate has been about 42 percent nationally since 1980 (Giovannoni 1987). [5] In other words, almost 60 percent of all reports of suspected child maltreatment are not confirmed each year. Therefore, over 900,000 cases of child maltreatment (involving somewhat fewer numbers of children) out of the 2.2 million reports in 1987 were substantiated. Quite understandably, this overall low substantiation rate has become the source of great concern and controversy among critics and supporters of this country's CPS system.

Some critics concentrate their attention on the functioning of the current CPS system by arguing essentially that already scarce CPS staff and resources are being wasted in the investigation of many "frivolous" reports and that CPS agencies must drastically narrow the criteria for accepting cases for investigation and intervention (Besharov 1985:540). In fact, a number of agencies, not necessarily in response to these criticisms but largely because of serious case overloads, have developed a screening system for weeding out those reports that clearly do not warrant the use of CPS professionals.

Another group of statistics of the CPS system has gained considerable political influence through advocacy work for reform of the mandatory-reporting laws. Many of these critics have been falsely accused as child abusers, referred to authorities as alleged perpetrators of child maltreatment, and then investigated. Using a national lobbying group, Victims of Child Abuse Laws (VOCAL),[6] they strenuously argue that many innocent parents and caretakers have been falsely accused, investigated, and often prosecuted for child abuse because of inadequate reporting systems, which are incapable of identifying and screening out bogus complaints and protecting the innocent. CPS staff are also criticized by supporters of VOCAL for not being objective and for not having been trained as skilled investigators. The major goal of VOCAL seems to be to change child-abuse laws so that they are more effective and efficient than they currently are in identifying false allegations. Given that nearly 60 percent of all child-maltreatment allegations are unsubstantiated nationally each year, it is not difficult to assume that, across the country, innocent persons are indeed accused of child abuse or neglect.

Current Policies and Professional Practices

FUNDING

Both public and private funds are used to address the problem of child abuse and neglect in the United States. Public funds include those that are appropriated each year by the Child Abuse Prevention and Treatment Act, as well as those that are expended by state and local governments, primarily to augment federal funds. Private funds include those spent by private foundations and corporations, as well as donations by private citizens and corporations that are distributed by philanthropic organizations. It is, however, extremely difficult to obtain accurate information about how much money the United States spends to support a wide variety of treatment, protective, and prevention programs; advocacy activities; research and demonstration efforts; and other activities in the field of child abuse and neglect. I present in this chapter, therefore, only a rough estimate of the amount of money spent to curtail child-maltreatment problems.

Public Funds

Public funds come from two major sources: the federal government, and state and local governments. Data on federal funding are readily available, but national information about state and local expenditures cannot be obtained. A recent study by the American Public Welfare Association (1988) estimates that a total of $806 million was spent by federal, state, and local governments to support CPS during fiscal year 1985. Although there is a clear indication that spending for CPS has increased significantly since then, it is not possible to make a meaningful trends analysis of expenditures for any specific social service because reliable national data are not available.

Over the years, federal funding under the Child Abuse Prevention and Treatment Act increased somewhat, as these figures for selected fiscal years show (Select Committee on Children, Youth and Families 1987):

1981	$22.9 million
1984	$16.2 million
1986	$24.8 million
1987	$25.9 million

As Table 7.1 indicates, the number of reports of child abuse and neglect rose from 1.23 million in 1981 to almost 2.18 million in 1987—an increase of 77.8 percent. As a result the caseloads of CPS agencies also rose nearly 80 percent nationwide during the same period. However, funding for the only federal program designed solely to prevent, identify, and treat child maltreatment went up only 13.1 percent. The 1988 amendments to the Child Abuse Prevention and Treatment Act authorized $48 million, but only $26 million were actually appropriated, as had been the case in the previous several years. Efforts by the National Child Abuse Coalition, the advocacy group comprising nearly thirty national organizations serving the interests of children, and other organizations to lobby for full funding at the authorized levels have not been successful.

The federal funds available under the Child Abuse Prevention and

Treatment Act are divided into two major types of grants: formula grants to states, which are allocated to support training, information-systems development, and design and implementation of innovative programs; and discretionary grants, which are awarded to public agencies and private organizations on a competitive basis to support various research and demonstration projects. In the 1980s Congress consistently allocated more money for the discretionary grants than for the formula grants. However, recognizing the critical need for additional resources, especially for handling cases involving child sexual abuse, Congress created a new state grant program to assist in establishing and operating programs to improve the investigation and prevention of child-abuse cases, particularly sexual-abuse cases. Neither type of federal grant can be used to finance direct services to victims of child maltreatment and their families. The provisions of the Child Abuse Prevention and Treatment Act indicate that Congress did not intend to pay for direct-service programs and expected that state and local governments would find funds from other sources to support these programs.

The main source of public funds that state and local governments use to finance their direct-service programs is the Social Services Block Grant (SSBG), which had been known as Title XX of the Social Security Act Social Services Program until the Reagan administration transformed it to a block grant in 1981. The figures for select fiscal years indicate the level of funding for the SSBG (Select Committee on Children, Youth and Families 1987):

1981	$3.0 billion
1984	$2.7 billion
1986	$2.6 billion
1987	$2.7 billion

As can be seen, funding for the SSBG declined during the period in which the caseloads of CPS agencies went up dramatically. Therefore, state and local governments had to increase their spending to keep up with the increased demand for CPS.

Furthermore, the only federal funding support to states aimed solely at the prevention of child abuse comes from the Child Abuse Prevention Challenge Grants Act (P.L. 98–473) of 1984. The expressed purpose of this unique law is to "encourage states to establish and maintain trust funds or other funding mechanisms, including [state] appropriations, to support child abuse and neglect prevention activities," and the law authorizes the federal government to match 25 percent of a state's budget for the prevention of child abuse and neglect. Forty-seven states have established some form of children's trust fund. Information from thirty-eight states indicates that a total of $16 million was collected by these trust funds in 1986.[7] Small grants are awarded on a competitive basis to community-based organizations providing services for child-abuse prevention, but competition is extremely keen for these grants.

A controversy has arisen concerning this program because, first, Congress appropriated only $4.8 million for fiscal year 1989 in spite of the total need of $7 million to fully match the $28 million that states had set aside for prevention efforts. Even though the Bush administration proposed elimination of the federal program when the Act expired on September 30, 1989, Congress appropriated $4.93 million in 1990. Although advocacy groups have launched massive campaigns to apply pressure on both Congress and the administration to save the program, the future of the Child Abuse Prevention Challenge Grants is uncertain at the present time.

In addition to these major programs, which directly affect efforts of state and local governments and communities to prevent or treat child maltreatment, several other federal programs finance various child welfare services that are, in some unique way, related to CPS. These federal programs include the program for child welfare services under Title IV-B of the Social Security Act; the family violence program created as Title III of the Child Abuse Prevention and Treatment Act in 1985; and the adoption assistance program under Title IV-E of the Social Security Act.

Private Funds

Private foundations and the United Way of America are the major sources of private funding for programs to fight the problems of child abuse and neglect in the United States. In addition, many private corporations donate funds to support various child welfare programs. However, national information about corporate giving specific to programs for child abuse and neglect programs is not available.

The Foundation Center, a nonprofit organization that collects and disseminates information about the funding and program activities of private foundations, has collected some funding information related to child-abuse programs since 1981. As shown in Table 7.5,

Table 7.5. Foundation Funding Related to Child Abuse, Key Years

	Number of foundations providing grants	Number of grants	Total amount
1981	57	84	$1,980,051
1985	74	129	$2,602,295
1986	87	186	$3,553,086

Source: Foundation Center, "Comsearch Printouts," no. 95, for 1981, 1985, 1986. Washington, D.C.

the amount of foundation giving for child-abuse programs increased greatly from 1981 to 1986, as did the number of grants, and the number of private foundations that provided grants also increased significantly during the same period. Because not all foundations report their data to the Foundation Center, it can be assumed that the actual involvement of the foundation community in programs for child abuse is greater than the figures indicate.

Funding information available from the United Way of America does not specify the amount for child abuse and neglect. However, if the information about the amount of funds allocated for all child welfare programs, including CPS programs, is used as a proxy measure for reference purposes, it can be shown that a total of $23.2 million was used for such purposes during 1985.[8] However, the child welfare field is only a small part of the United Way program; thus, this amount accounts for only about 1.6 percent of the total United Way allocation of more than $1.5 billion in 1985.

On the whole, private funding accounts for a small portion of the total funding in the field of child abuse and neglect. State and local governments, therefore, must depend on federal funding, particularly SSBG funds, to support treatment, CPS, and prevention programs. Many states and localities, however, have had their share of SSBG funding reduced in the past several years, and this reduction has resulted in layoffs of staff and drastic curtailment in services for abused children and their families. Furthermore, some states are beginning to express concern about their inability to investigate reports of child abuse and neglect in a timely manner because of the severe shortage of staff and the unrealistic caseload burden.

TYPES OF SERVICES AVAILABLE

Because child maltreatment is a multidimensional problem, a variety of agencies and services is necessary to provide its victims with treatment, to ensure the safety and protection of children in at-risk families, and to help prevent further occurrences of the problem. Across the United States, therefore, communities' social service, medical, mental health, educational, legal, and law enforcement resources are mobilized to address the challenges of child abuse and neglect. The multidisciplinary approach to treatment, protection, and prevention is the most popular method of professional intervention today. A brief summary of how child-abuse treatment, CPS and abuse-prevention efforts are generally carried out with the active participation of several different professions follows.

Treatment

Since the discovery of the "battered-child syndrome" (Kempe et al. 1962), the medical profession has played a key role in the diagnosis and treatment of victims of child abuse (Ellerstein 1981). Although statistics are not available, most major children's hospitals across the country operate programs designed to diagnose and treat the problems associated with child abuse and neglect. Physicians, mostly pediatricians, are providing leadership in many of these programs. Some (Boston Children's Hospital, San Diego Children's Hospital and Health Center, Washington, D.C., Children's Hospital, New York Hospital, to cite only a few) are better than others, primarily because they are either led by well-known physicians or engage in research in addition to providing clinical services. It appears that hospitals identify and treat more serious cases of child maltreatment than do other agencies in the community. Furthermore, one study discovered that hospitals identified "many more cases of physical abuse than did other agencies" (Hampton and Newberger 1988:212–221).

Because the abusive or neglecting parent generally exhibits some degree of psychological impairment that requires the attention of a mental health professional, these professionals have also been active in the field of child abuse and neglect. Psychiatrists, psychologists, psychiatric social workers, and psychoanalysts intensified their own training programs in the 1980s to understand the causes and dynamics of abusive acts against children. Either independently or as a part of an interdisciplinary program, mental health personnel offer evaluation, consultation, and therapeutic intervention—for example, individual and family counseling—to victims of child abuse, as well as to abusive and neglecting parents. Today, most community mental health centers are providing various types of services related to the problem of family violence and are also participating in interdisciplinary programs.

Because the abusive or neglecting family exists in a social context (Pelton 1981), intervention must include consideration of the family's sociocultural environment as well. The social work profession has made a significant contribution to ameliorating the adverse conditions that often overwhelm abusive and neglecting families. In a variety of settings that address problems of child abuse and neglect, professional social workers play an important role as support service providers, family therapists, advocates, researchers, and trainers, either working directly with clients or assisting experts from other professions.

Recognizing the critical role of the social work profession in the field of child abuse and neglect, NCCAN provided the National Association of Social Workers with a three-year grant in 1978 to establish and operate a National Professional Resource Center on Child Abuse and Neglect for Social Workers and Public Welfare Workers. In cooperation with the American Public Welfare Association, this resource center conducted a range of activities to help raise professional awareness of child abuse and neglect, improve the skills of social work practitioners, foster interdisciplinary collaboration, promote the cultural responsiveness of social workers to child maltreatment, and enhance resources (Antler 1982).

Given rapidly increasing caseloads, insufficient resources, and growing tension between child welfare agencies and the public concerning the appropriate role of these agencies, there is little doubt that the child welfare job is one of the most difficult to perform in the field of human services today. It is quite understandable, therefore, that turnover rates among child welfare staff, particularly direct-service workers, are extremely high. In one study, with eighteen states reporting, the average turnover rate among direct-service workers was 18 percent in 1986, but the highest rate was 40 percent (Russell n.d.: 36). Interestingly, the study found that the turnover rates were consistently higher in states that do not require a college degree for child welfare workers but lower in states that require a master's degree in social work (M.S.W.) (Russell n.d.). These findings strongly suggest a relationship between turnover rate and degree requirements, particularly the M.S.W. requirement, with respect to child welfare positions in public human service agencies. Therefore, the importance of the social work profession looms large in the field of public child welfare (National Child Welfare Resource Center for Management and Administration 1987).

Finally, there is the role of the legal system in the treatment of child abuse and neglect; in this system the police, the public prosecutor, the family courts, and private attorneys play a critical part. The involvement of law enforcement agencies in cases of child maltreatment has become frequent, as public sentiment toward child abuse and neglect has begun to favor prosecution and criminal punishment of offenders. Human service professionals generally prefer to take a nonpunitive approach to the treatment of child abusers. However, the police and public prosecutors in many states are training themselves to become experts and are beginning to handle some child-maltreatment cases, particularly physical-injury and sexual-abuse cases (Lanning 1968).

Protective Services

Although child-abuse treatment takes place largely in private organizational settings, CPS is almost exclusively in public agency settings, as the federal child-abuse statute and most state child protection laws stipulate. All states designate a specific unit of their human service agencies to serve as a CPS agency. The main objective of CPS is to design and deliver a range of services aimed at ensuring the health and safety of children who come to the attention of public agencies as alleged victims of maltreatment. In most jurisdictions, the state-level CPS agencies are responsible for operating the mandatory reporting system and responding to reports of suspected child abuse and neglect.

Specifically, CPS agencies in state and local governments engage in the following major activities: the operation of a system to receive reports and referrals of child maltreatment by gathering evidence from the child, parents, other family members, neighbors, and appropriate personnel from other professions involved in a particular case (physician, police officer, school official, psychologist); the substantiation or unsubstantiation of reports of child maltreatment based on evidence; the provision of emergency or short-term services to the child and family, as needed; the preparation of court proceedings, if necessary; the referral of cases to treatment or rehabilitation programs in the public or private sector; and the removal of the child or the perpetrator from the home, when needed.

All these activities significantly affect the lives of the people who are involved and, therefore, are critically important to the communities in which the CPS agency exists. For example, as mentioned earlier, nearly 2.2 million reports of suspected child maltreatment were made to the states' mandatory reporting systems in 1987; it was the responsibility of the CPS agencies to investigate and determine whether these reports could be confirmed or not. Furthermore, each year, more than 180,000 children are removed from their homes and placed in foster care, and almost 70 percent of these children have to be separated from their parent(s) for a protective reason (Tatara 1989a, 1989b). CPS workers play a key role in making these decisions about child removal and placement. It is the responsibility of other child welfare workers to ensure that the needs of children residing in foster care are fully met and families are given all services needed for reunification with their children.

Prevention

Increased emphasis on the prevention of child maltreatment has been identified by Congress as a priority. Early efforts in the field of child abuse and neglect were directed almost exclusively toward helping families in which abuse or neglect had already occurred. Pointing out that the National Center on Child Abuse and Neglect was devoting little attention to prevention, the General Accounting Office (GAO) suggested in a 1989 report that the federal government "identify and disseminate information about practical and effective programs or approaches for preventing child abuse and neglect and help states and localities implement such approaches" (1980:53). Subsequently, Congress incorporated these GAO suggestions into the Child Abuse Prevention Challenge Grants Act, as described earlier.

There is no disagreement in the professional community that the alternative to preventing child abuse and neglect is costly in both economic and human terms. For a long time, however, attempts at prevention were often met with skepticism, and they were generally considered ineffective. Some argued that the prevention of child abuse would require the total philosophical and political reorientation of society and doubted seriously the effectiveness of the Child Abuse Prevention and Treatment Act in curtailing the incidence of child maltreatment (Gil 1981:291–324; Zigler 1979:171–213). Mainly because of the dramatic increase in the numbers of child-abuse reports and the enormous cost of supporting treatment and rehabilitation programs however, public and professional attention eventually turned to child-abuse prevention. Although a complete social change may make perfect sense theoretically, as it relates to child-abuse prevention, such a drastic step is not likely to occur in the immediate future. For now, therefore, child-abuse prevention must rely on collaborative efforts by professionals and the public to create a chain of small changes at the community level.

Prevention programs are defined roughly as those designed to provide education and information to help create a social environment in which the use of violence of any kind in interpersonal relationships is unacceptable (primary prevention), and as those aimed at providing specific support services to families considered to be at risk of child abuse or neglect (secondary prevention). Professionals in the field generally agree with the following points concerning primary prevention efforts: Such efforts should be directed toward the general population; they should attempt to eliminate sociocultural factors that condone violence; they should promote ways to resolve conflict at the interpersonal level through nonviolent and peaceful means; they should focus particularly on the development of healthy parent/child relationships and sound family functioning; and they should be sustained for a long time to create changes in the behavior of individuals, as well as changes in social institutions.

In sum, the ultimate aim of primary prevention is to create a nonviolent society. But, given the history of the United States, in which the use of force was often justified, and the current sociocultural climate, which tolerates violent behavior, the success of primary-prevention programs will be limited.[9] Simply, compared with the situation in other developed countries, there is too much violence in the United States, a country that has not been able to ban the possession of small firearms and that has not been able completely to prevent violence toward children. Although most other developed countries have enacted stiff laws against the possession of handguns, it appears that the United States is moving backward when it comes to gun control. Furthermore, it probably has more violent crime than any other developed country in the world. Some years ago, Sweden adopted a national policy making all forms of corporal punishment for children illegal. However, although data are somewhat dated, reports from ten thousand middle-class respondents to a national survey conducted in the United States indicated that 77 percent thought that "children should be disciplined by physical punishment whenever necessary" (Zigler 1977).

Secondary prevention efforts are aimed mainly at families that, although not yet abusive, are more likely to become so than families in the general population. Some of the characteristics of secondary prevention programs are that services are provided to an already defined group of vulnerable families; services are more problem focused than are primary prevention services; services are designed to help prevent future parent/child problems by focusing on the alleviation of particular stresses and frustrations; and services are aimed at helping to strengthen overall family functioning.

Several different types of secondary child-abuse prevention programs are provided either by public or private agencies. *Prenatal and perinatal support programs* for expectant and new parents help prepare them for the task of rearing children. They learn about child development, parent/child relationships, and community resources available to families. Agencies frequently assist in forming peer support groups for first-time parents, teenage parents, and single parents. Because children are likely to be at risk of abuse in families in which the parent/child relationship is weak, these programs are used to strengthen the bond between the parents and the child at birth by humanizing the delivery experience, bringing the father into the delivery room, and emphasizing the importance of parental responsibility for rearing the child.

It is often observed that abusive families tend to be socially isolated and lack knowledge about health and social services in the community. *Creating networks of new parents* or *pairing first-time parents with experienced parents* can help to enhance their understanding of the child's early years because such arrangements encourage the sharing of information and advice on child care, nutrition, and home management.

Identifying and treating health and behavioral problems early in life are important in preventing child-abuse problems, as professionals have observed that children who are sick or handicapped may be more vulnerable than those who are not to abuse or neglect.

Good childcare programs can achieve many of the goals of child-abuse prevention because these programs can enhance emotional ties and communication between parents and children, increase parents' ability to cope with the stresses of caring for their children, reduce family isolation, increase peer support, and improve access to social and health services for the family. Many professionals argue that day care helps alleviate stress and increases family well-being. The rising number of families with both parents or with single parents in the work force brings with it a rise in stress among family members, particularly between parents and children. Because several child sexual-abuse cases at day-care centers have been reported nationally, many parents are concerned about the quality of childcare services available in their communities.

Many elementary and secondary schools are now offering *child-abuse prevention programs as part of their curriculum*. Such programs are supposed to provide children with practical skills to protect themselves from being abused and to provide adolescents with accurate information about human sexuality, pregnancy prevention, and the parental role.

In addition to their therapeutic effects, *programs for abused children* are considered to be valuable prevention resources because abused children may become abusive parents. Therefore, it is common today that treatment programs for abused children give a great deal of emphasis to the minimization of the long-term adverse effects of abuse or neglect and the provision early in life of positive parent role models, in addition to attempting to alleviate the immediate effects of maltreatment.

Families under stress with no place to turn in times of crisis are at increased risk of becoming abusive or negligent. *Crisis-assistance programs for at-risk families* are available in many communities, and such programs, frequently equipped with a twenty-four-hour telephone hotline and trained staff, provide families facing a crisis with counseling, temporary care of children, and other services.

The purpose of *public-awareness programs* is generally twofold: to provide at-risk parents with information about the locations of needed services and to promote an understanding that potential violence is in all persons, that all parents experience stress sometimes, and that it is all right to seek help. Both public and private agencies participate in a variety of information and education programs at the community level by publishing brochures and posters, broadcasting public-service announcements on the radio and television, sponsoring seminars, and giving speeches at various civic functions.

In summary, for families at risk two general approaches are incorporated into most child-abuse prevention programs with varying degrees of emphasis. One approach is directed toward effecting changes in the parents, strengthening their ability to cope with stress, and modifying their relationships to their children. Attempts are made to bring about changes in parents' patterns of behavior through education, behavior modification, and self-help groups, and through counseling, psychotherapy, and group work. These activities and their objectives are consistent with those of a traditional psychotherapeutic approach.

Another approach, which can be defined as a sociotherapeutic approach, is directed primarily toward reducing stress in families at risk of dissolution or in dysfunctional families through provision of tangible benefits, social support, facilitative services, and increased socioeconomic opportunities. Day care, family support, job training, employment services, services for caregivers, transportation, and adequate housing are examples of services provided under this approach.

EFFECTIVENESS OF PROGRAMS

Despite the thousands of child-abuse treatment, rehabilitation, and prevention programs of various types, the number of published studies concerned with the effectiveness of these programs is not large. In fact, the most extensive and most recent data on the results of these programs come from the evaluation of various federally funded demonstration projects in the 1970s. Because of severe funding cuts in the 1980s, few studies of note in the field of child abuse and neglect have been produced since then.

In addressing the question of whether specific CPS programs have achieved their objective of reducing maltreatment, available outcome data provide answers that are not complimentary to the professions involved in the programs. Furthermore, no reliable information points to any prevention programs that have produced desired outcomes. Using recidivism (or recurrence of abuse) as the basic criterion of success, one study found that treatment, rehabilitation, and protective services were successful in about half the cases (Berkeley Planning Associates 1977).

Some studies have found success rates much lower than 50 percent. For example, although the data are somewhat dated, Johnson concluded in 1977, following a detailed study of recidivism in two cities, that approximately 60 percent of the children treated by various programs were subsequently abused again—that is, the success rate was only 40 percent. Based on her findings, she noted that "there is no question that efforts to rehabilitate parents and prevent further neglect and/or abuse have generally failed" (1977:162). Other data from longitudinal studies of abusive families who have received services from treatment or rehabilitation programs corroborate these discouraging observations (Sudia 1981:268–290).

Most professionals in the field are aware that their interventions can achieve only some modest level of success in producing desired changes. Child abuse, like any other social problem, is caused by complex factors, and a single program is probably going to have rather limited success. On the whole, however, they remain committed to continuing efforts to bring about positive changes in the lives of children.

Future Prospects

Given present circumstances, child abuse and neglect will not be reduced significantly in the near future. Reports of child maltreatment show no sign of any declining. Federal funding under the Child Abuse Prevention and Treatment Act and the SSBG will probably not increase greatly. Furthermore, resources for prevention, protection, and treatment programs at the state and local levels are becoming scarce at a rapid pace. Concerned that there may be a serious crisis in the field of child abuse and neglect unless some fundamental changes are made, political advocates for children's issues and human service professionals are desperately lobbying for increased federal funding and involvement in the provision of technical assistance and training for state and local CPS agencies.[10]

Many professionals agree, however, that although additional funding and increased federal involvement are important, the present near crisis in the CPS system cannot be alleviated only by such increases and that a number of specific changes must also occur, particularly in state and local CPS agencies, to avert the worsening of the situation. Some of the recommendations frequently discussed are outlined here.

DEVELOPMENT OF A CLEAR STATEMENT OF THE MISSION OF CPS AGENCIES

The dramatic increases in, as well as the increased social and political significance of, the caseloads of CPS agencies require that CPS administrators collectively assess the current situation, redefine the philosophy and principles of the CPS profession, reformulate their intervention strategies, and develop and disseminate nationwide a CPS manifesto. In various communities the CPS agency has become the front-end, all-purpose agency for solving problems of children and families, largely because of the community's overwhelming tendency to refer these problems initially to the CPS agency without regard to the nature of the problems. As a result, many CPS agencies today suffer from a lack of both a distinct identity and a clear sense of mission. This situation has a negative effect on the morale and work performance of CPS workers. Given these circumstances, it is imperative that the nation's CPS administrators define clear lines of demarcation for the areas of their professional and statutory responsibility and articulate them to the public through effective public relations efforts.

DEVELOPMENT AND DISSEMINATION OF NATIONAL STANDARDS FOR INTERVENTION AND DECISION MAKING

There are no national standards for CPS practices that state and local agencies all use to design their CPS systems. The Child Abuse Prevention and Treatment Act provides basic definitions of various types of child maltreatment, but the operationalization of these definitions is left to each state. Moreover, this federal statute does not present in detail standards for professional social work practices in the field of child abuse and neglect. CPS practices, therefore, vary considerably from one state to another, and from one locality to another even in the same state. The interpretation of child-maltreatment definitions, guidelines for investigating reports of suspected abuse or neglect, criteria for assessing risks for children and families, and procedures for making decisions related to the removal of children from their own homes are only a few of the CPS practices that vary widely. Unfortunately, these variations in CPS practices have given the public an impression of a lack of professionalism and have led to the erosion of public confidence in a number of communities. CPS agencies have been criticized by various citizens' groups for their ineffectiveness in protecting children from maltreatment.

If the CPS system is to restore public confidence and support, without which it cannot function, and is to improve the effectiveness of its services, CPS administrators as a group must develop national standards. These standards should clearly delineate the guidelines for their professional activities, define the types and extent of core services available from CPS agencies, and set forth realistic lines of demarcation for CPS interventions.

IMPLEMENTATION OF AGGRESSIVE
EDUCATION CAMPAIGNS
ABOUT THE APPROPRIATE ROLE
AND FUNCTION OF CPS

It is essential that the public be correctly informed about the purpose, types, and limits of CPS programs, as well as the problems and issues in the CPS field, so that it will better understand the present system, its strengths and limitations, and form realistic expectations at the community level. It is particularly important that CPS administrators inform the public of key features of the national standards for professional practices that frequently tend to be controversial—for example, the criteria for an investigation and the guidelines for the removal of a child or perpetrator. Furthermore, the public must be informed that child–maltreatment cases are extremely complex and involve a number of social and psychological problems, but that the CPS program is not designed or empowered to resolve all these problems.

EXPANSION OF FAMILY-BASED SERVICES

By nature, the CPS system is reactive in that professional intervention usually begins with an investigation of reports of alleged child maltreatment. In order to augment this reactive function, state and local agencies must expand their existing family-based services to help strengthen the functioning of families at risk of abusing or neglecting their children. The federal government has recognized the importance of family-based services and their critical role in preventing child maltreatment in at-risk families as well as in preventing the unnecessary removal of children from their homes, and has supported a number of research, demonstration, and training projects.[11] Family-based programs should alleviate the pressure placed on CPS agencies by the increased number of reports of child abuse and neglect.

STRENGTHENING AND IMPROVEMENT
OF EXISTING SERVICES

There is no doubt that existing CPS services must be improved significantly in order to treat victims of child maltreatment in a timely manner, to rehabilitate families with abuse and neglect problems, and to help prevent recurrences of child maltreatment in at-risk families. Many CPS administrators acknowledge that the quality of CPS services has suffered for a long time largely because of such factors as the unrealistically large workloads, low worker morale, high worker turnover, lack of training for workers, and ineffective working relationships with other community agencies. Some aspects of the current critical situation in CPS—for example, lack of federal funding—are certainly beyond the immediate capability of CPS administrators to rectify, but CPS administrators could, for example, make a significant contribution by providing their workers with training and development opportunities on an ongoing basis to help them develop and maintain their intervention skills.

ENHANCEMENT OF THE CULTURAL RESPONSIVENESS OF CPS PERSONNEL AND SERVICES

Although some research has found that race/ethnicity is not a major factor in the incidence or prevalence of child maltreatment, African American children are greatly overrepresented in the reported cases, as mentioned earlier. In addition, there seems to be a strong relationship between socioeconomic class and child abuse and neglect. Some researchers even argue that, in fact, the problems of poverty are causes of the abusive and negligent behaviors of parents and of the "resultant harm to children" (Gil 1970; Pelton 1978). Regardless of whether it can be firmly proven that there is a causal relationship between poverty and child maltreatment, data on reported cases show that families in the lower economic classes, as measured by public-assistance status, account for nearly 50 percent of such cases (American Humane Association 1988).[12] Given these facts, it is clear that CPS staff must work effectively with children and families of color who receive public assistance. Increased efforts are needed to help workers enhance their cultural responsiveness and sensitivity in handling clients. In order to be effective, these efforts must include specific, ongoing in-service and on-the-job training programs and must require the participation of supervisors and agency administrators. At the same time, administrators must carefully reexamine agency policy and procedures in such critical areas as reporting, investigation, substantiation, risk assessment, child-removal decisions, and service planning and delivery, as well as staffing and recruitment, to eliminate any cultural bias from CPS practice at the institutional level.

Although CPS professionals can do little directly to reduce the social problems that affect child abuse or neglect, the preservation of a well-functioning, effective CPS system is essential to every community because such a system can ensure at least a minimum level of protection for children. If the CPS system becomes totally ineffective, society would be deprived of any mechanism to protect children in at-risk families from maltreatment and to rehabilitate families with abuse or neglect problems. Recognizing the grave situation of the CPS system, several national organizations, including the National Association of Public Child Welfare Administrators (one of the affiliate organizations of the American Public Welfare Association), the American Association for Protecting Children (a division of AHA), and the Child Welfare League of America, have developed national CPS guidelines and are now working on various training curricula for use in state and local agencies (National Association of Public Child Welfare Administrators 1988). These organizations frequently work with one another during the process of developing their own material, but they seldom collaborate with one another to work on one project jointly. In fact, these organizations have prepared these documents, which will have an impact on the future of CPS practices, almost independently of one another, a source of concern among public child welfare administrators. Nonetheless, it appears that all the requisites outlined have been studied closely by experts, have been further elaborated and included in the CPS guidelines, and are likely to be reflected in training curricula and other documents that are now being developed.

Conclusions

Child abuse and neglect are serious national problems that constantly threaten the health and safety of millions of children and disrupt the functioning of thousands of families in the United States. With the enactment of the Child Abuse Prevention and Treatment Act of 1974, the federal government firmly established its commitment to providing states and localities with funding and technical assistance to curtail the incidence of child maltreatment. In the 1980s the nation spent billions of dollars to finance a variety of treatment, rehabilitation, protective, and prevention programs in the field of child abuse and neglect.

However, although the country spends enormous amounts of money from public and private sources to combat the problems of child maltreatment, the number of reports of all types of alleged child maltreatment has continued to increase and has seriously eroded the ability of state and local agencies to provide adequate services to victims and their families. If these trends continue, the CPS system could become more and more ineffective.

Child maltreatment is a complex and difficult problem and requires the expertise and resources of many professions to treat victims, rehabilitate families, and prevent maltreatment. A variety of programs are available, but researchers have found that the effectiveness and success rates of these programs are limited. However, for the most part, professionals in the field maintain a positive attitude—that, even with modest success rates, their interventions have indeed produced some positive changes in the lives of many people.

Unfortunately, the prospects for greatly reducing child maltreatment in the near future are not good. The number of reports of child abuse and neglect is increasing steadily, and experts do not seem to be able to predict possible outer limits to the growth in the number of such reports. A serious national crisis may be imminent in the CPS system unless some fundamental changes are made to alter it and, at the same time, unless increased attention is given to ameliorating such social problems as poverty, unemployment, alcohol/substance abuse, adolescent pregnancy, inadequate housing, poor sanitation, inadequate nutrition, inadequate health care, and racial discrimination. If not the causes, these social problems are certainly antecedents to many cases of child abuse and neglect. Furthermore, the ability to effect significant solutions in these problems is simply beyond the scope of the CPS system. When a nation loses its war against these social problems, the chances of winning community battles against child abuse become slim.

Acknowledgment

This chapter is a revised version of T. Tatara, "Child Maltreatment in America: The Nature and Extent of the Problem and Current Policies and Professional Practices Designed to Address the Problem," *Kodomo to Katei* (Children and Families) 24 (1988):26–46.

Notes

1. The term *child maltreatment* is used interchangeably with the terms *abuse and neglect of children* and *child abuse and neglect*. The different types of child maltreatment, or abuse and neglect, are defined later in this chapter.

2. In addition to supporting AHA's efforts to regularly collect state data on abuse and neglect reports, NCCAN sponsored two research studies, in 1980 and 1986, to estimate the national incidence and prevalence of child abuse and neglect (National Center on Child Abuse and Neglect 1981, 1987).

3. See the studies cited in note 2. The 1987 study concluded that "there were no significant relationships between the incidence of maltreatment and a child's race/ethnicity."

4. Information about the relationships of abused children to alleged perpetrators is available for the 1986 data, but the categories of perpetrators were limited to only three: parents, other relatives, and unrelated.

5. The definition of substantiation varies from one state to another. Also, the substantiation rate varies depending on who reports a suspected child maltreatment. Reports made by law enforcement officials or physicians have always resulted in substantiation rates higher than 50 percent. Reports made by private persons have always had lower substantiation rates.

6. VOCAL was organized in the wake of one of the most widely reported child sexual-abuse scandals in the United States, which took place in the small rural community of Jordan, Minnesota, in 1984. At first, a total of twenty adults (parents of the alleged victims) were charged. When the person who had incriminated these adults recanted his initial testimony however, two were acquitted. Subsequently, charges against all others were dropped but not without acrimonious accusations and counteraccusations among the residents (including many professionals) of Jordan.

7. Information about the children's trust fund was obtained from states through an informal survey of staff of the American Public Welfare Association.

8. This figure was obtained from the national office of the United Way in Alexandria, Virginia.

9. The factors that determine behavior, psychological makeup, and attitudes are numerous and complex, and require an analysis of a wide range of historical, sociocultural, religious, political, and economic data to be understood. Although somewhat oversimplified, this characterization of the United States is, I believe, supported by factual data and intended only to capture some of the major manifested problems related to the difficulty of successfully implementing child-abuse prevention programs.

10. For example, the National Child Abuse Coalition has unsuccessfully lobbied for funding of the Child Abuse Prevention and Treatment Act at the authorized level, which has always exceeded $40 million a year.

11. Most notably, the federal government has assisted the University of Iowa School of Social Work in developing and operating a National Resource Center on Family-Based Services, which has been providing public state and local child welfare agencies with training and technical assistance as well as conducting research activities related to family-based services.

12. The 1986 data are the most recent published data on the public-assis-

tance status of families involved in the abuse and neglect reports. Of 87,600 families, for which the information was available, 48.3 percent were on public assistance.

References

Alfaro, J. D. 1988. "What Can we Learn from Child Abuse Fatalities? A Synthesis of Nine Studies." In *Protecting Children from Abuse and Neglect: Policy and Practice*, edited by D. Besharov, 219–264. Springfield, Ill.: Charles C. Thomas.

American Humane Association, 1984. *Trends in Child Abuse and Neglect: A National Perspective*. Denver.

———. 1988. *Highlights of Official Child Neglect and Abuse Reporting: 1986*. Denver.

American Public Welfare Association. 1988. *Analysis of Child Welfare Expenditure Data and Child Day Care Expenditure Data*. Phase II Report. Washington, D.C.

Antler, S., ed. 1982. *Child Abuse and Child Protection: Policy and Practice*. Silver Spring, Md.: National Association of Social Workers.

Berkeley Planning Associates. 1977. *Evaluation: National Demonstration Program in Child Abuse and Neglect*. Berkeley, Calif.

Besharov, D. J. 195. "Doing Something about Child Abuse: The Need to Narrow the Grounds for State Intervention." *Harvard Journal of Law and Public Policy* 8:540, 542–550.

Campagna, D. S., and D. L. Poffenberger. 1988. *The Sexual Trafficking in Children: An Investigation of the Child Sex Trade*. Dover, Mass.: Auburn House.

Daro, D. 1989. *Child Abuse Fatalities Continue to Rise: The Results of the 1988 Annual Fifty State Survey*. Working Paper 8808. Chicago: National Committee for the Prevention of Child Abuse.

Edna McConnell Clark Foundation. 1985. *Keeping Families Together: The Case for Family Preservation*. New York.

Ellerstein, N. S., ed. 1981. *Child Abuse and Neglect: A Medical Reference*. New York: Wiley.

Finkelhor, D. 1984. *Child Sexual Abuse: New Theory and Research*. New York: Free Press.

Finkelhor, D., with S. Aragi. 1986. *A Source Book on Child Sexual Abuse*. Beverly Hills, Calif.: Sage.

Gelles, R. J., and C. P. Cornell. 1985. *Intimate Violence in Families*. Beverly Hills, Calif.: Sage.

General Accounting Office. 1980. *Increased Federal Efforts to Better Identify, Treat, and Prevent Child Abuse and Neglect*. Washington, D.C.

Gil, D. G. 1970. *Violence against Children: Physical Child Abuse in the United States*. Cambridge: Harvard University Press.

——. 1981. "The United States versus Child Abuse." In *The Social Context of Child Abuse and Neglect*, edited by L. H. Pelton, 291–324. New York: Human Sciences Press.

Giovannoni, J. M. 1987. *Private Individuals' Reports of Child Abuse and Neglect*. Los Angeles: University of California.

Goldstein, S. L. 1987. *The Sexual Exploitation of Children: A Practical Guide to Assessment, Investigation and Intervention*. New York: Elsevier.

Hampton, R. L., and E. H. Newberger. 1988. "Child Abuse Incidence and Reporting by Hospitals: Significance of Severity, Class, and Race." In *Coping with Family Violence: Research and Policy Perspectives*, edited by G. T. Hotaling, D. Finkelhor, J. T. Kirkpatrick, and M. A. Strauss, 212–221. Beverly Hills, Calif.: Sage.

Hutchinson, J. R. 1983. *Family-Centered Social Services: A Model for Public Child Welfare Agencies*. Oakdale, Iowa: National Resource Center on Family-Based Services.

Johnson, C. 1977. *Two Community Protective Service Systems: Nature and Effectiveness of Service Intervention*. Athens, Ga.: Regional Institute of Social Welfare Research.

Kempe, H. C., F. N. Silverman, B. T. Steele, W. Droegemueller, and H. K. Silver. 1962. "The Battered Child Syndrome." *Journal of the American Medical Association* 181:105–112.

Lanning, K. V. 1986. *Child Molesters: A Behavioral Analysis of Law Enforcement Officers Investigating Cases of Child Sexual Exploitation*. Washington, D.C.: National Center for Missing and Exploited Children.

Magri, M. R. 1984. *Key Legislation to Preserve the Family: The Reasonable Efforts Determination*. Denver: National Conference of State Legislators.

National Association of Public Child Welfare Administrators. 1988. *Guidelines for a Model System of Protective Services for Abused and Neglected Children and Their Families*. Washington, D.C.: American Public Welfare Association.

National Center on Child Abuse and Neglect. 1981. *National Study of the Incidence and Severity of Child Abuse and Neglect: Study Findings*. OHDS 81–30325. Washington, D.C.: U.S. Department of Health and Human Services.

——. 1987. *Study Findings—Study of National Incidence and Prevalence of Child Abuse and Neglect*. Washington, D.C.: U.S. Department of Health and Human Services.

National Child Welfare Resource Center for Management and Administration, University of Southern Maine. 1987. *Professional Social Work Practice in Public Child Welfare: An Agenda for Action*. Portland.

Pelton, L. H. 1978. "Child Abuse and Neglect: The Myth of Classlessness." *American Journal of Orthopsychiatry* 48:608–617.

——, ed. 1981. *The Social Context of Child Abuse and Neglect*. New York: Human Sciences Press.

Petit, M., and D. Overcash. 1983. *America's Children: Powerless and in Need of Powerful Friends*. Augusta: Maine Department of Human Services.

Russell, M. n.d. "1987 National Study of Public Child Welfare Job Requirements." Portland: National Child Welfare Resource Center for Management and Administration, University of Southern Maine.

Salter, A. C. 1988. *Treating Child Sex Offenders and Victims: A Practical Guide.* Beverly Hills, Calif.: Sage.

Select Committee on Children, Youth and Families. 1987. *Federal Programs Affecting Children.* Washington, D.C.: Government Printing Office.

Sudia, C. E. 1981. "What Services Do Abusive Families Need?" In *The Social Context of Child Abuse and Neglect,* edited by L. H. Pelton, 268–290. New York: Human Sciences Press.

Tatara, T. 1989a. *Characteristics of Children in Substitute and Adoptive Care for FY 86 Data.* Washington, D.C.: American Public Welfare Association.

———. 1989b. "Substitute Care Flow Data and National Estimates of Children in Care." In *VCIS Research Notes,* vol. 1, 1–6. Washington, D.C.: American Public Welfare Association.

Younes, L. A. 1987. *State Child Abuse and Neglect Laws: A Comprehensive Analysis—1985.* Washington, D.C.: Clearinghouse on Child Abuse and Neglect Information.

Zigler, E. 1977. "What's Happening to the American Family: Attitudes and Opinions of 302,602 Respondents." *Better Homes and Gardens,* September and October.

———. 1979. "Controlling Child Abuse in America: An Effort Doomed to Failure?" In *Critical Perspectives on Child Abuse,* edited by R. Bourne and E. H. Newberger. Lexington, Mass.: Lexington Books.

8

ROBERT L. HAMPTON

Child Abuse in the African American Community

He that spareth his rod hateth his son; but he that loveth him chasteneth him betimes.
—PROVERBS 13:24

It is difficult to relinquish illusions about the family. Many people are saddened to learn that their image of the family never existed for the majority. For years family violence was unrecognized as the pervasive social problem we now know it to be. Since the 1970s family violence has received increased scientific and public attention. Scores of professional papers and books have reviewed the state of knowledge about this important topic. In spite of the impressive amount of work being done in this area, several issues await thorough examination. The gap between mainstream family-violence research and research on African American families is one such issue. Several factors contribute to this gap, including inadequate or inappropriate models in the literature for addressing such issues as economic factors, cultural differences, political pressures, and social realities.

Those who are concerned with bridging the gap between research and practice must also be concerned with understanding violence in African American families. This chapter begins by examining the extent of child abuse in African American families. It then assesses the current conceptual knowledge of child abuse in general, with a particular focus on African Americans. Finally, it uses an ecological perspective to link conceptual notions about abuse to the cultural-variance and Africentric perspectives.

Incidence and Severity of Violence toward
African American Children

Between 1965 and 1970 all fifty states enacted laws mandating the reporting of suspected child abuse and neglect. The purpose of these laws was to ensure that all children at risk come to public attention so that intervention could occur when deemed appropriate. In the early 1970s, the need for a coherent federal role in the identification, prevention, and treatment of abused and neglected children stimulated the drafting of new legislation. In February 1971 the U.S. Senate Subcommittee on Children and Youth was created, and the Child Abuse Prevention and Treatment Act of 1974 (P.L. 93–247) was one major product of the committee's work. Among the many benefits associated with this legislation was its requirement that child and family data be collected on each reported case.

Figures on the incidence of child abuse are obtained from child-protective agencies. Statistics on reported cases of child maltreatment are then compiled annually by the American Humane Association and reported in *Highlights of Official Child Abuse and Neglect Reporting*. This report provides national information on the number of families, alleged perpetrators, and children involved in official reports of child maltreatment. It also provides data on characteristics of these families, perpetrators, and children, and, where possible, provides comparative data for the general population. The data were first available for detailed analyses in 1976.

African American children have been overrepresented in this tabulation since its inception. According to the 1980 census, about 15 percent of all children in the United States were African American; from 1976 to 1980, however, reports involving these children remained fairly constant at about 19 percent. Furthermore, in 1982 almost 22 percent of all child-maltreatment reports concerned African American children. This figure declined to 20.8 percent in 1984 (American Humane Association 1986), then rose to 26.8 percent in 1985 (American Humane Association 1987). Thus, of the approximately 1,928,000 reports of child abuse and neglect were made to child-protective services agencies in 1985, approximately 516,704 concerned African American children.

It is risky to draw conclusions from official reports about the rates of child maltreatment among African American families because the poor and racial minorities are typically overrepresented in official reports of deviant behavior (Gelles 1975; Newberger et al. 1977). Several studies have found that children from poor and minority families are more likely to be labeled "abused" than children from more affluent and majority homes with comparable injuries (Gelles 1975; Hampton 1986; Hampton and Newberger 1985; Nalepka, O'Toole, and Turbett 1981; Turbett and O'Toole 1980). These studies and others show that race and social class are as important in determining which cases will be labeled child abuse as the nature of the injury, and sometimes they are more important (Katz et al. 1986).

NATIONAL INCIDENCE STUDY

Official statistics on child abuse (and other forms of family violence) best reflect the workings of the system as it attempts to measure the extent of abuse. Official statistics do not provide a true measure of the full extent of child maltreatment in families because such statistics, like other data on deviant behavior, are limited to cases that come to official public attention. These data are frequently biased in terms of who is reported, what is reported, and by whom.

Given the limitations of official statistics, other research has been conducted to obtain estimates of the prevalence of child abuse. The first National Study of the Incidence and Severity of Child Abuse and Neglect (NIS) was designed from a simple conceptual model.[1] This model suggests that although substantial numbers of abused and neglected children are recognized as such and reported to protective services, reported cases represent only the tip of the iceberg. The model assumes that additional cases are known to other investigatory agencies such as the police, public-health departments, courts, corrections agencies, schools, and hospitals (U.S. Department of Health and Human Services 1981). As a result, even an unambiguous case of child maltreatment may go unreported and never be included in the official records.

The NIS study, conducted from April 1979 to May 1980, was a large, systematic effort to gather information on cases of child abuse and neglect in the United States. The study collected family data for each suspected case reported to county child-protective-services (CPS) agencies during the study period. In addition to CPS caseworkers, professional staff in other agencies were asked to participate in the study. The NIS study collected case data from CPS and non-CPS agencies located in twenty-six counties throughout the United States; the counties were chosen by stratified random sampling. To compensate for unequal probabilities of selection and to provide the basis for computing national estimates, each case was weighted by a complex procedure that enabled researchers to estimate the percentage and distribution of cases in the general population.

A secondary analysis of the data estimated that of the 172,800 cases of African American children reported to CPS agencies during the study year, 74,503 (roughly 43 percent) were substantiated. Substantiated cases (also termed confirmed cases) were those for which CPS had concluded the investigation and had determined that the allegation was supported by the evidence. Compared with substantiated cases among whites and Hispanics, substantiated cases among African Americans included families who were poorer, more likely to be on public assistance, and more likely to be in father-absent households. Three-quarters of the African American families had incomes of $7,000 or less, compared with 50 percent of the white families. Three-fifths of the African American families but only one-third of the white families received public assistance. Physical neglect was the most frequently diagnosed form of maltreatment for all groups, followed by physical abuse. Almost 45 percent of the African American sample were reported to have experienced physical neglect, in contrast to the 29 percent who experienced physical abuse. Compared with other children, African American children were less likely to be classified as victims of emotional injury (Hampton 1987a).

Because physical abuse receives the most emphasis by professionals, the media, and the general public, a separate analysis of physical abuse cases by ethnicity was conducted. As can be seen in Table 8.1, compared with whites, African American victims of assaultive maltreatment were more likely to be in the six- to twelve-year-old category, live in urban areas, have mothers who had not completed high school, and suffer more serious injuries. More than half (52 percent) the African American victims of physical abuse received injuries from implements (knife, gun, stick, cord). In comparison, 27.4 percent of white and 44.4 percent of Hispanic victims of violence suffered injuries inflicted by implements. Table 8.1 also contains information regarding the caseworkers' assessments of caretaker problems associated with the abuse. Although these are subjective evaluations grouped into large categories, they provide some valuable insights. For example, caseworkers reported that caretaker stress was strongly associated with physical abuse, particularly among nonwhites. Stress was also related to the use of an implement.

These data provided some important insights concerning similari-

Table 8.1. Physical Abuse by Ethnicity, Substantiated Cases

| | Percentage of sample | | | |
	White	African American	Hispanic	Total
Age of child				
0–5	36.5	21.6	41.6	33.8
6–12	45.8	59.9	53.4	48.6
13–17	18.0	18.5	5.0	17.5
Sex of child				
Male	55.2	42.9	41.8	52.4
Female	44.8	56.9	58.2	47.6
Mother's education				
0–8 years	4.8	17.5	12.6	7.2
9–11 years	40.7	50.1	62.3	43.1
12 or more years	54.5	32.4	25.2	49.7
Mother's employmnent				
Employed full time	30.1	36.9	20.0	30.8
Employed part time	63.4	53.9	67.7	61.9
Unemployed	6.5	9.3	12.3	7.3
Father in household				
Yes	68.7	48.7	83.7	65.7
No	31.3	51.3	16.3	34.3
Family income				
Less than $7,000	36.4	43.7	31.2	37.5
$7,000–$14,999	48.5	37.8	39.4	46.2
$15,000–$24,999	10.5	11.5	24.6	11.3
$25,000 or more	4.6	7.0	4.8	5.0
Receiving AFDC[a]				
Yes	25.5	38.4	23.9	27.7
No	74.5	61.6	76.1	72.3
Severity of abuse[b]				
Serious	9.2	11.7	9.3	9.7
Moderate	57.6	42.8	75.7	55.6
Probable	33.2	45.5	15.1	34.7
Caretake problems associated with abuse[c]				
Alcohol/drugs	16.8	12.0	8.2	15.6

ties and differences among African American and other victims with respect to demographic characteristics. In addition, these data were examined to assess differences within a sample of African American victims. Among these were (1) low socioeconomic status was more closely associated with physical neglect than with any other form of child maltreatment; (2) physical abuse was more prevalent among families residing in urban areas and in households where the mother was employed full time; and (3) physical and sexual abuse cases accounted for a higher than expected proportion of serious injuries to children, and occurred more frequently in two-parent than one-parent

Table 8.1. (*continued*)

Variable	Percentage of sample			
	White	African American	Hispanic	Total
Physical disability	5.0	0.9	0.0	1.2
Child rearing	16.0	23.1	15.1	17.1
Emotional	9.1	13.1	6.3	9.6
Stress	32.3	40.3	52.2	34.5
History of abuse	11.0	3.3	12.5	9.8
Other	9.9	7.4	6.3	9.3
City size				
SMSA^d over 200,000	36.5	59.6	80.6	42.6
Other SMSA	26.9	18.4	16.8	24.9
Non-SMSA	36.5	22.0	2.6	32.4
Injury caused by implement^c				
Yes	27.4	52.0	44.4	32.6
No	72.6	48.0	55.6	67.4
N	734	205	34	973
Weighted N^f	(92,008)	(21,654)	(5,008)	(118,671)

Source: Adapted from Hampton (1987b).
Note: Percentages are based on weighting and may not add to 100 percent because of rounding.
^{a}Aid to Families with Dependent Children.
^{b}An injury or impairment was defined as serious when there was reasonable cause to believe that the act/omission caused or materially contributed to the occurrence or unreasonable prolongation of an injury or impairment that (a) produced significant, long-lasting impairment of bodily functions or of mental or psychological capacities or (b) required professional medical or other rehabilitative care to relieve acute present suffering or to prevent significant long-lasting impairment. Moderate injuries were those that persisted in observable form for at least forty-eight hours. The *Probable* implied that injury/impairment had probably occurred; it would be misleading to assume that "probable" is always less serious than "moderate" in these data.
^{c}Caretaker problems were assessed on intake by CPS workers.
^{d}Standard Metropolitan Statistical Area.
^{e}Implements used in the abuse included common household items ranging from brooms, hair-brushes, and belts to potentially lethal weapons.
^{f}Data were weighted to compensate for the sampling design and to allow for the computation of national rates.

families. Although this study permitted the examination of a broader range of issues than is usually possible from data obtained in official reports, the data are based on substantiated rather than reported cases (Hampton 1987b).

NATIONAL SURVEYS

The limitations of official data outlined so far have led to several attempts to measure the incidence of child abuse and spousal abuse through nationally representative sample surveys (Gelles and Straus

1988; Harris and Associates 1979; Straus, Gelles, and Steinmetz 1980; U.S. Department of Justice 1980). Although these studies derive data that are generalizable, the information elicited is frequently limited (Gelles 1985). A national probability sample of 2,143 households constituted the first National Family Violence Survey of 1975 (Strauss, Gelles, and Steinmetz 1980). *Violence* was defined as an act carried out with the intention, or perceived intention, of causing physical pain or injury to another person. The injury could range from slight pain, as in a slap, to murder. The motivation might range from a concern for a person's safety (as when a child is spanked for going into the street) to hostility so intense that the death of the person is desired (Gelles and Straus 1979). Violence was measured by the violence, or physical-aggression, items on the Conflict Tactics Scales (CTS).[2] *Abuse* was defined as those acts of violence that had a high probability of causing injury to the person (an injury did not actually have to occur).[3]

The sample included 147 African American families, 75 of whom had at least one child aged three to seventeen living at home. The results did not support the contention that African American parents are more violent and abusive than white parents. The survey found little difference between African Americans and whites in the rate of severe violence toward children (15 percent in African American families and 14 percent in white families). This finding was similar to an earlier observation by Billingsley (1969).

Given the associations among unemployment, low income, and violence toward children, African American families were expected to report higher rates of violence. Cazenave and Straus (1979) found that the aid and support, especially childcare, provided by extended-family ties, seemed to reduce the risk of abusive violence in African American families. When income and husband's occupation were controlled for, African Americans were less likely than whites to engage in acts of severe violence toward their children.

The second National Family Violence Survey, conducted in 1985, had two primary goals: to provide current estimates on the prevalence of family violence and to assess changes in the rates of family violence since the previous survey. African American and Hispanic families were oversampled in order to allow for separate analyses. In order to make an appropriate comparison between the two surveys, it was necessary to compare the same types of families. Therefore, the more restrictive 1975 categories were used—that is, households with a couple or with a couple and at least one child three to seventeen years

Table 8.2. Comparison of 1975 and 1985 Violence Indexes

	Rate per 1,000 African American children age 3 through 17[a]		
	---	---	---
	1975	*1985*	*Percent change[b]*
Overall violence	541	652	+20.5
Severe violence	145	221	+48.3
N	75[c]	277	

Source: Adapted from Hampton, Gelles, and Harrop (1988).
[a]For two-caretaker households with at least one child three to seventeen years of age living at home.
[b]Although there may be substantial differences in rates between the two surveys, few changes achieve statistical significance because of the low base rate for abuse. See Straus and Gelles (1986).

living at home. The 1985 sample had 576 African American couples, 277 of whom had at least one child three to seventeen years of age living at home, compared with the 1975 sample, which contained 147 African American couples, 75 of whom had at least one child in the age category of interest living at home.

As Table 8.2 shows, there was a 20 percent increase in the rate of overall violence toward African American children between 1975 and 1985 (Hampton, Gelles, and Harrop 1988). Table 8.2 also shows that the rate of severe, or abusive, violence increased. The change was due entirely to an increase in the number of parents who reported hitting or trying to hit their children with something. Although the increase in neither overall nor severe violence was statistically significant, the rates were of substantive importance. These data were not consistent with the decline in the rate of severe violence toward children reported elsewhere (Straus and Gelles 1986). Yet they do suggest that the level of violence toward African American children remains uncomfortably high. In an analysis of data from the second National Family Violence Survey using the entire sample of African American families with children aged zero to seventeen years, Hampton and Gelles (1988) estimated that approximately 379,000 of these children were victims of abuse in 1985.

Overall, national surveys provide better estimates of the prevalence of abuse than data based on official reports. On balance, these data suggest that a large number of African American children are abused each year by their parents. A major limitation of this approach to the study of family violence is that it does not address child neglect. Given the number of abused children, however, it is important to understand some of the factors that appear to be associated with family violence. The next two sections address this issue.

Understanding the Origins of Child Abuse

Child maltreatment and family violence are perhaps best thought of as indicators of families in trouble. Many factors can place a family in jeopardy and lead to violence. This multiplicity of causes complicates the task of understanding the origins of family violence. One must take into account particular vulnerabilities in a child, parent, or family that heighten their susceptibility to particular stresses that, in turn, might eventuate in violence toward a family member. The task of understanding the origins of family violence becomes even more complex when race is considered. Nonetheless, several factors have been related to abuse and violence in the literature consistently, and they are discussed here.

INTERGENERATIONAL TRANSMISSION

Research and clinical findings indicate that parents who use violence against their children have frequently been subject to violence as children (Newberger et al. 1977; Straus, Gelles, and Steinmetz 1980). Steinmetz (1977) reports that even less severe forms of violence are passed on from generation to generation. Straus, Gelles, and Steinmetz (1980) found support not only for the hypothesis that "violence begets violence" but also for the hypothesis that the greater the frequency of violence in childhood, the greater the chance the victim will grow up to be a violent partner or parent. Caution must be exercised in drawing conclusions from the association so often reported between violence experienced as a child and the subsequent use of violence. Many individuals who experienced violence in their childhood are not violent adults, but violent background is a significant contributor to the likelihood that a person will be violent toward a child (Gelles and Cornell 1985). Although exposure to violence as a child may predispose some children to grow up to be abusers, the majority do not.

The reason proffered for the observed intergenerational nature of violence is that parents provide models for conflict resolution and child rearing for their children. Hence, physically violent parents may lack the behavioral skills to respond nonviolently under stressful conditions. It has also been argued that parents who were physically abused as children are frequently emotionally deprived as well (Steele and Pollock 1968) and consequently suffer from low self-esteem, depression, and feelings of powerlessness as adults. These feelings account in part for their reliance on coercive tactics and the tendency to use them on those weaker and less powerful than they (Straus, Gelles, and Steinmetz 1980).

SOCIAL CLASS

Family violence is found at all socioeconomic levels. Officially reported cases of child abuse, however, are much higher among the poor than among the upper strata in our society, in part because the poor must use public rather than private medical facilities and the police and other officials are quicker to press charges against the poor (Hampton and Newberger 1985; Newberger et al. 1977). Survey data also report social-class differences in rates of family violence (Straus, Gelles, and Steinmetz 1980). The interclass difference is, however, much less than that reported in other studies. Many factors are associated with these class differences, including relative deprivation, differential perceptions of the use of physical punishment, and a differential understanding of family dynamics.

Studies of social-class differences in family violence have examined issues related to social position and family-life experiences. Households where the husband was unemployed or underemployed had the highest rates of violence between spouses and violence by parents toward children. Unemployed men were twice as likely to be severely violent toward their wives as males employed full time, and men employed part time had a rate of wife beating three times that for men employed full time. The rate of child abuse among fathers employed part time was nearly twice as high as the rate for fathers employed full time (Straus, Gelles, and Steinmetz 1980).

Clearly, several correlates of social class appear conducive to violent behaviors, one being the lack of available resources when a father does not have full-time employment. Another is the amount of time that is at risk. Unemployed and part-time-employed fathers have more hours to spend in interaction, both nonviolent and violent, with other household members. Finally, there is the stress associated with the lack of employment.

STRESS

Interest has been increasing since the 1960s in the effects of stress on human well-being. It has been suggested that overzealous physical punishment of children by parents may be as much a result of the various stresses experienced by the parents as it is a result of the desire or need to control behavior. Gil (1970) explains socioeconomic differences in child abuse as resulting, at least partially, from the differential number and severity of stressful experiences that characterize family life at different socioeconomic levels. More than twenty different social stress factors were found to be associated with the use of aggressive physical force in the first National Family Violence Survey (Straus, Gelles, and Steinmetz 1980). Other studies have also documented the association between stress and maltreatment. Stress was found to differentiate families who provided good care from those who provided inadequate care (Egeland, Breitenbucher, and Rosenberg 1980). Specifically, highly stressed mothers who were also aggressive, anxious, and low in help-seeking behaviors were more likely to abuse their infants than mothers with the opposite traits. Stress was significantly correlated with high maltreatment risk in another study (Altemeier et al. 1979).

Stress has typically been measured by the presence or absence of events deemed to be stressful, using measures similar to Holmes and Rahe's Social Readjustment Scale (Holmes and Rahe 1967), rather than by examining individual differences in response to stress. This research has focused on stress resulting from change per se, hypothesizing that any change that requires readjustment in one's life causes stress (Holmes and Masuda 1974). For example, the recent loss of a loved one, a divorce, an unplanned pregnancy, or a sudden change in economic well-being is frequently classified as a stressful life event irrespective of an individual's coping resources. The level of stress experienced will vary depending on the presence or absence of these resources.

Although life events must be considered, they are not the only source of stress. A considerable amount of stress comes not from the necessity of adjusting to sporadic change but from steady, unchanging (or slowly changing) oppressive conditions that must be endured daily (Fried 1982; Makosky 1982; Peters and Massey 1983). Research in this area suggests that stressful life conditions, as well as discrete events, contribute to the stress experienced by individuals and families. For example, in a sample of low-income women, Makosky (1982) found that those who had endured the most difficult stable conditions (parenting problems, poverty, living in a high-crime neighborhood, physical-health problems) for the two years prior to the study were at the greatest risk for mental health problems.

One of the difficulties with much of this research lies in its failure to differentiate between types and sources of stress. It is quite useful to categorize stress according to type (endemic versus acute) and to source (external versus internal). A simple typology is suggested in Table 8.3, which attempts to capture the interaction between type and source of stress.

Endemic stress is a condition of continuous and manifest changes, demands, threats, or deprivations in daily life (Fried 1982). This cate-

Table 8.3. Sourse of Family Stress

Endemic life conditions	Acute life conditions
Internal	
Parental:	
Single parent	Divorce, separation, desertion
Discord	Recent death in family
Unhappiness	Marriage or remarriage
Low self-esteem	Physical assault
Depression	Sexual difficulties
Abused as child	Pregnancy (parent)
Substance abuse	Child leaving home
Child:	Loss of childcare
Discipline problems	Illness
Attachment problems	Pregnancy (child)
Perinatal stress	
Unwanted or excess	
Disabled	
Developmentally delayed	
External	
Poverty	Job loss
Unemployment	Eviction
Poor housing	Loss of welfare
Social isolation	Serious accident
Social impoverishment	Incarceration
Racism	Household moves
Underemployment	Child suspended
Problems with in-laws	Being arrested
Social policies	Economic changes
Classism	Social policies
	Victim of crime

gory of stress has also been labeled "mundane stress" (Peters and Massey 1983) and "life conditions stress" (Bellie 1982; Makosky 1982). It has been suggested that several structural features of family life may create endemic stress and thus contribute to the occurrence of conflict within families. Among the structural characteristics is a high level of emotional involvement. Another characteristic is that family members spend more time interacting with each other than with others, and the quality of this interaction is unique. As a primary group, the family has a greater commitment to interaction with each other than with others. Close family interaction may make a family warm, supportive, and intimate, but it also can enhance the likelihood of violence. Another characteristic that can lead to conflict is family size. Large families place more demands on parental resources than small families. Holding resources constant, increasing the membership of a family usually results in fewer resources per family member and thus increases the likelihood of conflicts over those resources. Such a pattern may be even more problematical in low-income than in higher-income families because resources in low-income families may already be relatively scarce.

Many other endemic stressors are directly attributable to internal family process. Children who require special care, perhaps because they were premature or had a low birth weight Dubowitz and Egan 1988) or because they are hyperactive or disabled (Groce 1988), place heavy demands on families. These, along with parent-produced stressors, can be quite formidable for a family. Some of these problems are intensified in single-parent families. It has been found that single parenthood in lower-socioeconomic-status families contributes to the occurrence of family interaction patterns found to be associated with child abuse and neglect (Burgess, Anderson, and Schellenbach 1980).

Extremely endemic stresses on the family are frequently related to poverty, long-term unemployment or underemployment, social isolation, housing, and neighborhood/community development. Although each of these conditions is stressful in and of itself, Garbarino (1981) suggests that they interact to produce "social impoverishment." The literature supports the premise that economic impoverishment has many negative consequences for families; it undermines health and well-being. Chronic poverty and economic deprivation both on the familial and community level interfere with normative functions. Economic forces are thus significant to the degree that they produce social impoverishment (Garbarino 1981).

To be effective, families depend on a supportive context—that is, support from the community and larger society. Garbarino (1981) and others, using an ecological perspective, have been instrumental in promoting the proposition that environmental stress, particularly that produced by neighborhood characteristics, is an important correlate of child maltreatment. Concentrations of socioeconomically distressed families are most likely to be high-risk areas for child maltreatment. This analysis suggests that those who need the most tend to be clustered together in settings where they must struggle the most to meet their needs. The high need level is compounded by the problem of scarce social resources. In such a stressful environment families are often inclined to seek an advantage by getting all they can from others while giving little. Social isolation seems to be mutually encouraged because of ambivalence about neighborly exchanges. High-risk neighborhoods are socially impoverished neighborhoods; in them characteristics associated with family stress and lack of support are perceived and reported by family members (Garbarino 1981).

Research on acute stress has been a central focus in the field of family studies since the late 1940s. Hill's (1949) ABCX family-crisis framework has continued to serve as a foundation for research and theory-building efforts. This framework focuses on the interaction among stressful events and family resources in producing a perceived level of stress. It is apparent to most who work in this field that crisis-like, or acute, stress is quite different from the continuous or recurrent series of small stresses in the lives of many people. Frequently, acute and endemic stress flow into one another so that distinguishing between the two can be difficult, although close examination of a series of episodes can reveal a number of clear differences in their quality, duration, intensity, clarity, and immediate effects (Fried 1982).

Life changes such as the death of a loved one, marital disruption, becoming pregnant, illness, or having a child disrupt routines and require adjustments. Adaptations to such internal acute stress often involve rather severe role transitions.

Recent job loss, the incarceration of a family member, a child suspended from school, and sudden shifts in the social, economic, or political climate are all external acute stresses. These stressful events generally invoke a sense of shock, followed by anxiety or grief. These reactions, in turn, result in a gradual process of marshaling adaptive resources (Fried 1982)

Strong evidence indicates that recent unemployment in particular is highly associated with child abuse. In an examination of the relationship between changes in employment and child abuse over time in two metropolitan areas, Steinberg, Catalano, and Dooley (1981) found that reported abuse increases when work-force size declines, supporting the hypothesized causal role of unemployment in maltreatment. This finding is similar to that of an earlier analysis that used census-tract data for reported child abuse and economic conditions (Garbarino and Crouter 1978).

The distinction between types and sources of stress permits a good conceptualization of the role of stress, including stress that results from socioeconomic factors, and family violence. Family characteristics may provide a family with the ability to cope with some stressors and reduce their ability to cope with others. Although there is substantial variability in responses to stress, some negative responses include depression, withdrawal, rigidity, confusion, and violence. Each of these responses has deleterious implications for family life.

SOCIAL ISOLATION

Social support can often reduce the impact of stressful events (Brownell and Shumaker 1984) and promote a sense of identity, self-esteem, and physical well-being. A support network can provide assistance with childcare, access to information, and resources. It can be one of the major factors distinguishing high-risk from low-risk families (Newberger et al. 1986). Similarly, some researchers consider social isolation to be one of the key causal factors in child abuse (Garbarino and Gilliam 1980; Newberger et al. 1977). The basic hypothesis is that an individual with a strong, supportive social network has an enhanced ability to cope with stress. In a study comparing two neighborhoods matched for social class but differing in reported rates of child maltreatment, Garbarino and Sherman (1980) found that one of the characteristics of families in the low-maltreatment neighborhood was that they had more extensive social networks. Social isolation is often a major characteristic of samples of abusive parents. Social isolation can be identified by examining organizational memberships, amount of contact with family, friends, and neighbors, and frequency of moves. Abusive families often belong to few or no organizations, have limited contact with others, and do not reside in the same community for a long time. Consequently, they remain unconnected and uninvolved.

Generally these four factors—intergenerational transmission, class, stress, and social isolation—have been found to be related to child abuse and neglect. It should be clear that in all instances these relationships are probabilistic, not deterministic. Frequently, the publicly perceived strength of an association is based on how often the finding is cited, not how strong the statistical association is or how well the research conforms to standards of scientific inquiry. No single factor such as social class or growing up in a violent family has been shown to account for more than a small percentage of the incidence of violence toward children.

Toward an Understanding of Violence against African American Children

Since the 1960s research has been increasing on the nature of African American family life. Although accepting the premise that there is no single African American family type, the cultural-variant and Africentric perspectives acknowledge that certain family functions are universal. Both perspectives, however, recognize that various constraints may produce culturally distinct structures and dynamics (Johnson 1981). Consequently, they do not necessarily use white middle-class norms as the primary referent, and they explain the family according to African American values and experiences. In this way they emphasize cultural relativity.

A certain level of family violence and child abuse will always exist given both the structure and the nature of family life in the United States. As is increasingly recognized, family violence is the product of multiple factors, rather than a single factor. In many ways, family violence involves the interaction of the whole system—parents, children, and society—and must be addressed as a multilevel problem. From an Africentric perspective, an ecological approach, as advocated by Garbarino (1977, 1982) and Bronfenbrenner (1977, 1979), provides a useful framework within which to assess the dynamics of family violence in both its origins and consequences. This approach also blends well with the cultural-variant perspective on African American family life.

Three key areas of the ecological framework can be illuminated for discussion. First, this approach focuses on the progressive, mutual adaptation of organism and environment (Bowles 1983). The interdependent interaction of systems is viewed as a dynamic force affecting perceptions of social reality (Garbarino 1982). Second, the ecological approach stresses the importance of quality of life for families and the

importance of socially rich environments in creating that life (Garbarino, Stocking, and Associates 1980). This emphasis frequently implies some concern with "social habitability" and raises questions not
only about the environment per se but about the means to achieve a
desired quality of life. Third, the ecological perspective states that
many of the most important aspects of human behavior take place as
a result of interactions that are shaped, even controlled, by forces not
directly touching individuals as they interact (Garbarino 1981; Garbarino, Stocking, and Associates 1980). Bronfenbrenner (1977) called
these indirect effects "second order effects" to indicate the something
beyond the individuals is setting the agenda for their interactions. In
other words, it can be argued that factors outside the parent/child
dyad have a significant, even controlling, impact on the dynamics of
maltreatment (Justice and Justice 1976). Relations between family
members within an African American family are clearly influenced by
a number of external forces.

One principal theme that emerges from an ecological analysis is
that the ability of a family to achieve a satisfactory level of functioning
depends in large part on the social context in which they live. It depends on the extent to which families can receive support from outside
the household as well as the extent to which outside forces intrude
into family life and set the agenda for household interactions (Garbarino, Stocking, and Associates 1980). For African American families,
outside forces have intruded into the household on several different
levels. One could ask which factors among those that directly affect
the lives of families increase the risk for child maltreatment. Although
a number of variables immediately come to mind, an appropriate
starting point is the operational definition of child abuse.

PERCEPTIONS OF CHILD ABUSE

The current concept of child abuse in the United States is perhaps
more political than scientific. It implies behavior that is considered
immoral or improper but fails to provide a specific definition of the
nature of the behavior (Gelles 1987). Definitions of abuse almost always rely on value judgments. For example, if one defines as abuse
hitting, spanking, and slapping children, then over 90 percent of
Americans are abusive (Straus and Gelles 1988). Any conclusions
about who abuses and how much depend on a culturally validated
definition of abuse (Garbarino and Gilliam 1980).

Giovannoni and Becerra (1979), in the most comprehensive attitudinal research on ethnicity and violence, explored ethnic and professional differences in definitions of child maltreatment. A series of case vignettes presented to subjects described specific incidents of child maltreatment: the incidents were drawn from a range of behaviors that might be considered maltreatment, and they varied in degree of severity. Professional and lay people in metropolitan Los Angeles were asked to rate each vignette according to the "seriousness of its impact on the welfare of the child" (p. 24). With an ethnically diverse sample, the study sought to test the idea that the poor and ethnic minorities are "more tolerant of mistreatment and likely to have a higher threshold for considering actions as mistreatment" (p. 175). The results, however, showed just the opposite: In 94 percent of the cases, African Americans and Hispanics gave more serious ratings to the vignettes than did whites. Contrary to the original expectations, education and income (the prime indicators of socioeconomic status) were related inversely to ratings of seriousness. Ethnic differences among respondents were not merely a product of social-class differences; they persisted even across educational levels. African Americans at all educational levels, for example, rated certain categories of neglect as more serious than others. Analysis by income showed similar but less consistent trends.

This research suggests that poor and nonwhite families may hold different attitudes toward maltreatment than do white and more affluent families. Analysis of intraracial differences further illuminates ethnic differences in perception. Among the African American respondents, there were no differences according to income, education, or gender, suggesting that responses were influenced primarily by ethnicity rather than socioeconomic status (Giovannoni and Becerra 1979). African Americans showed greater concern than other groups for failure to provide supervision and, unlike other ethnic groups, demonstrated greater consensus as a group without regard to social class. There were no real disagreements on the direction of their evaluations, only on degree. This is not the first study to question the utility of traditional social-class categories when applied to African Americans (Bronfenbrenner 1979). In general, however, this research supports the proposition that all groups share some common definitions of maltreatment, albeit with differences in emphasis (Garbarino and Ebata 1983), and that it is not attitudes and values about abuse and neglect per se that differentiate ethnic groups in the United States.

While acknowledging the weak relationship between attitudes and behaviors as demonstrated by decades of social psychological research, Garbarino and Ebata (1983) suggest that the Giovannoni and Becerra research highlights the importance of social conditions in producing behavior. They argue that given the relative uniformity of condemnation for maltreatment, actual behavioral differences are probably attributable to the balance of social stress and support. A complete ecological explication is required to assess the significance of ethnicity on child maltreatment.

SOCIAL FACTORS THAT INCREASE
THE RISK OF ABUSE

The ecological perspective suggests that one should approach the topic of child maltreatment by analyzing factors at different levels. The ecological and Africentric perspectives allow for the assessment of African American values and experiences as a central element in this analysis. Both perspectives also ask questions about the extent to which outside forces intrude on the family and set its agenda. What are the social conditions that operate to produce various family behaviors?

One cannot examine parent/child relations among African Americans without acknowledging that these parents must socialize children to survive in an environment that is often hostile, racist, and discriminatory. In other words, an environment of subtle-to-overt racism influences how these families live and raise their children (Peters 1981). Disciplinary techniques in African American families have often been described as direct and physical in contrast to the psychological approach preferred by mainstream families. This strict approach, however, has been shown to constitute functional, appropriate discipline by caring parents. The stress often associated with child abuse in general is often a factor in parental disciplinary practices that become abusive (Lassiter 1987).

On the family level, research in the area of child abuse and neglect has found that certain structural arrangements of families and caretakers increase the risk that children will be abused. For example, child maltreatment tends to be associated with marital disruption. Although being married is important to most African Americans, the fact that a near majority are not married and living in traditional nuclear family units is noteworthy (Staples 1985). It can be argued that the structural conditions that prevent the establishment of a normative family are closely related to those that sustain high rates of parental violence against children.

One of these structural conditions is male joblessness, which has an indirect effect on child maltreatment through its ties to family disruption. Sampson (1987) discusses this connection between male joblessness and urban violence. Just as persistently high rates of African American crime appear to stem from the structural links among unemployment, economic deprivation, and family disruption in urban communities, household violence is probably similarly associated with these factors. The scarcity of employed African American men increases the prevalence of families headed by females (Sampson 1987; Staples 1985). Female-headed families are projected to constitute 59 percent of all African American families (Joe and Yu 1984). Almost 75 percent of African American children live in such families, and 70 percent of African Americans with incomes below the poverty level belong to these families. The factors correlated with this family structure are precisely those that are central to child maltreatment. Such contextual variables contribute to both stressful life conditions and stressful life events.

To move beyond the level of the individual family, although there were a number of improvements in the social and legal status of African Americans and in the quality of their family life in the 1960s, race is still an important determinant of life chances in the United States. In an analysis of data from the General Social Survey from 1972 to 1985, Thomas and Hughes (1986) show that African Americans score consistently lower than whites on measures of psychological well-being and quality of life, even after controls have been introduced for social class, age, and marital status. Furthermore, racial differences remained constant during this period. These authors also state that the probability of being in a stable marriage, an advantage whites have over African Americans, is partially attributable to the stresses American society places on nonwhite as opposed to white marriages. Therefore, when controlling for marital status in the analyses, they were also in part controlling for the effects of race. And Thomas and Hughes argue that the effects of race on quality of life and psychological well-being were even stronger than was found in their research.

Similarly, any analysis of maltreatment in families must acknowledge social-policy factors. Budgetary retrenchment and reallocation policies can affect both the amount of violence in families and the programs designed to assist families. The full impact of the shift in federal priorities since 1981 cannot be measured at this time or in the foreseeable future. During the 1960s and early 1970s many federal programs were established to address major social problems such as poverty. Government income-transfer programs, manpower and employment programs, and support for education constitute the major efforts to decrease the amount of poverty, and, in fact, government transfer programs have played the single most important role in reducing measured poverty (Smolensky 1982). These programs also usually affect those families that, according to most research, tend to be violent.

Money problems, more often than any other stressor, are significantly correlated with problems in other areas of life. Money stressors correlate with other stressors such as mental health, education, and parenting, and are marginally associated with physical health (Makosky 1982). Some argue that cuts in programs such as family planning; Medicaid; food stamps; school lunch; the Women's, Infants', and Children's nutrition program; Aid to Families with Dependent Children; and public housing, by reducing economic aid directly or indirectly, impinge on the quality of family life in real and symbolic ways. As a result, some people live their entire lives or long periods of their lives with a sense of economic scarcity. The current sense of scarcity experienced by many African American families is exacerbated by the expectation that public officials will do little to resolve this problem. Cuts in social programs disproportionately affect socially marginal groups, such as African Americans and female-headed families. With fewer resources, public and private, the quality of life of these families may decline. Poor families will be required to cope with higher levels of acute and mundane (endemic) stress, while operating in an environment that may offer fewer supports. Within this context, dramatic increases in the rates of child maltreatment can be expected.

Child abuse may thus be a second-order indirect effect of social impoverishment, which, in this instance, is greatly influenced by factors that operate outside the parent/child dyad. It should not be surprising, therefore, that data suggest that violence toward African American children has not decreased since 1975, even though there has been a decrease in violence toward other children. In other words, child maltreatment in African American families may be a secondary effect of societal violence against these families (Daniel, Hampton, and

Newberger 1983). At least some of these families and children are at risk for maltreatment because their values, beliefs, norms, roles, and relationships have been consciously and unconsciously undermined by white America.

Conclusions

The field of family violence has advanced on several fronts, including mandatory-reporting laws for child abuse; research to improve knowledge of the family dynamics that contribute to violence; and programs to intervene in families where violence has been recognized as well as programs to prevent violence. It is clear to some observers that these programs often fail to acknowledge the cultural experiences and expectations of African American families. The fact that child-abuse rates for white Americans decreased between 1975 and 1985, while child-abuse rates for African Americans did not seems to suggest that many programs did not reach African Americans. Although the true incidence of family violence remains unknown, a major social problem exists within the African American community if recent estimates are accepted.

Child maltreatment, like other forms of violence, is a problem of environments as well as of individuals. Policies to enhance the quality of family life and to provide families with meaningful choices are policies that will, in the long run, reduce the level of abusive violence. Policies that provide socially impoverished environments and leave families choiceless will increase the level of maltreatment. Efforts to reduce family violence must recognize the social ecological system within which African American families reside and the Africentric perspective. Without culturally relevant efforts for prevention, it is unrealistic to expect major reductions in the rates of violence.

Notes

1. NIS was designed and conducted by Westat, Inc., under the sponsorship and direction of the National Center on Child Abuse and Neglect.

2. The CTS asks respondents to think of the times when they had a conflict with their child or just got angry with them. Respondents are then given a list of tactics they might have used in these situations. The tactics range from calm discussion to attacks with a knife or gun. The violent acts are throwing

something at the child; pushing, grabbing, or shoving; biting or hitting with a fist; hitting or trying to hit with something; beating up the child; burning or scalding (1985 version only, not used in the 1975–85 comparison); threatening with a knife or gun; using a knife or gun.

3. Abuse, or *severe violence*, was defined as acts that have a relatively high probability of causing an injury. For example, kicking is classified as severe violence because it has a much greater potential for producing an injury than spanking or slapping. The acts making up the severe-violence index are kicking, biting, punching, hitting with an object, beating up, threatening with a knife or gun, using a knife or gun.

References

Altemeier, W. A., III, P. M. Vietze, K. B. Sherrod, H. M. Sandler, S. Falsey, and S. O'Connor. 1979. "Prediction of Child Maltreatment during Pregnancy." *Journal of the American Academy of Child Psychiatry* 18:205–218.

American Humane Association. 1986. *Highlights of Official Child Neglect and Abuse Reporting: 1984.* Denver.

————. 1987. *Highlights of Official Child Neglect and Abuse Reporting: 1985.* Denver.

Belle, D. 1982. "Introduction." In *Lives in Stress,* edited by D. Belle, 11–23. Beverly Hills, Calif.: Sage.

Billingsley, A. 1969. "Family Functioning in the Low-Income Black Community." *Casework* 50:563–572.

Bowles, R. T. 1983. "Family Well-Being, Family Violence and Rapid Community Growth: An Ecological Perspective." In *Proceedings of the Alaska Symposium on the Social, Economic, and Cultural Impacts of Natural Resource Development,* edited by S. Yarie. Fairbanks: University of Alaska.

Bronfenbrenner, U. 1977. "Toward an Experimental Ecology of Human Development." *American Psychologist* 32:513–531.

————. 1979. *The Experimental Ecology of Human Development.* Cambridge: Harvard University Press.

Brownell, A., and S. A. Shumaker. 1984. "Social Support: An Introduction to a Complex Phenomenon." *Journal of Social Issues* 40(4):1–9.

Burgess, R. L., E. A. Anderson, and C. J. Schellenbach. 1980. "A Social Interactional Approach to the Study of Abusive Families." In *Advances in Family Interaction, Assessment, and Theory: An Annual Compilation of Research,* vol. 2, edited by J. P. Vincent. Greenwich, Conn.: JAI.

Cazenave, N. A., and M. A. Straus. 1979. "Race, Class, Network Embeddedness and Family Violence." *Journal of Comparative Family Studies* 10:281–300.

Daniel, J. H., R. L. Hampton, and E. H. Newberger. 1983. "Child Abuse and Accidents in Black Families: A Case Controlled Comparison." *American Journal of Orthopsychiatry* 53:645–653.

Dubowitz, H., and H. Egan. 1988. "The Maltreatment of Infants." In *Abuse and Victimization across the Life Span,* edited by M. A. Straus, 32–53. Baltimore: Johns Hopkins University Press.

Egeland, B., M. Breitenbucher, and D. Rosenberg. 1980. "Prospective Study of the Significance of Life Stress in the Etiology of Child Abuse." *Journal of Consulting Psychology* 48:194–205.

Fried, M. 1982. "Endemic Stress: The Psychology of Resignation and the Politics of Scarcity." *American Journal of Orthopsychiatry* 52(January):4–19.

Garbarino, J. 1977. "The Human Ecology of Child Maltreatment: A Conceptual Model for Research." *Journal of Marriage and the Family* 39(November):721–735.

———. 1981. "An Ecological Perspective on Child Maltreatment." In *The Social Context of CHild Abuse and Neglect,* edited by L. H. Pelton, 228–267. New York: Human Sciences Press.

———. 1982. *Children and Families in the Social Environment.* New York: Aldine.

Garbarino, J., and A. Crouter. 1978. "Defining the Community Context of Parent-Child Relations: The Correlates of Child Maltreatment." *Child Development* 49:604–606.

Garbarino, J., and A. Ebata. 1983. "The Significance of Ethnic and Cultural Differences in Child Maltreatment." *Journal of Marriage and the Family* 45:773–783.

Garbarino, J., and G. Gilliam. 1980. *Understanding Abusive Families.* Lexington, Mass.: Lexington Books.

Garbarino, J., and D. Sherman. 1980. "High-Risk Neighborhoods and High-Risk Families: The Human Ecology of Child Maltreatment." *Child Development* 51:188–198.

Garbarino, J., S. H. Stocking, and Associates. 1980. *Protecting Children from Abuse and Neglect: Developing and Maintaining Effective Support Systems for Families.* San Francisco: Jossey-Bass.

Gelles, R. J. 1975. "The Social Construction of Child Abuse." *American Journal of Orthopsychiatry* 43:363–371.

———. 1985. "Family Violence." In *Annual Review of Sociology,* edited by R. H. Turner and J. F. Short, 347–367. Palo Alto: Annual Reviews.

———. 1987. "What to Learn from Cross-Cultural and Historical Research on Child Abuse and Neglect: An Overview. In *Child Abuse and Neglect: Biosocial Dimensions,* edited by R. J. Gelles and J. B. Lancaster, 15–30. Hawthorne, N.Y.: Aldine.

Gelles, R. J., and C. P. Cornell. 1985. *Intimate Violence in Families.* Beverly Hills, Calif.: Sage.

Gelles, R. J., and M. A. Straus. 1979. "Determinants of Violence in the Family: Towards a Theoretical Integration." In *Contemporary Theories about the Family,* vol. 1, edited by W. R. Burr, R. Hill, F. I. Nye, and I. L. Reiss, 549–581. New York: Free Press.

——. 1988. *Intimate Violence.* New York: Simon & Schuster.

Gil, D. G. 1970. *Violence against Children in the United States.* Cambridge: Harvard University Press.

Giovannoni, J. M., and R. M. Becerra. 1979. *Defining Child Abuse.* New York: Free Press.

Groce, N. E. 1988. "Special Groups at Risk of Abuse: The Disabled." In *Abuse and Victimization across the Life Span,* edited by M. A. Straus, 223–239. Baltimore: Johns Hopkins University Press.

Hampton, R. L. 1986. "Race, Ethnicity, and Child Maltreatment: An Analysis of Cases Recognized and Reported by Hospitals." In *The Black Family: Essays and Studies,* 3d ed., edited by R. Staples, 172–185. Belmont, Calif.: Wadsworth.

——. 1987a. "Race, Class and Child Maltreatment." *Journal of Comparative Family Studies* 18(1):113–126.

——. 1987b. "Violence against Black Children: Current Knowledge and Future Research Needs." In *Violence in the Black Family: Correlates and Consequences,* edited by R. L. Hampton, 3–20. Lexington, Mass.: Lexington Books.

Hampton, R. L., and R. J. Gelles. 1988. "Physical Violence in a Nationally Representative Sample of Black Americans." Paper presented at the annual meeting of the National Council on Family Relations, Philadelphia.

Hampton, R. L., R. J. Gelles, and J. W. Harrop. 1988. "Is Violence in the Black Family Increasing? A Comparison of 1975 and 1985 National Survey Rates." Paper presented at the annual meeting of the American Sociological Association, Atlanta.

Hampton, R. L., and E. H. Newberger. 1985. "Child Abuse Incidence and Reporting by Hospitals: The Significance of Severity, Class, and Race." *American Journal of Public Health* 75:56–60.

Harris, L., and Associates. 1979. *A Survey of Spousal Abuse against Women in Kentucky.* New York.

Hill, R. 1949. *Families under Stress.* New York: Harper & Row.

Holmes, T. H., and M. Masuda. 1974. "Life Changes and Illness Susceptibility." In *Stressful Life Events: Their Nature and Effects,* edited by B. S. Dohrenwend and B. P. Dohrenwend, 45–72. New York: Wiley.

Holmes, T. H. and R. H. Rahe. 1967. "The Social Readjustment Scale." *Journal of Psychosomatic Research* 11:213–218.

Joe, T., and P. Yu. 1984. *The "Flip-Side" of Black Families Headed by Women: The Economic Status of Black Men.* Washington, D.C.: Center for the Study of Social Policy.

Johnson, L. B. 1981. "Perspectives on Black Family Empirical Research: 1965–1978." In *Black Families,* edited by H. P. McAdoo, 87–102. Beverly Hills, Calif.: Sage.

Justice, B., and R. Justice. 1976. *The Abusing Family.* New York: Harper & Row.

Katz, M. H., R. L. Hampton, E. H. Newberger, R. T. Bowles, and J. C. Snyder. 1986. "Returning Children Home: Clinical Decision Making in Cases of Child Abuse and Neglect." *American Journal of Orthopsychiatry* 56:253–262.

Lassiter, R. T. 1987. "Child Rearing in Black Families: Child-Abusing Discipline." In *Violence in the Black Family: Correlations and Consequences,* edited by R. Hampton, 39–54. Beverly Hills, Calif.: Sage.

Makosky, V. P. 1982. "Sources of Stress: Events or Conditions?" In *Lives in Stress: Women and Depression,* edited by D. Belle, 35–51. Beverly Hills, Calif.: Sage.

Nalepka, C., R. O'Toole, and J. P. Turbett. 1981. "Nurses' and Physicians' Recognition and Reporting of Child Abuse." *Issues in Comprehensive Pediatric Nursing* 5:33–34.

Newberger, E. H., R. L. Hampton, T. J. Marx, and K. M. White. 1986. "Child Abuse and Pediatric Social Illness: An Epidemiological Analysis and Ecological Reformulation." *American Journal of Orthopsychiatry* 56(4): 589–601.

Newberger, E. H., R. Reed, J. Daniel, J. Hyde, and M. Kotelchuck. 1977. "Pediatric Social Illness: Toward an Etiologic Classification." *Pediatrics* 60:178–185.

Peters, M. F. 1981. "Parenting in Black Families with Young Children: A Historical Perspective." In *Black Families,* edited by H. P. McAdoo, 211–224. Beverly Hills, Calif.: Sage.

Peters, M. F., and G. Massey. 1983. "Mundane Extreme Environmental Stress in Family Stress Theories: The Case of Black Families in White America." *Marriage and Family Review* 1/2:193–215.

Sampson, R. J. 1987. "Urban Black Violence: The Effect of Male Joblessness and Family Disruption." *American Journal of Sociology* 93:348–382.

Smolensky, E. 1982. "Poverty in the United States: Where Do We Stand?" *Focus* 5(2):1–12 (Institute for Research on Poverty, University of Wisconsin, Madison).

Staples, R. 1985. "Changes in Black Family Structure: The Conflict between Family Ideology and Structural Conditions." *Journal of Marriage and the Family* 47:1005-1014.

Steele, B. F., and C. Pollock. 1968. "A Psychiatric Study of Parents Who Abuse Infants and Small Children." In *The Battered Child,* edited by R. Helfer and C. Kempe, 103–147. Chicago: University of Chicago Press.

Steinberg, L. B., R. Catalano, and D. Dooley. 1981. "Economic Antecedents of Child ABuse and Neglect." *Child Development* 52:975–985.

Steinmetz, S. L. 1977. *The Cycle of Violence: Assertive, Aggressive, and Abusive Family Interaction.* New York: Praeger.

Straus, M. A., and R. J. Gelles. 1986. "Societal Change and Change in Family

Violence from 1975 to 1985 as Revealed in Two National Surveys." *Journal of Marriage and the Family* 48:465–479.

———. 1988. "Violence in American Families: How Much Is There and Why Does It Occur?" In *Troubled Relationships,* edited by E. W. Nunnally, C. Chilman, and F. M. Cox, 141–162. Beverly Hills, Calif.: Sage.

Straus, M. A., R. J. Gelles, and S. Steinmetz. 1980. *Behind Closed Doors: Violence in the American Family.* New York: Doubleday.

Thomas, M. E., and M. Hughes. 1986. "The Continuing Significance of Race: A Study of Race, Class, and Quality of Life in America, 1972–1985." *American Sociological Review* 51:830–841.

Turbett, J. P., and R. O'Toole. 1980. "Physicians' Recognition of Child Abuse." Paper presented at the annual meeting of the American Sociological Association, New York.

U.S. Department of Health and Human Services. 1981. *National Study of the Incidence and Severity of Child Abuse and Neglect: Study Findings.* OHDS 81–030326. Washington, D.C.: Government Printing Office.

U.S. Department of Justice, 1980. *Intimate Victims: A Study of Violence among Friends and Relatives.* Washington, D.C.: Government Printing Office.

9

BOGART R. LEASHORE,
HARVEY L. MCMURRAY,
AND BARBARA C. BAILEY

Reuniting and Preserving African American Families

> Teach us to know that failure is as much a part of life as success—and
> whether it shall be evil or good depends upon the way we meet it. . . . The
> race is not to the swift—nor the battle to the strong.
> —W.E.B. DU BOIS,
> *Prayers for Dark People*

This chapter focuses on the resource needs of poor and near-poor African American parents who can be reunited with children placed in foster care if adequate services and resources are acquired or provided. Special emphasis is given to how African American voluntary groups, organizations, and individual volunteers can provide these resources.

This emphasis is consistent with several features of the Africentric perspective. It assumes that children should be nurtured and protected by their natural family network, which includes the extended family and nonrelatives who can meet affiliative needs. It also assumes that problems in family relationships can be successfully resolved, and that the African American community can provide supports and resources for the resolution of family problems. The maintenance of the nurturing unit through collective efforts, self-help, and mutual aid is inherent in the Africentric perspective. Developing resources within the African American community, through its various social, civic, fraternal, and religious groups and organizations, and utilizing these resources to promote family reunification and preservation are forms of collective responsibility for survival. Collective efforts, self-help, and mutual aid to promote the well-being of children and families can also promote community development by building and strengthening the capacity of community groups and organizations to help reunite and preserve families.

Although federal legislation—that is, the Adoption Assistance and Child Welfare Act of 1980 (P.L. 96–272)—mandates services to promote the return or reunification of children in foster care with their families, adequate services are frequently not provided. For example, a study of children who were returned to their biological families after temporary foster-care placement found that a majority of the families needed housing, medical and dental services, income, counseling, special education, legal services, recreation services, and employment training or counseling (Fein et al. 1983). Similarly, a study of foster-care recidivism found that few community services were afforded parents and children either while the children were in foster care or after they were returned to their biological families. Among other conclusions, this study recommended that "additional and more creative use of community services while children are in care may increase the frequency with which biological parents show improvement in existing problems, thereby reducing the risks of recidivism" (Turner 1984:504).

This chapter examines the negative effects of removing children from their families and child welfare policies and practices related to reuniting and preserving African American and other families. It provides an illustration of how community resources can be developed and used to reunite children in foster care with their families. Attention is also given to how policies and practices can promote the preservation of families.

Removing Children from Their Families

Child welfare practitioners and policymakers are gradually recognizing that many children in foster care can and should be reunited with their natural or biological families. Separating children from their families and communities is a drastic measure to take in the name of protecting or rescuing them. In addition, the emphasis in child welfare on removing children from their families has restricted the scope and use of services for African American children (Billingsley and Giovannoni 1972).

Unnecessary removal of children from their families can occur when child welfare practitioners and policymakers fail to recognize cultural differences and variations in parenting and caregiving (Stehno 1982). For some, this negligence represents another source of oppression toward those who have the fewest material resources. Poverty, racism, and sexism necessitate special sensitivity in designing and delivering appropriate and effective child welfare services. For example, differences in language, child-rearing patterns, parental roles, and responsibilities of family members should not be narrowly viewed as deficits. In the context of child abuse and neglect specifically, and child and family services generally, assessment and subsequent intervention should build on the strengths of culturally based values and traditions of family structure and functioning. These include the extended-family and informal ties of single-parent or nuclear families; the individual and family values that are or can be used for problem resolution; and the beliefs, attitudes, and behaviors that can promote the well-being of families and the growth and development of children.

Sanctions for removal of children from their families are provided by family jurisprudence based on conceptualizations about children and families that have not been systematically or scientifically investigated (Melton 1984). Moreover, for children and families of color, cultural beliefs and norms may be ignored or contradicted. Inadequate and vague laws too often result in placing children in foster care because of relatively minor incidents where appropriate child rearing is at issue. Some of these situations require little more than educating parents, for example, about the legal ramifications of certain forms of disciplining children, about developmental needs of children, and about how these needs can be adequately met.

Foster care can be used when parents have engaged in immediately harmful behavior. However, cumulatively harmful behavior need not require foster care (Besharov 1986). Immediately harmful behavior involves parental or caregiver actions that are a continuing threat to the child and can cause an immediately serious injury, "except that *serious injury* [*is*] *averted* by the intervention of an outside force or perhaps simple good luck" (Besharov 1986:24–25). Cumulatively harmful behavior involves parental or caregiver actions that are a continuing threat to the child and can cause cumulatively serious harm to the child if continued over sufficient time. In either case, the evidence needs to be clear and sufficient with appropriate consideration given to the cultural contexts in which children live.

In the case of cumulatively harmful behavior, parents should be helped to provide adequate care without removing the child. Positive parenting and caregiving patterns and behavior should be recognized and reinforced; compensatory child-oriented services can be used when parental deficiencies persist. Such standards for state intervention can have the following benefits: a reduction of child welfare practitioners' caseloads by as much as 25 percent; an increase in protection for those children in immediate danger of serious injury; and a reduction in the number of children placed in foster care by as much as 40 percent (Besharov 1986). Tax dollars saved can be redirected to or appropriated for programs and services that promote stability and the well-being of children. These include adequate, accessible, and quality health and child care, income-support programs, and adequate and affordable housing.

An estimated 275,756 children were in substitute care in the United States during 1984; nearly one-third (32 percent) of these children were African American; 53 percent were white; and the remaining 15 percent were Hispanic, Native American, and members of other racial groups (U.S. Department of Health and Human Services 1984). Approximately two-thirds of these children were in foster or adoptive homes; most of the remaining one-third were in group homes, emergency shelters, and other child-care facilities or arrangements. Parental rights had not been terminated or relinquished in 88 percent of the cases (U.S. Department of Health and Human Services 1984). These data indicate a disproportionate involvement of children of color, particularly African American, in substitute care; an overreliance on foster care and adoption; and a significant number of parent/child relationships that have not been legally terminated.

Although some research has shown no statistically significant difference in rates of child abuse among African American and white families (Straus, Gelles, and Steinmetz 1980), multivariate analyses of 1981 national data specific to hospitals indicate that African American families may be the victims of a decision-making system for removing children from their birth families that is based on personal characteristics rather than actual behavior (Hampton 1986). Typically, socioeconomic differences between the clinician or service provider and the alleged child abuser create social distance, with the service provider in the authoritative role of diagnosing and treating the child's symptoms and assessing the family's caregiving capacity (Hampton 1986). Judgments are made on the basis of physical symptoms or "evidence" and personal characteristics without much regard for the cultural traditions and social conditions in which families and children live. For example, the violent reaction of a twenty-four-old, African American, single mother on Aid to Families with Dependent Children reflects the social conditions in which the family lived. She said, "He [her eight-year-old son] would come to me and say, 'Momma, I don't like this neighborhood.' . . . I would say, 'I know, but Momma doesn't have money.' He said, 'They sell drugs around here.' I said, 'I know, but they sell drugs everywhere. You just stay away from them.' Then I would feel bad the rest of the day" (Gaines-Carter 1986:B7). This young, unemployed mother of three children subsequently "clenched her teeth and with all her might struck her eight-year-old son in the mouth" (p. B1). Frightened by the injury inflicted, she immediately took him to the hospital. The child was placed in foster care for seven months before he was returned to his mother. Although this temporary placement of the child was probably perceived as being in his best interests, it may have been unnecessary.

Among the poor, parenting can sometimes be secondary to providing food and clothing and meeting other basic needs of the children. For example, inadequate income and few financial resources can make providing adequate shelter problematical, particularly for single-parent mothers. In short, instrumental as well as expressive family functioning can be influenced by economic status (Billingsley 1968; Kriesberg 1970; McEaddy 1976; Wilkinson 1984). Although being poor does not necessarily lead to poor family functioning or child abuse or neglect, it can make children and families vulnerable. Thus, like race, social class can influence involvement in the child welfare system. Failure to recognize these influences leads to the proliferation of child welfare practices and policies that are ineffective in the short run and damaging in the long run.

Others have concluded that other factors—such as environmental stress and sexism—in addition to race and social class place many children and families at risk for alleged abuse (Garbarino 1982; Peters and Massey 1983). For example, analysis of reported and unreported cases of abuse by a hospital staff showed that African American and Hispanic children were more likely to be reported as abused than white children. Families with younger children, single parents, and families supported by public assistance were more likely than their counterparts to be reported for alleged abuse. Furthermore, physical abuse was more likely to be reported than emotional abuse or neglect.

Case reporting seemed most affected by income, mother's role in the alleged mistreatment, race, whether the harm was physical rather than emotional, child's sex, whether the case was one of sexual abuse, and mother's level of education. Interestingly, higher-income white mothers alleged to have emotionally abused their children were disproportionately represented among unreported cases (Hampton 1986).

The negative consequences of separating children from their birth families have been documented in the child welfare literature (Jenkins 1969; Littner 1975; Pollock 1957). The separation trauma, guilt, sense of loss, devaluation of self, and identity conflicts experienced by children and their biological families are real, as are the emotional bonds and attachments between them. The ties are not easily broken, nor should they be in most cases. The family is often the only source of a child's sense of belonging, security, and identification, despite parental behavior. Research has shown that children who are involuntarily placed may hold the child-placement agency and staff responsible for separating them from their families. Even separation resulting from voluntary placements was sometimes viewed by children as perpetrated by the agency (Pollock 1957). Children who have been separated from their families and communities and placed in foster care are rendered subject to behavioral and emotional problems including depression (Zimmerman 1988).

The removal of a child from his or her family has been found to be equally devastating for the parents. In one study, both mothers and fathers of children placed in foster care experienced sadness, worry, nervousness, anger, bitterness, guilt, and shame. No statistically significant differences were found between parents, except for feelings of shame, which were experienced by more fathers than mothers (Jenkins 1969). Too often, child welfare practitioners fail to recognize the responses of parents, siblings, and other family members when children are removed. Recognition of these responses and the provision of adequate family support services to deal with them are consistent with working in the best interests of the child.

Reuniting Children with Their Families

Inadequate resources and supportive services continue to be barriers to family reunification and preservation, especially for families of color. Successful interventions include social services such as parent support groups, parenting classes, adequate health care, income support, education, day care, transportation, job training, employment opportunities, and family counseling services. The results or outcomes of the provision of these services include improved parent/ child relationships, a reduction in child abuse and neglect, increased school attendance, and a decreased need for special services (Miller 1981).

In accordance with the provisions of the Adoption Assistance and Child Welfare Act of 1980 that authorized funds for demonstration projects, a two-year family-reunification project was conducted through the Howard University School of Social Work in 1985.[1] A major assumption of the project was that there were untapped community-based resources that could be used to help reunify families with children in foster care. The goal of Project VCIN (Volunteers for Children in Need) was to utilize a community-based volunteer network to help reunite African American children in the foster-care system of Washington, D.C., with their natural families. At the time of this initiative, 98.5 percent of the children in care were African American.

Specifically, the objectives of VCIN were to identify and recruit minority, voluntary, community-based groups and organizations; to strengthen the capacity of minority leaders and organizations to develop resources; to establish links between the minority volunteer network and child welfare agencies; and to develop a model that would enable community groups and organizations to assist minority families. The major activities of the project were (1) recruitment and training of affiliates for the network, (2) referral of children and families to the project, (3) assessment of resource needs, and (4) resource allocation for reunification purposes. The project was staffed by a full-time coordinator, secretary, graduate social work students, consultants, and a project director. The local public child welfare agency assigned a management-level staff liaison to the project.

As an initial activity, individuals, groups, and organizations were identified for participation in the project through published directories of groups, churches, and organizations, and through personal contacts, and referrals. Nearly two hundred primarily African American community groups, organizations, churches, and individuals expressed a desire to participate in the project.

Prior to accepting referrals, the project conducted a needs assessment to determine specific resources needed to facilitate the reunification of children in foster care with their families. The assessment indicated the following most frequently needed resources: housing, family counseling, drug treatment, day care, furniture, employment, financial assistance, and parenting-skills training. This information was shared with participating groups and organizations who were asked to identify resources they could provide.

For outreach, information, and orientation purposes, an initial community-awareness forum was held to formally introduce the project to community groups and organizations. Presentations were made by staff of the local child welfare agency and by the project staff with follow-up audience discussion and participation. Representatives from a wide range of groups and organizations attended: churches, sororities, fraternal organizations, clubs, grass-roots organizations, neighborhood centers, youth groups, and advocacy organizations. At the close of the forum, each representative completed an "organizational biography," a short form used to collect pertinent information for a resource directory that was later produced by the project. This directory was disseminated to local child welfare administrators and practitioners for use in securing resources and services for children and families. Representatives were also asked to give information about other groups and organizations that might be interested in participating in the project. Evaluation of the forum indicated an improved understanding of child welfare services, problems faced by children in foster care and their families, and the project's goals and objectives.

In addition to this community forum, a project announcement, fact sheet, and poster were developed and disseminated for outreach purposes to numerous groups, organizations, and churches. Written materials about the project were distributed at local conferences, meetings, and other community activities. A press release announcing the project was prepared in collaboration with the university's public relations office and distributed to local radio stations and newspapers, especially those with significant African American audiences and subscribers.

Initial efforts of Project VCIN included training to strengthen the capacity of the African American voluntary community groups and organizations that had the capacity to provide assistance to families with children in foster care. Training and technical-assistance workshops were held on Saturday mornings and covered the following areas: information about local child welfare services and the needs of children and families; recruiting, retaining, and motivating volunteers for social-action programs; fund raising; public relations; and proposal writing and grantsmanship. The workshops were conducted at various community locations by staff as well as consultants. Project staff also attended meetings of some groups and organizations to solicit support and resources for families.

Sixty-two African American families, with 115 children in foster care, were referred to the project by the Child and Family Services Division of the D.C. Commission on Social Services and a consortium of private agencies in the metropolitan area. The criteria for case acceptance included a goal of returning the children to their families; a specific time frame for achieving this goal, usually one year; a need for resources; and written parental consent to participate in the project. Only cases with reunification as the permanent plan were accepted for project services based on a brief referral form used by participating agencies.

Accepted referrals were assigned to paid project consultants, who convened case conferences and served as case managers for meeting resource needs. Typically, each conference was attended by the consultant, the agency social worker, parent(s), project staff, and others as appropriate—for example, children, significant others, and volunteers. Comprehensive family-centered assessments were made to identify and reinforce family strengths and to determine the resources needed to facilitate reunification, stabilization, and self-sufficiency. Goals, tasks, and responsibilities were identified and time frames were delineated. Follow-up conferences were held regularly to monitor progress in meeting family needs and ultimately achieving reunification. The project was subsequently expanded to include the development and utilization of community resources to prevent the placement of children in foster care.

To facilitate uniformity in the implementation phase of the project, all the consultants were given an orientation on the approach to be used, the expectations of them as experts, and the available resources for families. The project's conceptual framework of empowerment emphasized a family-centered approach for problem resolution and family stabilization (Hutchinson 1983; Solomon 1976). Project consultants were also informed about the resources that some groups and organizations offered. All the consultants were African American social workers with knowledge of African American family life and of local child welfare services. The objective was alleviating resource deprivation, which prevented family reunification and stabilization, by utilizing a team approach with the consultants serving as team leaders.

Written summaries of all case conferences were required and shared with agency workers, as well as parents. Neither the consultants nor project staff assumed primary responsibility for cases. This responsibility remained with the referring social worker and agency.

Because housing was needed by approximately three-fourths of the families, a special brain-trust luncheon was held to identify practical housing alternatives. Representatives of voluntary groups and organizations, community leaders, and local government officials, including the city's housing director, attended this luncheon. As in many large urban areas, a shortage of adequate and affordable housing for low-income families was a major barrier to reunification. Recognizing this shortage, the city had recently developed a special tenants' assistance program, which provided housing-subsidy vouchers and, on request, direct payment to participating landlords. The program sought, among other things, to expand the housing market for low-income families. The city agreed to set aside 10 to 15 percent of the housing allocations for special-needs families including those participating in the family-reunification project. Inclusion of the project in this set-aside occurred when parents participating in the project met as a political constituency with a member of the city council and expressed their need for housing. They also expressed the desire to have their children returned from foster care and openly discussed circumstances related to the removal of the children from their homes. Responding to their housing need, the city councilman facilitated the inclusion of these families in the set-aside.

Other groups also helped with housing. A representative of a voluntary organization expressed interest in lobbying for five apartment units of a new housing development that the organization was sponsoring for low-income families. An organization of African American real estate agents assisted some families in locating and securing housing, and real estate consultation was available for those families interested in home-ownership programs.

Other needs of families referred to the project were also met through the community. A physician provided free medical services. Some individuals and organizations donated furniture and other household items, money, food, and clothing, while others volunteered supportive services—for instance, "surrogate sisters" for single mothers and family recreational activities. All donations of money were deposited in a special account with the public child welfare agency's Office of Volunteer Services and were used exclusively for family reunification and preventive services—for example, to replace broken windows in apartments during the winter. Several organizations "adopted" a family and provided supportive services as well as assistance with tangible needs.

Characteristically, all the families referred to the project maintained strong desires to be reunited with their children. Strong bonds between children and their families existed despite placement in foster care. Most families regularly visited and otherwise kept in contact with their children. Some strongly resented the agency for removing them. Generally, parents maintained cooperative attitudes about participation in the project. They frequently contacted their agency social workers and project staff to discuss difficulties and to share the successes they experienced in undertaking responsibilities and tasks related to reunification. Over the course of their participation, many parents viewed the project and its staff as their advocates, which reduced hopelessness and increased their motivation to actively engage in the reunification effort.

In all, the project helped reunite or prevented placement for eighteen families and assisted others in working toward the return of their children from foster care. Most (94 percent) of the families served by the project were African American single mothers who received public assistance. Nearly half the families had only one child in foster care, while the remaining had two or more children in care. Some families were providing care for other children who had not been removed from their homes. Although the length of time in foster care varied, the average time was 2.7 years. The majority of the children in foster care were male; the average age of the children was eight years. Thirty-nine percent of the mothers lived alone, while 61 percent lived with relatives or nonrelatives.

Financial and job needs were also addressed by the project. Limited financial resources were a major problem for most of the families who were either poor or near poor. Thus, economic constraints had to be considered and surmounted. Although most of the families received public assistance, a few parents were gainfully employed and able to support themselves and their children, usually at marginal levels. Household budgeting was covered as needed with parents individually, as well as through group sessions with project staff, consultants, and volunteers. Parents were generally responsive to assistance in this area. Several receiving public assistance were actively looking for work; they received help in securing employment or job training.

Interest in occupational mobility was not uncommon among those who had a high school education. Typically, these parents were interested in job training that would provide them with additional skills, job opportunities, and income.

In some instances, the children placed in foster care had special needs that were difficult for their birth families to meet. Unaware of available services and unable adequately to mobilize resources, some parents simply did the best that they could until something went wrong and child protection services became involved. For example, a thirty-year-old African American mother of three children, one of whom was born with a physical disability, was forced to quit her job because of a lack of adequate childcare. Unable to manage on public assistance, the family was subsequently evicted from their apartment and moved into a shelter for the homeless. Because of the child's special needs and the mother's eventual inability to meet them, the child with the disability was placed in foster care. Another young mother placed her young deaf daughter in foster care, as she felt unable to provide special care. This mother stated: "Being a single parent, I couldn't give her [the daughter] all the care she needed. . . . She was born premature, and she needed a lot of doctor care. I couldn't give it to her, and I didn't have anyone to go to for help" (Reddick 1986).

With help from this project, these mothers were able to secure adequate housing, furnishings, and moving assistance. They also received clothing for their children and such supportive services as respite care, which afforded them some relief from the constant needs of their children for attention, especially those who had physical disabilities. On an intangible level, these mothers also gained skill in accessing services within their own communities and increased their abilities to handle similar circumstances in the future.

Parents received support from varied sources. Some found that religious beliefs helped them cope with separation and provided hope for the return of their children. As one mother stated, "I prayed a lot for them to come home"; another mother felt that going to church and praying helped a great deal. In other instances, extended family and friends provided support and encouragement in planning for the return of children. Some parents felt that their agency social workers were helpful and they tried to do things that the workers advised them to do.

Having their children taken away from them and the subsequent submission to the authority of the court and the child welfare agency had made many parents feel powerless. The project motivated and supported them so that they were able to achieve or make significant progress toward reunification. Motivation to reunite their families prompted some parents to be flexible and resilient in their role as parent and to assume various self-help tasks necessary for reunification. These tasks included assuming active roles in searching for housing and employment, participating in parent-training classes and counseling for specific problems, and increasing and maintaining contact with their children during placement.

Promoting Family Preservation and Reunification

Relatives and significant others are sometimes overlooked or not permitted to provide needed care for children despite strong family ties. Failure to utilize these resources contributes to unnecessary placement in foster care and other forms of substitute care—for instance, group homes and institutions. Failure to use other people as care providers occurs for several reasons: Sometimes child welfare workers do not fully explore the possibilities of using relatives and others as resources; in some instances, child welfare workers make arbitrary and value-laden decisions about the life-styles of relatives and significant others (as they do about the life-styles of the children's parents); and sometimes other people are not willing to provide care because of the unrealistic and general assumption that relatives should provide for children because they love them and should therefore not be given financial support (Children's Defense Fund 1978). Needed services should be available to all significant others so that if placement becomes necessary, children can be moved to the homes of people who know them.

Among African Americans, fictive kin, or nonrelatives, who know the family can be resources for children and families (Billingsley 1968; Stack 1974), as can godparents among Hispanic Americans (Vidal 1988). These nonrelatives can provide support for the family and adequate care for children.

In some cases, legal guardianship may be the most desirable option, although it is generally underutilized by the courts and child welfare practitioners. This arrangement may be particularly suitable for African Americans who have absorbed individuals, especially children, into their households on a temporary or permanent basis without the benefit of court action. Legal guardianship involves court-assigned authority over and responsibility for children during a specified time period. Parental rights are not terminated. As with some adoptions, guardianship subsidies should be provided when needed (Leashore 1984). This living arrangement is consistent with the Africentric perspective, and it can reduce the anxiety, fear, anger, and hostility that emerge when separation of parents and children occurs.

Children need to be involved in decisions about their care. Research shows that they often know who might provide for them in their extended family and community. One study looked at children removed from their biological families who did not want another set of parents and therefore resisted adoption; some maintained contact with their parents despite knowing that they might never return home to live. Adoption was viewed as destructive of the relationships with their parents; and agreeing to be adopted, as a betrayal of their families (Bush and Gordon 1982).

Attempts to reform or humanize child welfare services for African American children and families require recognition that these services are the result of a complex blend of racism, professionalism, sectarianism, and bureaucracy (Billingsley and Giovannoni 1972). If African American children and their families are to be adequately served, radical changes need to be made in public policy, in the attitudes of service providers, and in service delivery. Standards regarding childcare need to be realistic, with increased appreciation for and understanding of the social context and life experiences of African Americans in a predominantly white society (Billingsley and Giovannoni 1972) Education, understanding, and recognition of the strengths of African American families, translated into action, can contribute much to the development of culturally sensitive human service systems.

However, in the absence of adequate health insurance, housing, employment and income support, and other services for families and children, the reunification of African American families as well as of other families with children in foster care, will be difficult if not impossible to achieve. Comparative analysis of U.S. social policy and services for children with those in other Western industrialized nations indicates an embarrassing lack of adequate prenatal and postnatal care for women and children, among other things.

In response to this and other needs, coercive social-policy and child welfare practices should be replaced by some form or combination of a minimum guaranteed income for families, a negative income tax, or a children's allowance, which could ensure a higher quality of life without humiliating those who received them (Edelman 1978). In addition, a policy agenda for children should include these recommendations: reduce homelessness for families with children through supplemental family housing allowances, improve child health through universal health services or insurance for children, protect family income during pregnancy and childbirth so that babies are given a good start, and protect the well-being of children while parents work, enhance their social development, and prepare them for school through quality childcare services (Kamerman 1989).

The structural conditions of poverty—poor and inadequate health care, substandard housing, unemployment, racism and discrimination, drug abuse, and poor education—must be addressed if the well-being of African American children and families is to be significantly enhanced. Removing children from families whose dysfunctioning is directly related to these structural conditions only creates additional problems. Instead, laws and regulations that offer substantive solutions to the problems discussed in this chapter should be developed by the federal and state governments and complied with; vague laws and regulations need to be clarified; adequate funds for reform should be appropriated; and close monitoring of state services for compliance should be undertaken. Well-defined standards should specify what constitute "reasonable efforts" to avoid placement and what services are available; similarly, services rendered to families, as well as the quality of these services, should be adequately documented. Full legal representation should be provided for children and their parents. Caseloads of child welfare workers should be manageable so that children and families who need services can receive them; flexible working hours should be permitted with around-the-clock services (Edna McConnell Clark Foundation 1985).

A shortage or lack of resources has been identified as the most important immediate obstacle to providing services that would prevent the placement of children. Other factors related to this problem are eligibility requirements, which dictate entitlement to services; a lack of information about services; and the absence of effective lobbying for services (Miller 1981). There is also a need to target additional funds for resource development. Removing these obstacles is essential because as Kamerman and Kahn (1976) have stated, there is no primary prevention for such a vaguely defined phenomenon as abuse and

neglect except sound social policy for children and families in interaction with their communities.

Conclusion

African American children are disproportionately separated from
their families by the American child welfare system and placed in foster or other substitute care. This government intervention, undertaken
in the name of protecting or rescuing children, can impair the social
and psychological development of children and impose yet another
threat to or assault on the well-being of families. As a result, families
and children may feel powerless, threatened, vulnerable, hostile, and
angry. Civil liability for inadequate foster care, costly and inappropriate institutional care, and adoption disruption are other negative
consequences of separating children from their biological families. Increasingly, public child welfare agencies are being confronted with liability charges—for example, negligence in the selection of foster
parents or supervision of the placement. Legally, foster parents have
few specific powers and uncertain rights. Their relationships with
children placed in their homes may create conflict and questions of
loyalty to the biological family, especially for the children.

Child welfare policies and practices should be oriented toward
strengthening families. The mobilization and utilization of community-based support services can allow children to remain with their
families and in their communities. These actions can be cost-effective
and ensure healthy child development. The family reunification project at the Howard University School of Social Work demonstrated
that African American children placed in foster care can be reunited
with their families without jeopardizing their welfare. The project also
demonstrated that African American voluntary groups, organizations,
and individuals can help these families by providing tangible and intangible resources. The project is based on a family-support model
that can be replicated. The emphasis on volunteer services in collaboration with public services illustrates the kind of public/private partnership that can be developed for African American children and their
families as well as for others. Community-based partnerships and self-
help can facilitate education about the needs of African American
families and the development of resources to meet those needs. Knowledge, understanding, skills, and the ability to help can be enhanced so

that child welfare services are sensitive to and effective in strengthening African American families.

The threat of or actual removal of children from their families can be devastating and traumatic. When inflicted on those who are already the victims of poverty, inadequate health care, substandard housing, poor education, and limited employment opportunities, hopelessness and powerlessness can be inevitable consequences. Without the economic means to provide basic care for dependent children, African Americans and other families of color are more likely than others to be reported for child abuse and neglect. Public policies and services are needed to break this cycle—to provide economic support and opportunities for poor and working-class families. These should include job training and employment opportunities, national health insurance, day care, increased wages and benefits, improved education, affirmative action, and a minimum guaranteed income.

Acknowledgment

The authors express appreciation to Kathy Cunningham for assistance in the preparation of this chapter.

Note

1. This project was funded by the Administration for Children, Youth and Families, Office of Human Development Services, U.S. Department of Health and Human Services (Grant 90-CW0742). Funds for data analysis were provided by the Howard University Sponsored Faculty Research Program. A manual for replication of the project is available on request.

References

Besharov, D. J. 1986. "Right versus Rights: The Dilemma of Child Protection." *Public Welfare* 42(2):19–27.

Billingsley, A. 1968. *Black Families in White America.* Englewood Cliffs, N.J.: Prentice-Hall.

Billingsley, A. and J. M. Giovannoni. 1972. *Children of the Storm: Black Children and American Child Welfare.* New York: Harcourt Brace Jovanovich.

Bush, M., and A. Gordon, 1982. "The Case for Involving Children in Child Welfare Decisions." *Social Work* 27(4):309–314.

Children's Defense Fund, 1978. *Children without Homes: An Examination of Public Responsibility to Children in Out-of-Home Care.* Washington, D.C.

Edelman, M. W. 1987. *Families in Peril: An Agenda for Social Change.* Cambridge: Harvard University Press.

Edna McConnell Clark Foundation. 1985. *Keeping Families Together: The Case for Family Preservation.* New York.

Fein, E., A. Maluccio, J. Hamilton, and D. Ward. 1983. "After Foster Care: Outcomes of Permanency Planning for Children." *Child Welfare* 62: 485–560.

Gaines-Carter, P. 1986. "Counseling Service Helps Write a Happy Ending." *Washington Post.* August 21.

Garborina, J. 1982. *Children and Families in the Social Environment.* New York: Adine.

Hampton, R. L. 1986. "Race, Ethnicity, and Child Maltreatment: An Analysis of Cases Recognized and Reported by Hospitals." In *The Black Family: Essays and Studies,* 3d ed., edited by R. Staples, 172–185. Belmont, Calif.: Wadsworth.

Hutchinson, J. 1983. *Family-Centered Social Services: A Model for Child Welfare Agencies.* Ames: University of Iowa Press.

Jenkins, S. 1969. "Separation Experiences of Parents Whose Children Are in Foster Care." *Child Welfare* 48:334–340.

Kamerman, S. B. 1989. "Toward a Child Policy." *Child Welfare* 48:371–390.

Kamerman, S. B., and A. J. Kahn. 1976. *Social Services in the United States: Policies and Programs.* Philadelphia: Temple University Press.

Kriesberg, L. 1970. *Mothers in Poverty.* Chicago: Aldine.

Leashore, B. R. 1984. "Demystifying Legal Guardianship: An Unexplored Option for Dependent Children." *Journal of Family Law* 23(3):391–400.

Littner, N. 1975. "The Importance of the Natural Parents to the Child in Placement." *Child Welfare* 54:175–182.

McEaddy, B. J. 1976. "Women Who Head Families: A Socio-Economic Analysis." *Monthly Labor Review* 99(6):3–9.

Melton, G. B. 1984. "Development Psychology and the Law: The State of the Art." *Journal of Family Law* 22:445–482.

Miller, C. 1981. "Primary Prevention of Child Mistreatment: Meeting a National Need." *Child Welfare* 60:11–23.

Peters, M. F., and G. Massey. 1983. "Mundane Extreme Environment Stress in Family Stress Theories: The Case of Black Families in White America." *Marriage and Family Review* 1/2:193–215.

Pollock, J. C. 1957. "The Meaning of Parents to the Placed Child." *Child Welfare* 36:8–17.

Reddick, T. 1986. "Families Reunited under New Program." *Washington Times.* October 8.

Solomon, B. B. 1976. *Black Empowerment: Social Work in Oppressed Communities.* New York: Columbia University Press.

Stack, C. B. 1974. *All Our Kin: Strategies for Survival in a Black Community.* New York: Harper & Row.

Stehno, S. M. 1982. "Differential Treatment of Minority Children in Service Systems." *Social Work* 27:39–45.

Straus, M. A., R. J. Gelles, and S. Steinmetz. 1980. *Behind Closed Doors: Violence in the American Family.* New York: Doubleday.

Turner, J. 1984. "Reuniting Children in Foster Care with Their Biological Parents." *Social Work* 29:501–505.

U. S. Department of Health and Human Services. 1984. *Child Welfare Statistical Fact Book 1984: Substitute Care and Adoption.* McLean, Va.: Maximus.

Vidal, C. 1988. "Godparenting among Hispanic Americans." *Child Welfare* 67:453–459.

Wilkinson, D. Y. 1984. "Afro-American Women and Their Families." *Marriage and Family Review* 7:125–142.

Zimmerman, R. B. 1988. "Childhood Depression: New Theoretical Formulations and Implications for Foster Care Services." *Child Welfare* 46:37–47.

10

CAROL C. WILLIAMS

Expanding the Options in the Quest for Permanence

And the King said, divide the living child in two, and give half to the one
and half to the other.
                —1 KINGS 3:25

The quest for permanence in the placement of children initially focused on securing adoptive homes for children needing out-of-home
care, but more recently this quest has come to focus on the need to
preserve families of origin. These two strategies, while an essential
part of an effective permanency effort, will not, by themselves, provide security for those children at risk of out-of-home placement. An
analysis of each of these areas is needed in order to develop a holistic
approach for meeting the permanency needs of African American
children.

Adoption

Although adoption services were established in this country prior
to the 1930s, African American children were excluded from these
institutionalized services. However, adoption was not unknown in African American communities. In fact, patterns of informal adoption
existed as far back as the time of slavery. The community's response
to the disruption of family bonds, a common occurrence during slavery, was to absorb children into existing family networks. Building

on the African experience of extended family and community, children who were separated from their parents were cared for by the slave community, which established kinship relationships among persons who were not related by blood (Billingsley and Griovannoni 1972; Blassingame 1979; Gutman 1976).

Family within African American communities has thus meant the extended family rather than the nuclear family and has included persons related by blood as well as persons without blood or marital ties (Hill 1972; Martin and Martin, 1978). For African Americans, the family is defined by functional relationships as well as by sanguinity. These patterns of child caring and family building continue and are reflected in the patterns of informal adoption and child sharing documented by Stack (1974, 1985), Hill (1977), Billingsley (1968), and Nobles (1982).

One of the characteristics of informal adoption is that custody and responsibility for the child are transferred without the severance of parental rights. In the past, children and caretakers knew who the parents were, and in postslavery times they often maintained a relationship with the birth parents. Even during slavery, efforts were made to know the whereabouts of parents who had been separated from their children and to communicate with them. There was a notion of shared parenting, with the actual or implied permission of birth parents.

Thus, in contrast to the exclusiveness of nuclear families, the African American family is inclusive, taking into its boundaries in-laws, kin, and nonrelatives. Kinship networks that include unrelated persons compensate for the socioeconomic stressors African American families encounter. The building of families in this manner allowed for the pooling of social, financial, and psychological resources. Shared childcare, informal exchange of goods and services, and a network of emotional support provided buffers against family crisis, poverty, and racism.

In the twentieth century, this pattern of extended family care and child sharing continued as the great urban migrations occurred and parents moved north or sent their children north to relatives and close family friends, where they could find opportunities for work and education. In recent times, however, these patterns have been challenged by changes in the social environment, including the increased mobility of families, the high cost of rearing children, the increase in the proportion of single-parent families, and the escalating economic and social vulnerability of African American families.

In spite of these trends, the pattern of child sharing continues to be a response to family crisis. In one study of African American children in foster care, a significant number had been living with relatives and had exhausted the resources of the extended family prior to formal placement by the child welfare agency (Malson and Williams 1989). Similarly, as a response by families in the African American community to the devastating effects of drugs and acquired immune deficiency syndrome, many grandparents, aunts, and uncles are providing primary care to children whose own parents are disabled, have died, or have disappeared. A study in California documented the rapid growth of kinship placement among African American children (Kemper, Simonds, and John 1990).

Contemporary child welfare practices intersect with this familiar pattern. Often African American children come into the child welfare system after being "abandoned" with a nonrelative caretaker. A parent leaves the child in the care of a relative or family friend. In many instances, the caretaker has had a relationship with the parent and is considered a suitable person to care for the child. The parent who assumes the right to give the child to someone and feels that this is a good decision, may be surprised to find that child welfare authorities view these actions as "abandonment."

Dwanna Smith, age six, has been living with the Jones family since she was five months old. Dwanna was placed with Mrs. Jones by her mother. Ms. Smith was sixteen when Dwanna was born, and she was in intense conflict with her own parents. As a result, she and Dwanna stayed for short periods of time with friends, relatives, and acquaintances. During Dwanna's infancy, Ms. Smith often left Dwanna with Mrs. Jones for several hours. Eventually she asked the Joneses to take care of her full time.

The birth mother visits the Joneses from time to time and brings gifts to Dwanna. Her visits are sporadic, sometimes weekly, sometimes as long as six months apart. Although Mrs. Jones does not see the mother regularly, she has a system for getting in touch with Ms. Smith, who regularly changes living arrangements. Mrs. Jones leaves a message at the neighborhood store, and the mother gets in touch within several days.

Dwanna calls the Joneses "Mom" and "Dad" and calls her birth mother by her first name. She understands that Ms. Smith is her first mom. Dwanna seems to be thriving, achieving in school, and comfortable in her family.

The Joneses and the mother have an amicable relationship. They see Ms. Smith as a troubled young woman who needs help. Mrs. Jones tries to listen and make constructive suggestions to the mom, but she doubts the mother will stabilize. Ms. Smith is pleased with Dwanna's care and often expresses gratitude to Mrs. Jones. There appears to be a tacit agreement that Dwanna will grow up with the Joneses.

The only public-agency contact in this case is related to Aid to Families with Dependent Children (AFDC) for Dwanna. The Joneses receive nonneedy caretaker benefits. After the AFDC application, Dwanna's case was referred to the adoption unit of the local department of social services to explore the feasibility of adoption by the Joneses. In the adoption discussions, the Joneses indicated a high level of commitment to Dwanna but reluctance to pursue adoption. They felt that the adoption would require them to take Dwanna away from her mother and that they had a relationship and an "understanding" with the mother. They did not want to be placed in an adversarial relationship with the mother and felt that asking her to surrender the child or having legal action taken to terminate parental rights would jeopardize the relationship and the placement of the child. [1]

Another example of parenting patterns is reflected in the number of adoptions that are completed by African American foster parents after children have lived with them for a while. Many of these families would be reluctant to adopt an "unknown" child but are comfortable with legal adoption once the child is incorporated into the family (Spaulding for Children 1990). Conversely, many relatives are reluctant to legalize an informal adoption because of the necessity of terminating the parental rights of someone who is part of their familial network.

One of the major dilemmas in developing an Africentric approach to permanency is the difference in legal and social definitions of the family. In the common-law tradition, familial rights and responsibilities are limited to the relationship between parents and the child. In most procedural law, this means that legal actions relating to custody, adoption, and termination of parental rights require the notification of parents only, not grandparents or the siblings of the parents. In other words, the extended family and unrelated kin are viewed by law as having no rights to participate in decisions affecting the child. Foster parents in many jurisdictions are seen as having a greater interest than unrelated kin in such decisions and are required to receive notification. In the American approach to permanency, little substantive attention has been given to the development of legal and social strategies that legitimate the use of extended-family members as permanent care-takers or co-parents.

Patterns of Formal Adoption

Formal agency-based adoption services developed to serve white couples who were unable to have children. Because adoption had little social acceptance and was viewed as a confidential matter, emphasis was placed on physical matching of the child to the adoptive parents and assurances that the child was healthy with no undesirable genetic or physical traits. Initially, African American couples and children were not served by this approach to adoption and were, in fact, systemati-cally excluded from it (Billingsley and Giovannoni 1972; Day 1979). While informal adoption and child sharing were major responses to the need of children for alternative care, a pattern of third-party, stranger adoption also occurred in the African American community. It remains unclear whether these adoptions were legalized or remained informal. During the early twentieth century, children were placed by third-party intermediaries on an interstate basis. The placements were accomplished by black lawyers and other professionals to help young, middle-class black women avoid the stigma of unwanted pregnancies (W. R. Wilson II, personal communication, November 1989).

The civil rights struggles, most visible during the 1960s and early 1970s, raised issues of equal access to services. As the human services sector began to address issues of desegregation, adoption services were extended to African American infants. Based on pilot projects developed in the voluntary sector during the 1950s and 1960s, efforts were made to adapt these services to the needs of the African Ameri-can community (Billingsley and Giovannoni 1972). Strategies to serve these children through public and voluntary agencies have included modifying the assessment criteria and process; providing community-outreach and child-advocacy services; eliminating fees and providing subsidies; emphasizing public education and child-specific recruit-ment; and increasing the proportion of African American staff. Addi-tionally, a number of specialized African American adoption agencies and adoption advocacy programs based in the community were developed. These strategies increased credibility for adoption services in the community, informed the public of the needs of waiting children, and resulted in improved placement outcomes for children. Although these efforts have secured permanence for many African American children, they have failed to meet the needs of all the children who are bereft of families of their own (Tatara 1989).

During this same period, the public system of child-protective services developed. Increased numbers of African American families came to the attention of child welfare authorities with the passage of mandatory reporting laws and the implementation of a system for investigating and responding to suspected child abuse and neglect. There was a general recognition in the 1970s of an overreliance on out-of-home care as the protective-services program expanded. Children were lingering in the foster-care system, and a disproportionate number of these were African American children. In response to the concerns about the insecurity and the psychosocial problems experienced by foster children, permanence through adoption was sought for all children without safe and functioning families. To make services responsive to the needs of African American children, renewed efforts were made to deliver adoption services in a culturally appropriate manner (Billingsley and Giovannoni 1972; Day 1979).

Underlying these efforts were three interwoven assumptions. The first was that the criteria and procedures used to select families for white infants were neither appropriate for African American families nor responsive to their cultural and economic experience, and they therefore resulted in the screening out of potential families. The traditional approach to adoption assumed there were more families wanting to adopt than there were adoptive children. This approach was based on an elitist strategy in which the very best families were sought from a large pool of applicants. The criteria used were both psychosocial and economic. Adoption agencies were able to choose the most affluent and well-functioning families for their white infants. The threshold for acceptance was high. When adoption services were extended to African American families and the criteria remained the same, many families did not get through the process (Day 1979). Concerned agencies and professional groups redefined the qualities needed to adopt and established new criteria and approaches that would screen African American families appropriately (National Black Child Development Institute 1987).

The second assumption was that adoptions were not occurring because the African American community was not aware of the needs of African American children in out-of-home care (Day 1979). Concerns that the African American community did not know that the children needing permanent families were well founded. In the past, the needs of families and vulnerable children were visible to family members, neighbors, churches, and communities (Ross 1978). With the geographic mobility of families, the changing structure of communities, and the emergence of the public child welfare system, which valued confidentiality and relied on out-of-home placement, it became increasingly difficult to identify the needs of children. The lay person in the community was unlikely to understand that many children had become social and legal orphans. Outreach and education efforts were appropriate responses and resulted in increased adoptions.

The large numbers of African American children awaiting adoption contributed to the third assumption: that African Americans do not adopt. Numerous articles published in the professional literature addressed this issue. Empirical data, however, documented a proclivity within the African American community to take in the children of others. Hill (1977) noted that over one million African American children were adopted without legal sanction by relatives, most notably grandparents, aunts, and uncles. Gershenson (1984), using another approach, compared the actual rate of adoption by nonpoor African American and white families with the rate of adoption needed to place all the waiting children. The actual rate of adoption for nonpoor African American families was 18 per 10,000 families compared with 4 per 10,000 families for whites. To secure the number of families needed to adopt the African American children awaiting, the rate would have to be 44 per 10,000 nonpoor families. The data indicate the high rates of formal and informal adoption within the African American community. The question that emerges from the data is: Why do so many African American children find themselves without parents and in need of permanent substitute care?

Social and Systemic Factors That Lead to Out-of-Home Placement

Achieving permanence and family stability for African American children is critical. The public-policy response has focused on identifying and seeking additional adoptive resources for these children.

Little attention has been directed to the social and systemic factors that place them at greater risk of family disruption than whites. The issue of permanency has been addressed as if it were exclusively an adoption problem and not the outcome of weaknesses in other parts of the service-delivery system. The result of this simplistic approach has been to reinforce a deficit view of the African American family and the African American community. Families were presumably not functioning well enough to take care of their own children. When children were without parents, the community was portrayed as being unwilling to care for them. To deal effectively with the issue of permanence, a systemic perspective needs to be taken to examine the way in which children enter care, the availability of services to prevent placement, the accessibility of reunification services, and the need for additional permanency options.

Children enter the child-protective-services system because of suspected abuse or neglect, with the vast majority being targets of intervention because of neglect. Unlike physical and sexual abuse, where there is often concrete evidence to substantiate maltreatment, neglect is complicated to assess. For the most part the definitions are vague and difficult to operationalize. For example, the National Association of Public Child Welfare Administrators (1988: 23) defines child abuse and neglect as "any recent act of failure on the part of a parent which results in the death or serious physical, sexual, or emotional harm, or presents an imminent risk of serious harm to a person under the age of 18." Child welfare workers are expected to make distinctions between poverty and neglect and to evaluate situations with an understanding of the cultural factors that influence child rearing.

Workers' abilities to make judgments and decisions are critical skills. Giovannoni and Becerra (1979) found variations in the ways different groups of professionals and different cultural communities evaluate the severity of abuse and neglect. Research on worker decision making indicates that decisions are more likely to be made on the basis of deficits in available resources, accepted agency practice, personal values and biases, and notions of an ideal family than by application of consistent rules to the facts of the case (Stein and Rzepnicki 1984). The factors that workers consider in making risk assessments vary as do assessments of the severity of risk and levels of intervention indicated. Given the documented inconsistency in decision making, there is justifiable concern about bias.[2]

Once children come into the child-protective-services system, pub-

lic policy mandates that "reasonable efforts" be made to prevent placement (Adoption Assistance and Child Welfare Act of 1980). Since the
mid-1980s several states have begun to provide family-preservation
services to the families of youngsters at imminent risk of placement.
These services are family-centered, home-based, intensive, and short
term, and include a mix of concrete and psychoeducational assistance
(Kinney et al. 1988). One study showed that in more than three-
fourths of the families, placement had been avoided, and children were
able to remain at home safely for a year after intervention. Families
have also shown improvement on a number of indicators of family
functioning (Fraser, Pecora, and Haapla 1988). One additional outcome is the assurance that the placements that are made are necessary
for the protection of the child. Family-preservation services are available on a limited basis in a few jurisdictions. Given high workloads
and the primary need to carry out investigations, the absence of
family-preservation services may result in the unnecessary placement
of African American children.

The absence of resources families may need to resolve the problems
confronting them also is a barrier to family stability. In African
American families inadequate housing and substance abuse are placing children at risk (Malson and Williams 1989; National Black Child
Development Institute 1989; Williams 1990). Because of the lack of
an adequate supply of low-income housing and of substance-abuse-
treatment services that are family-focused and accessible, out-of-home
care is frequently utilized. Lacking prevention resources, families are
given available services even though these services may not be what
they need. Often the most available service is out-of-home placement.
Because of shortages of the resources necessary to meet the needs of
families, one can speculate that worker expectations for change in
troubled families is diminished, resulting in reduced efforts on their
behalf (Malson and Williams 1989; Stein and Rzepnicki 1984). The
absence or shortage of resources increases the unnecessary placement
of children and the length of time they remain in care once placement
has occurred.

After placement, the expectation is that families will receive services that promote reunification. Strategies for helping families include the development and implementation of service plans, regular
meetings with family members, and assurances of visits between parent and child when appropriate. Close (1983), in a study of the expe-

riences of families during the first three months after placement, found differential patterns of service delivery for white and African American families. The presence of a service plan varied by racial group and age of the child. For children age six or younger, service plans were found for 74 percent of the African American children as compared with 56 percent of the white children. For children over the age of six, the reverse was true, with 81 percent of the white children having service plans and 64 percent of the African American children having none. A comparison of the number of contacts between the agency and the principal childcaring person revealed that the parents of white children were seen an average of 3.7 times within the first three months after placement, while the parental figures of African American children were seen an average of 1.8 times. The frequency of contact with children also varied by race. White children were seen an average of 1.0 times and African American children were seen an average of 0.66 times. An examination of the mean number of all contacts with the client system showed that the mean was 7.2 for white families and 2.9 for African American families.

In addition to having less contact with staff, African American families were linked to significantly fewer services. White children received an average of 2.7 services, while the average among African American children was 2.3 (Close 1983). Although effective reunification services are based on a partnership between agencies and parent, the data suggest that the child welfare system gives African American families few of the supports necessary for reunification. The National Black Child Development Institute's (1989) study of black children in urban foster-care systems demonstrated that parents were being held accountable for change, but agencies were not being held accountable for the provision of the services agreed to in the case plan.

Adoption is considered the solution to the parenting needs of children without ties to families who can protect them. Efforts to make adoption services responsive to the needs of African American children have been well intentioned and appropriate. However, the effect of the singular focus on adoption as the solution has been to blame the community for failing to assume responsibility for its children, while diverting attention away from the systemic issues that lead to disproportionately high rates of separation among African American families. In reality, the disproportionate number of African American children needing permanence is a function of both the complex problems that African American families encounter and the operation of a child welfare system that does not serve these families appropriately or equitably.

African American children are more likely than other children to be reported as neglected, to enter out-of-home care, and to have a prolonged duration of care, and they are less likely to secure permanence through adoption. The child welfare system has a funnel effect on these children: It is easy to get in and to stay in, but very difficult to get out. Adoption is a permanency resource for waiting children. However, the disproportionate number of African American children needing adoption is a symptom of failed policy implementation: failure to prevent unnecessary placement; failure to reunite families in a timely fashion; and failure to stabilize the lives of children lacking the protection of families.

Toward a Responsive Approach to Permanence

Assuring permanence for African American children requires a threefold approach: developing additional permanency resources that build on the strengths of the African American cultural experiences so that the lives of waiting children can be stabilized; strengthening the delivery of child welfare services to enhance family integrity and minimize the risk of inappropriate placement and excessive intervention; and altering the impoverished policy context for the delivery of services.

EXPANDING PERMANENCY OPTIONS:
LEGAL GUARDIANSHIP

For those African American children who have not secured permanence through adoption, the need for stability continues. Adoption is a preferred method of assuring stability because it most replicates the relationship between the child and the biological family in that all legal rights and responsibilities are transferred to the adopting party. Even with the availability of subsidies and postadoption services, adoption has not met the needs of all legally free children. Moreover, adoption is not always the appropriate permanency mechanism for children who can find substitute parents within their familial networks. Adoption services have been available to 8 percent of the children leaving foster care. An additional 21 percent of these children have other or unknown plans (Tatara 1989); other options need to be available to them.

One of these options is guardianship. A legal guardian is a person who has control over a minor's person or estate or both, by decree of the court. Legal guardianship has received little attention since the early 1980s (Appleberg 1970; Costin and Rapp 1984, ch. 2; Glassbergh 1973; Leashore 1984; Weisman 1964; Williams 1980) and has been underutilized as a mechanism for protecting the rights of dependent children to permanency and family stability.

Several trends suggest the need for guardianship as a permanency option. Placement in foster family care with relatives has increased dramatically in some states (Kemper, Simonds and John 1990). Case law and service strategies document the lack of services to children placed with relatives and have led to the development of specialized services that assure appropriateness, stability, and protection. The escalating entry of young, medically fragile children into care in the absence of appropriate foster homes will require increased mobilization of such kinship networks. Furthermore, guardianship complements the social and cultural reality of many African American children.

Guardianship is a legal institution known under Roman law. Developed as a way to substitute for absent parents, guardianship is based on the law of infancy, which recognizes minors as individuals who cannot make decisions or manage their own affairs because of age and immaturity. Like adoption, guardianship is a legal and social mechanism that compensates for a child's natural limitations by giving an adult personal responsibility for major decisions affecting the child's life.

Unlike in adoption, the appointment of a legal guardian by the court transfers some, but not all, responsibilities and rights of the biological parent to the guardian. The guardian is not responsible for the support or education of the child except from the resources of the minor's estate or socially provided income. The guardian and ward are not entitled to inherit from each other. The guardian is under the supervision of the court. Consequently any change in a child's living arrangements must be approved by the court. Guardianship does not require termination of parental rights. Parents retain residual rights and responsibilities, including the right to reasonable visitation, to consent to adoption, and to determine a child's religious affiliation. The parent, when living, remains responsible for financial support of the child. Guardianship, however, may be established when parental ties have been terminated by relinquishment or judicial action. Under these circumstances, the parents can no longer claim these residual rights and responsibilities, and the guardian assumes the right to consent to adoption (Costin and Rapp 1984, ch. 2; Social Security Administration 1961).

Despite the existence of a statutory base authorizing the judicial appointment of a guardian for a minor child, guardianship is rarely used for dependent children. Children are without guardianship for two reasons: the absence of the biological or adoptive parents, or the inability or unwillingness of the parents to fulfill their child-rearing responsibilities. The following situations illustrate the conditions under which children are without guardianship because of the absence of parents.

1. Orphans living within their family networks who are without testamentary nomination of guardians:

The mother of three children died of a drug overdose. The father of the children had abandoned them and did not support them. The mother's oldest sister informally assumed full responsibility for the children, but the relationship had no legal protection.

2. Children whose ties to their parents have been surrendered or judicially terminated and who have not been placed for adoption:

Frank, age sixteen, was abandoned by his biological mother at age five. He was found wandering in an amusement park on New Year's Eve. He was placed in foster care, and parental ties were involuntarily terminated when a family applied to adopt him. However, the adoption was disrupted and Frank was returned to foster care, where he remains.

3. Children whose adoptions have been annulled and whose custody has been returned to a public agency:

John was adopted as a nine-year-old. He had serious emotional problems. The adoptive family sought treatment and worked with John. However, by the time he was fourteen he was running away and was a threat to the safety of his parents. Frustrated, the parents had the adoption revoked and refused further contact with John, who is currently in residential care.

Legally, these children belong to no one. At best they are in the custody of an agency or an interested party. Where the agency assumes guardianship, it is administrative and lacks the personal commitment of an individual involved with the child who understands the child's situation intimately and can act on that knowledge in the child's behalf.

The next examples describe children who have legally recognized guardians who are either unable or unwilling to fulfill their guardianship role:

1. Children who are placed informally (without agency assistance) by their parents in the homes of friends, relatives, and sometimes strangers, on a long-term basis.

Dwanna, the youngster discussed earlier in this chapter, is a classic example of the situation. Legally, the mother could demand return of the child at any time. Dwanna's relationship with the Joneses is unprotected.

2. Children who are in placement and whose parents, although they visit regularly, are unable to provide twenty-four-hour care.

Mark, age five, has been in placement since he was eighteen months old, after having suffered physical abuse at the hands of the mother's boyfriend. Mark suffered brain damage and has developmental difficulties that require a high level of specialized care and continuous medical supervision. Currently, the mother maintains her own household and is caring for Mark's five older siblings. The care of these children taxes the mother to the maximum. The mother visits Mark weekly and takes him home for the weekend regularly. Mark is receiving good care and has a meaningful relationship with his mother and his siblings. It is anticipated that Mark will remain in care because of his special needs and the demands on the mother. The foster mother has agreed to keep Mark but does not want to adopt because of his special needs and his mother's active involvement. Because his mother maintains a significant relationship with him, there is no legal ground for terminating parental rights.

For children such as these, what is the potential of legal guardianship? Guardianship has both legal and psychosocial significance for such children. The legal appointment of a guardian provides the guardian/ward relationship with sociolegal sanction. This sanction makes the relationship permanent in that a judicial review is required to terminate the relationship in situations other than the child's majority. The legal sanction creates an expectation of continuity that may be absent in less formal arrangements.

The legal sanction also clarifies who is the major authority in the child's life and the extent of the powers that the authority figure can exercise. Many children find themselves in relationships with caretakers who are neither their parents nor their legal guardians and who consequently have no legal authority over them. The legal term for this kind of relationship is *in loco parentis*. The caretakers may act "in the place of the parents," but they have no continuing legal obligation toward the child, and the assumption of parental rights and responsibilities is not genuine or binding but simply the result of the situaton in which child and parent substitute find themselves at that point in time (Black 1968). This relationship is tenuous and without the legal standing that could formalize it and increase its stability. *In loco parentis* changes with any change in the physical custody of the child (Smith 1955). Children also find themselves in situations in which authority over them is divided between the caretaker and the state through a delegated public agency. In this situation it is not clear which rights and responsibilities are exercised by the caretaker and which are exercised by the designated agency.

The psychosocial significance of guardianship stems from the problems associated with the tenuousness of child/caretaker relationships and the ambiguity of authority. When a child's relationship with caretakers is without legal sanction, it can be disrupted at any time. This places a child in a dilemma that has consequences for psychosocial development. On one hand, the child may make a significant attachment to parental figures whose relationship may be disrupted, leading to the short-term trauma of loss and possible long-term trauma reflected in an inability to attach and to relate to others (Rutter 1972). On the other hand, the child may not attach to the caretakers or attach in a superficial manner in order to protect herself or himself from an anticipated separation. In this case, the developmental progress of the child will be limited in that maturation is fostered by nurturing and stable relationship. Legally sanctioned, socially safeguarded guardianship protects the relationship from casual disruption and can facilitate appropriate attachment between child and parent substitute.

The further significance of guardianship is tied to the clarification of authority. When the child is unclear about who is responsible for decision making in matters that affect him or her or when the child perceives that a caretaker is sharing responsibility with another person or entity, the child may have difficulty accepting authority and discipline from the caretaker. The internalization of limit setting is important in channeling the normal impulsiveness of children into socially sanctioned behaviors. The ability to achieve internalization is reduced when parental authority is diffused.

Finally, decision making that flows from having authority in a child's life ought to be based on a clear understanding of the child's unique strengths, limitations, interests, needs, and aspirations. Decision making is facilitated when the appointed guardian is an individual who is known to the child and with whom the child has a personal relationship. Under these conditions, the guardian can be an advocate for the child by assuring that decisions reflect the child's best interest (Costin and Rapp 1984, ch. 2).

The goal of guardianship is the establishment of a substitute parent/child relationship that is continuous and has qualities that facilitate the healthy development of the child. To achieve this goal, two findings are essential. First is a determination that guardianship is the plan of choice for the child. The requirements for guardianship as a service plan are that the child is without a natural guardian and that adoption is an inappropriate or unavailable option. The second major determination to be made is that the individuals who are assuming guardianship are capable of meeting the needs of the child on a long-term basis (Costin and Rapp 1984, ch. 2). Guardians must be able effectively to parent a child who is not their own. Guardians should have the ability to help the child accept both biological and social identities (Kirk 1964). These tasks require warmth, flexibility, emotional maturity, and the ability to accept the biological parents. When these characteristics are present, guardianship will achieve its protective function. In the absence of these characteristics, the child may be subject to abuse, neglect, exploitation, and poor socialization experiences.

The judicial appointment of guardians carries the implication that society has sanctioned the relationship and is assured of the appropriateness of the long-term parental substitutes. The appointment of guardians therefore requires the establishment and implementation of legal and social safeguards. To protect the legal integrity of guardianship, the appointment of a guardian for a dependent child should take place in a court that has jurisdiction over child–custody matters and thus the expertise to make appropriate decisions (Williams 1980). The guardian should be held accountable to the court for the care of the child. Provisions should be made for time-limited judicial supervision, and clear criteria and time frames should be established for ending court oversight. Guardianship policy should articulate specific grounds for the termination of the guardian/ward relationship to minimize the likelihood of easy disruption.

To protect the social integrity and the quality of guardian/ward relationships, guardianships should not be granted without a psychosocial study to determine the need for guardianship and the suitability of the proposed guardian for the child in question. This assessment should be based on the child's lack of access to biological or adoptive parents and the existence of a significant bond between the child and the proposed guardian. Similarly, to determine the suitability of the guardian, the quality of the existing relationship, the prospective guardian's commitment to the child, and the potential for a sustained relationship during the child's minority years should all be examined.

Although guardianship is designed to be a self-sustaining relationship, two additional social supports may be necessary in selected situations to ensure the stability of the relationship. Access to social services and financial subsidies may be needed by the guardian and ward. Like children in adoption, children in legal guardianship may have periodic crises that can be resolved or minimized with access to social services. Such service should be available based on need to prevent the disruption of the guardianship (Williams 1980).

Many of the children who are appropriate candidates for guardianship are poor children whose financial support comes from AFDC. They have no resources, and often potential guardians, relatives, and foster parents have limited abilities to provide total support. In some jurisdictions, the appointment of a guardian makes a child ineligible for income maintenance and thus creates a disincentive for permanence. Needy children protected by guardianship should have access to socially provided income as do children in foster care and subsidized adoption.

Guardianship has the potential for stabilizing the lives of children whose families of origin cannot be preserved but who have significant relationships with relatives who are willing to assume responsibility for their care. Guardianship may also be a resource for those children without biological parents, adoptive parents, or relatives who find themselves in long-term out-of-home care. For both groups of children, guardianship can bring clarity and authority to the relationship between caretaker and child, and a sense of permanence. As outlined above, achieving the potential of permanence through guardianship will require a strengthening of legal and social safeguards in guardianship policy. With acceptance of guardianship as a permanency option along with family reunification and traditional, open, and subsidized adoption, the opportunity for long-term care that reflects the social reality of African American family life will be increased, and few children will suffer the damaging effects of unplanned long-term foster care.

INCREASING THE ABILITY TO PRESERVE AND REUNIFY FAMILIES

The disproportionate need for permanent substitute care among African American children is driven in part by the limited ability of the child welfare system to intervene early, prevent placement, and reunify families. The quest for permanence requires changes in policy frameworks and service approaches. New programmatic directions must be supported by a fiscal strategy that provides incentives for strengthening families and disincentives for inappropriate use of out-of-home care.

Given the vague definitions of neglect, the preponderance of African American children entering care because of neglect, and the wide variation in intake decision making among social workers, careful attention should be given to both the statutory and operational definitions of neglect. Findings of neglect can be guided by risk-assessment protocols that offer a consistent framework for assessing the severity of neglect and the cultural issues that may affect neglect determinations (Horejsi 1988). To prevent inappropriate intervention, neglect determinations should be based on findings of more than one kind of neglect or abuse in the family (Giovannoni and Becena 1979). Consideration should also be given to the impact of neglect on the child's psychosocial functioning (Wald 1976).

Schorr's (1988) study of effective programs for multiproblem families who experience child placement, school failure, and adolescent pregnancy identified the characteristics of the programs that improve outcomes for children. No matter what the presenting problems, programs that worked were holistic, family-centered, flexible, intensive, based in the community, and focused on client strengths and empowerment.

The flexibility of the successful programs is based in a holistic, noncategorical approach. Families receive services based on need. A mixture of concrete and psychological services are provided in response to the specific needs of families. Workers are not hindered by categorical barriers for accessing resources. Services are intensive, involving a number of hours of direct contact between worker and family each week, and are delivered within the community and often within the home. The focal unit of treatment is the family rather than the child or the identified patient. The family as a system, with its unique definition of self, dynamics, values, and ways of operating, is the target for change. When the family is looked at as a system, intervention is focused on recognizing and building up the strengths within the unit. Empowerment is a common theme in this approach as opposed to the emphasis on problems in the deficit approach.

Family-preservation services that are now used to prevent placement in the child welfare, juvenile-justice, and mental health systems embody this approach. Being intensive, time-limited, family-focused, and home-based, they achieve remarkable outcomes for some of the most troubled African American families.

> The parents of a family living in a large urban community were addicted to crack cocaine. Their three children were the subject of neglect petitions because of extended school truancy. The family was living in a "crack house," with no furniture or utilities. And the oldest child, age thirteen, was acting as parent to the two younger children.
>
> Family-preservation services were provided to the family; they included making intensive outreach efforts, securing new housing outside the crack area, assisting the family to move and obtain furniture, returning the children to school with tutorial assistance, and providing family-focused drug counseling followed by couples therapy.
>
> Nine months later, the children were in school and achieving; the parents were drug free; and the parents married after thirteen years of cohabitation when they discovered the potential of their relationship. The mother, in describing how family-preservation services helped her, indicated that the persistence of the worker in telling her she "did not have to live this way" changed her view of herself, her family, and ultimately the way they live.

The child welfare system must increase its capacity to provide family-preservation services to those families for whom placement is imminent and those families who have been written off as failures. As the case example suggests, these families have the capacity to change when they are provided with intensive services that convey hope, respond appropriately to need, and offer skilled interventions.

As with family preservation, the reunification of families in which placement has occurred also requires the development of intensive strategies that deal with their real needs. For African American families, the lack of adequate housing and of family-focused, accessible substance-abuse-treatment services is a major cause of extended out-of-home care and a failure to reunify families. Family-preservation strategies for those families with children in placement offer promise for reunification and improved family functioning and stability.

As preservation and reunification services expand, every effort must be made to assure that these new services are not delivered in ways that reinforce past inequities. Safeguards must be in place to assure African American families access to services in proportions that reflect their out-of-home placement rates. Services must be developed in a culturally competent manner that reflects Africentric definitions of family and the cultural integrity of the group.

Within the child welfare profession, there is concern that extended-kin placements may impede the reunification of families or the adoption of children. This fear, coupled with the paucity of services available for the increasing number of extended-kin placements, raises new issues. If one could offer assurances that African American families did not enter the child-protective-services system unnecessarily and that culturally appropriate family preservation and reunification services were available, the need for permanent substitute care would be significantly reduced.

Even with these efforts, there needs to be an examination of the role of kinship care in child welfare services. As the number of African American children finding placements within kinship networks increases, analyses are required to assure the appropriate utilization of these placements. Among the issues requiring analyses are the role of placements with relatives in relation to reunification or adoption efforts (or both); the service strategies needed to support effective placements within families; and the role of short-term and permanent guardianship in extended-kin placements.

RESHAPING AN IMPOVERISHED POLICY ENVIRONMENT

The strengths and weaknesses in the delivery of child welfare services reflect not only the design and organization of the services but also the policy context in which services are provided. Since the early 1980s, rates of child and family poverty have been escalating, homelessness has been increasing, and the availability of early intervention services in the areas of nutrition, health care, employment and training, mental health, and substance abuse has been significantly reduced. African American families have been heavily affected by this decline in resources. The lack of supports for families within the community contributes to the escalating reports of abuse and neglect. Simultaneously, the impact of child welfare services is limited by the inaccessibility to these same resources. Improvement in the outcomes for children receiving services is in part dependent on creating a policy context that is supportive of families and that assures certain minimum outcomes: access to adequate income through training and employment, pre- and postnatal health care, housing, early intervention services to improve family functioning, and mental health and drug-treatment services based on need.

The quest for permanence for African American children is more than a demand for additional adoption resources. Rather it requires improving the policy provisions available to vulnerable families; restructuring the delivery of services to abusive and neglectful families so that more families are preserved and reunified; and finally expanding permanency options to reflect the social and cultural realities of African American family life. This public-policy agenda requires a reappraisal of the social contract in the context of a continuing quest not just for permanency but for equity and social justice for African American families. How long can we continue to separate children from their parents because our helping systems are flawed?

Notes

1. Cases in this study are drawn from the direct practice and consultation experience of the author. The names have been changed to protect the identity of the children and families described.

2. In studies of the impact of race on clinical judgments in mental health, racial status affected the number of pathological diagnoses. In this author's work in training child-protective-services managers, the introduction of race as a variable in situations of child maltreatment led to different assessments of both the seriousness of the risk and the level of intervention required. In some jurisdictions there is evidence that substantiation rates are considerably higher for children of color (State of Maryland 1989).

References

Appleberg, E. 1970. "The Significance of Personal Guardianships for Children in Casework." *Child Welfare* 49:6–14.
Billingsley, A. 1968. *Black Families in White America*. Englewood Cliffs, N.J.: Prentice-Hall.

Billingsley, A., and J. M. Giovannoni. 1972. *Children of the Storm: Black Children and American Child Welfare.* New York: Harcourt Brace Jovanovich.

Black, H. C. 1968. *Black's Law Dictionary.* 4th ed. St. Paul: West.

Blassingame, J. W. 1979. *The Slave Community: Plantation Life in the Antebellum South.* New York: Oxford University Press.

Close, M. M. 1983. "Child Welfare and People of Color: Denial of Equal Access." *Social Work Research and Abstracts* 19(4):13–20.

Costin, L. B., and C. A. Rapp. 1984. *Child Welfare; Policies and Practice.* 3d ed. New York: McGraw-Hill.

Day, D. 1979. *Adoption of Black Children.* Lexington, Mass.; Lexington Books.

Fraser, M., P. Pecora, and D. Haapla. 1988. *Families in Crisis: Findings from Family Based Intensive Treatment Project.* Salt Lake City: Social Research Institute; University of Utah School of Social Work, and Federal Way, Washington: Behavioral Sciences Institute.

Gershenson, C. 1984. *Community Response to Children Freed for Adoption.* Child Welfare Research Notes 3. Washington, D.C.: U.S. Department of Health and Human Services.

Giovannoni, J. M., and R. M. Becerra. 1979. *Defining Child Abuse.* New York: Free Press.

Glassberg, E. 1973. *Guardian Law and the Poor Child.* Social Work Process, Series 18, Monograph 1. Philadelphia: University of Pennsylvania.

Gutman, H. G. 1976. *The Black Family in Slavery and Freedom, 1750–1925.* New York: Random House, Vintage Books.

Hill, R. B. 1972. *The Strengths of Black Families.* New York: Emerson Hall.

———. 1977. *Informal Adoption among Black Families.* Washington, D.C.: National Urban League.

Horejsi, C. R. 1988. "Child Welfare and Native American Families." Unpublished report, Department of Social Work, University of Montana, Missoula.

Kemper, L., K. Simonds, and G. John. 1990. "Ten Reasons to Invest in Children in California." Publication of the County Welfare Directors Association of California, Chief Probation Officers Association of California, and California Mental Health Directors, Sacramento, Spring.

Kinney, J., D. Haapla, C. Booth, and S. Leavitt. 1988. *The Homebuilders' Model in Improving Practice Technology for Work with High Risk Families: Lessons from Homebuilders' Social Work Education Project.* Monograph 6. Edited by J. Whittaker. University of Washington School for Social Work. Seattle: Center for Social Welfare Research.

Kirk, H. D. 1964. *Shared Fate.* New York: Free Press.

Leashore, B. R. 1984. "Demystifying Legal Guardianship: An Unexplored Option for Dependent Children." *Journal of Family Law* 23(3):391–400.

Malson, M. R., and C. W. Williams. 1989. "Black Children in Placement in North Carolina." Report to the North Carolina Task Force on Permanent Families for Children.

Martin, E. P., and J. M. Martin. 1978. *The Black Extended Family*. Chicago: University of Chicago Press.

National Association of Public Child Welfare Administrators. 1988. *Guidelines for a Model System of Child Protective Services for Abused and Neglected Children and Their Families*. Washington, D.C.: American Public Welfare Association.

National Black Child Development Institute. 1987. *Guidelines for Adoption Services to Black Families and Children*. Washington, D.C.

———. 1989. *Who Will Care When Parents Can't?* Washington, D.C.

Nobles, W. W. 1982. "A Formulative and Empirical Study of Black Families." Unpublished research grant report, Westside Community Center, Oakland, Calif.

Ross, E. 1978. *Black Heritage in Social Welfare*. Metuchen, N.J.: Scarecrow Press.

Rutter, M. 1972. *Maternal Deprivation Reassessed*. Baltimore: Penguin.

Schorr, L. 1988. *Within Our Reach: Breaking the Cycle of Disadvantage*. New York: Doubleday, Anchor Books.

Smith, A. D. 1955. *The Right to Life*. Chapel Hill: University of North Carolina Press.

Social Security Administration. 1961. *Legislative Guides for the Termination of Parental Rights and Responsibilities and the Adoption of Children*. Children's Bureau Publication 194. Washington, D.C.: U.S. Department of Health, Education and Welfare.

Spaulding for Children, National Resource Center on Special Needs Adoption. 1990. "Adoption Data." Chelsea, Michigan. Mimeograph report.

Stack, C. B. 1974. *All Our Kin: Strategies for Survival in a Black Community*. New York: Harper and Row.

———. 1985. "Professional Wisdom, Cultural Realities: Cross Cultural Perspective on Child Welfare." In *Foster Care: Current Issues, Policies and Practices*, edited by M. J. Cos and R. D. Cox, 134–146. Norwood, N.J.: Ablex.

State of Maryland, Division of Child Protective Services. 1989. "Management Information Report."

Stein, T. J., and T. L. Rzepnicki. 1984. *Decisionmaking in Child Welfare Services: Intake and Planning*. Boston: Kluwer-Nijhoff.

Tatara, T. 1989. *Children in Substitute Care, FY87*. Washington, D.C.: Voluntary Cooperative Information System, American Public Welfare Association.

Wald, M. S. 1976. "State Intervention on Behalf of Neglected Children: A Search for Realistic Standards." In *Pursuing Justice for the Child*, edited by M. K. Rosenheim, 246–278. Chicago: University of Chicago Press.

Weisman, I. 1964. "Guardianship: Every Child's Right." *Annals* 355: 134–139.

Williams, C. W. 1980. "Legal Guardianship: A Minimally Used Resource for

California's Dependent Children: 1848–1980." D.S.W. diss., University of Southern California.

———. 1990. "Child Welfare and Homelessness: Issues in Philosophy, Policy and Practice." In *Homeless Children and Youth: A New American Dilemma,* edited by J. Kryder-Coe, L. Salamon, and J. Molnar, 285–291. New Brunswick, N.J.: Transaction Books.

11

SANDRA S. CHIPUNGU

A Value-Based Policy Framework

> How willingly in all these years and now, have thousands of mothers and
> fathers toiled and sweat and watched from dawn til midnight over these
> children here, only to be rewarded—not indeed by crime, but by persistent
> carelessness almost worse than crime.
>> —W.E.B. DU BOIS,
>> *Prayers for Dark People*

Current child welfare policies reflect the dominant values of society as
they relate to families and children in general and to the historical
oppression of African Americans in particular. An examination of the
values underlying child welfare policies can help in determining the
impact of these policies on significant numbers of African American
children. To improve the system of providing welfare services to African American children, a well-defined value base for policies is
needed. Here, traditional African American values, which fostered the
survival of African Americans during slavery and through past and
present discrimination, prejudice, and exploitation, can be useful.

This chapter examines the historical roots of the current child welfare system in the United States and its effect on African American
children. The impact of selected dominant values on child welfare services and African American children is described, and alternative African values are offered. Criteria for evaluating existing child welfare
policies are proposed. Finally, alternative policies are recommended to
improve child welfare services for African American children and ultimately for all American children.

Historical Roots of Child Welfare

Historically, African Americans were excluded from child welfare services, served in separate institutions, or offered forms of care developed for or by African Americans. Billingsley and Giovannoni (1972:22–23) argue that child welfare services in the United States were influenced by four crucial factors: conceptualizations of poverty; the secretarianism of autonomous religious groups; the domination of European American settlers, which led to ethnocentric child welfare policies; and slavery, which justified the exclusion of African Americans from child welfare services. These factors still influence the organization and delivery of child welfare services today.

Poverty has been and continues to be attributed to individual laziness and depravity (Day 1989; Johnson and Schwartz 1988). This view of individual flaws or personal defects persists, despite objective evidence to the contrary, precisely because it is based on values and perceptions. A strong belief is that no one in the United States needs to be poor because it is the land of opportunity. All one needs to do is work hard and live a decent life, and success will follow. Lack of success is due to personal flaws or frailties. Johnson and Schwartz (1988:73) argue that "many wrongly believe that poor people have low income not because of membership in an economic class, or from other circumstance beyond their control but because they are not useful to society, are less hard working, frugal, and responsible. Poverty then becomes a failure to adhere to the values about hard work and self-sufficiency confirming the flawed character argument of poverty."

The poverty of children is attributed to the weaknesses of their parents. Because poor families are viewed as defective, their children are also viewed as potentially weak and needing to be rescued from their parents so that they will not learn the bad habits that led to poverty. This view of poverty is best reflected in the forms of care provided to children during the early 1800s, such as almshouses and indenture (Day 1989; Jansson 1988; Johnson and Schwartz 1988).

Almshouses, an institutional form of care, were used to shelter those who could not care for themselves—the dependent. Children stayed in almshouses with their parents. Parents and children were required to work and to "follow a strict schedule, that was carefully planned and that included spartan meals, long hours, lectures on morality and religious observation" (Jansson 1988:54). The intent was to regenerate the moral fabric of families and children. "Social provisions for dependent children during the colonial period or the first two centuries of American history can be characterized as meager arrangements made on a reluctant, begrudging basis to guarantee a minimal level of subsistence. The arrangements were designed to insure that children were taught the values of industriousness and hard work and received a strict religious upbringing" (McGowan and Meezan 1983:48). Some free African American children were found in these almshouses after the Civil War (Billingsley and Giovannoni 1972).

Indenture, however, was the primary form of caring for poor children. "Indenture was a plan for apprenticing children to households where they would be cared for and taught a trade, in return for which they owed loyalty, obedience, and labor until the costs of their rearing had been worked off" (McGowan and Meezan 1983:48). Some free African American children as well as English children were in the indenture system. However, there is evidence that some colonial communities made the indenture of African American paupers harsher than that of other paupers (Billingsley and Giovannoni 1972). Johnson and Schwartz (1988) argue that the practice of apprenticeship reflected the belief that all individuals should be a part of a family. On a practical level, it provided a useful way to control and discipline children, reduce unemployment, provide skilled workers to meet the needs of the growing colonies, and relieve public officials from the responsibility of directly caring for needy children.

Orphanages were later established to house both dependent children whose parents were deceased and poor children whose families could not provide for them. Orphanages were viewed as an alternative to almshouses. Orphanages also complemented the indenture system because many orphans graduated from the orphanages into an indentured position (Billingsley and Giovannoni 1972). African American children were excluded from the orphanages established before the Civil War as a matter of policy. Separate orphanages were established by certain religious groups or African Americans themselves for African American children.

The free foster home was the next stage of innovation in child welfare services in this country. "The development of the free foster home was stimulated by the abolition of slavery. When, in fact, children of African descent were no longer being bought and sold, discomfort arose in the child welfare movement with the fact that children of European descent were still being sent into a state of serfdom through indenture" (Billingsley and Giovannoni 1972:34). The free foster home began as a form of indenture because parents were not paid for the care provided and children had to work for their upkeep. Free foster-home care was the prevailing form of care for poor children until the middle of the twentieth century. It was gradually replaced during the first half of the twentieth century by the foster boarding home, an arrangement in which the foster parents were paid for caring for children. Placement in foster boarding homes eventually extended to African American children. Interestingly, the modern foster-care system has been more open to African American children than the institutional system of care, despite its exclusionary beginnings.

The sectarian roots of many of the private voluntary child welfare agencies that currently offer services can be traced to the colonial period (Jansson 1988; Johnson and Schwartz 1988). The colonial desire for religious autonomy and the protection of religious beliefs resulted in the establishment of religiously affiliated, private agencies. The first orphanages were established by the Society of Friends, a religious group involved in the Abolitionist Movement. The Philadelphia Association for the Care of Colored Children was established in 1822 (Billingsley and Giovannoni 1972). Similar organizations were also founded in other northern cities.

Because the early settlers were predominantly English, the organization and provision of child welfare services reflected Anglo-Saxon cultural values, beliefs, and standards. Members of other ethnic and racial groups were expected to conform to these ethnocentric ideals.

The existence of slavery meant that child welfare services could develop with little concern for African American children; these children were simply not recognized by the larger society. As peculiar as it seems, the institution of slavery performed many social welfare functions. Slave masters had to provide food, clothing, health care, and services to the elderly and children to ensure the continued benefits of slave labor.

Because they were systematically denied access to child welfare services, African Americans established their own forms of care both prior to and following the Civil War. Prior to the Civil War, slave children were informally cared for or adopted by extended kin or other African Americans on the plantation. Those who were not slaves lived in almshouses. After the Civil War, the Freedmen's Bureau and African American churches, schools, women's clubs, a few religious groups, and individual philanthropy aided dependent children in orphanages and provided financial assistance, home care, and work opportunities (Morisey 1990).

Dominant Values

Dominant American values influenced the development and provision of child welfare services for African American children in the United States. Values are important in defining social problems, proposing solutions, and evaluating the outcomes of programs developed to address those problems. Thus, values help shape existing programs as well as proposed programs. Values influence how we define the needs of dependent children as well as the types of services we provide to them. An understanding of the underlying values is crucial in assessing the impact of the child welfare system on African American children.

Several writers emphasize the importance of values in shaping social policy in the United States (Gil 1976; Gilbert and Specht 1986; Kahn 1976; Prigmore and Atherton 1979). Values shape policy at various stages of its development and may not necessarily be consistent, with the result that value conflicts are often manifested in our policies. For example, the value placed on family privacy conflicts with society's value of protecting children from harm.

Beliefs, values, and ideologies of societies tend to be shaped and guarded by cultural and political elites recruited mainly from among the powerful and privileged (Dinitto and Dye 1987; Gil 1976). Some (Dinitto and Dye 1987, ch. 1; Kahn 1976; Prigmore and Atherton 1979) argue that large social changes are based not only on values but also on political considerations.

Although there are many dominant values in American society, no attempt is made here to examine all of them. Instead the most relevant values for understanding how African American children are dealt with in the welfare system are considered. The key dominant values here are individualism, the work ethic, the privacy of the family, the view of children as the property and responsibility of parents, and the view that society also has responsibilities toward children.

INDIVIDUALISM

The basis for individualism is the idea that any American can achieve success through individual effort and motivation. Everyone is expected to survive and make it on his or her own through hard work and perseverance (Day 1989). Williams (1967) argues that Americans are taught from birth that the individual personality is of high intrinsic worth. The individual is viewed as an independent unit and as responsible for the decisions he or she makes. Prigmore and Atherton (1979:25) argue that "American culture values the accumulation of money in the operations of one's business or profession. . . . Most Americans have a strong tendency to hold money and position as symbols of success." In other words, success derives from one's own efforts.

Because of the emphasis on individualism, parents are blamed if they fail to live up to societal expectations of parenthood. Parents are expected to meet the instrumental and expressive needs of family members. Instrumental needs include concrete items such as food, clothing, and shelter. Expressive needs are social and emotional—the need for love and care, and the need to be socialized. If parents fail to provide adequately for their children—that is, if they provide care below an acceptable community standard—they are viewed as dysfunctional, and the children may be removed from their care. For example, if parents are unable to provide adequate shelter, welfare agencies may remove a child from the care of the parents, rather than providing the parents with assistance in finding housing. The underlying assumption is that it is the parents' fault that they do not have adequate housing and they need to be punished. Even if no fault is assigned, public funds are available to provide care for the child in a foster home but not to assist the parents in caring for the child in their existing home or to assist them in finding improved housing.

Lack of housing has been identified as one of the primary reasons African American children are placed in care, as well as one of the primary reasons foster children cannot be reunited with their natural parents. Findings from a study of 1,003 African American children in foster care indicate (National Black Child Development Institute 1989:2):

> While the majority of the study population entered foster care because of abuse or neglect, many of these placements were also attributable to

environmental stresses caused by chronic poverty. In 25 percent of the cases, poverty itself was a significant factor in placement. Inadequate housing occurred in 30 percent of cases as a significant factor in placement. Homelessness or living in shelters was occurring among 11 percent of the families when their children were removed. This study revealed that even if families at risk did not suffer from other problems, such as substance abuse or mental illness, many of these children would still enter care due to lack of affordable housing for low-income families.

Although at the 1909 White House Conference on Children delegates recognized that a child's basic needs usually can be met by the natural family and argued that the child welfare system should no longer remove children from their homes solely on the basis of inadequate family income, this practice still persists. Documentation for this allegation is found in studies that indicate that the largest proportion of children placed in foster care have been found to be neglected, not abused.

WORK ETHIC

The work ethic focuses on individual worth as it relates to work. Day (1989:7) argues:

> The Protestant work ethic is the moral basis for the American capitalistic economic system—the search for profit through business enterprises mostly uncontrolled by the government. A social rather than an economic creed, Americans, regardless of religion, accept the Protestant work ethic as part of American life. Work for economic gain is the way to success, a sign of personal morality, and a moral obligation. Conversely, poverty and public dependency demonstrate immorality.

The concept of the worthy and unworthy poor was based on the Protestant work ethic. Those who were not expected to work—the aged, those with disabilities, women, and children—were considered among the worthy poor. Many who espoused indentured service thought they were saving children from learning habits that would lead to pauperism. Children were indentured in order to learn how to work and develop into productive citizens.

However, the initial philosophy of the Freedmen's Bureau, which was established to assist freed slaves, incorporated the work ethic in a different manner. The provision of land, work, and direct relief to the freed slaves was intended to prevent and eliminate poverty by strengthening and keeping families together. Billingsley and Giovannoni (1972:43) note that the efforts of the Freedmen's Bureau, though short-lived, were revolutionary developments in child welfare. Today, in most public programs, such as work-incentive programs, emphasis is still placed on preventing dependence and promoting self-sufficiency through work. Yet the experiences of African American children who have been removed from their families because their parents are poor and unable to provide adequate shelter, nutrition, and medical care suggest that society is more willing to pay for a substitute parent than it is to offer work and direct relief to the biological parents.

SANCTITY OF THE FAMILY

Belief in the sanctity of the family is deeply embedded in the provision of child welfare services to African American children. Miller (1989) argues that there are conflicting views about the role of women and children and the work world in this society. Those who advocate "separate spheres" believe there should be no public interference with the family or the "sacred" world of home. And the family has been traditionally viewed in the United States as an inappropriate target for government planning and intervention except for the most compelling reasons (Costin and Rapp 1984). If a family fails to provide for the safety and well-being of its children, then the state can and does intervene. But "as long as . . . care takes place in the child's own home and as long as it does not fall below a minimal standard demanded by a given community, in most instances a wide range in quality and kind of care is tolerated, . . . and the family is able to retain its privacy and independence" (Costin and Rapp 1984:8). Society is willing to accept some differences in the care of children because parents determine living patterns within culturally determined boundaries.

CHILDREN AS PARENTS' PROPERTY

In the United States the primary right to care for children rests with parents as does the responsibility to care for them. The rights of parents include the right to guardianship and the right to withhold consent to the child's adoption. The responsibilities of parenthood include financial support and the provision of physical care, emotional care, and guidance or supervision. Thus, parents are responsible for the overall well-being of their children and have certain rights relative to them. However, "the right of children to be dealt with as individuals continues to be given insufficient attention under the law, which is weighted in favor of the rights of adults and makes parents the owners of children rather than trustees who have a duty to care for and protect all children, not just their own" (Costin and Rapp 1984:9).

CHILDREN AS THE RESPONSIBILITY OF SOCIETY

Society also has responsibilities regarding children and carries them out through three avenues: regulations that govern the behavior of parents, such as compulsory school-attendance laws; legal statutes that enable the state to intervene in the relationship between parent and child on behalf of children, as in the case of the removal of a child to a foster home; and "authority to legislate for the development of various child welfare services" (Costin and Rapp 1984:9–10), as in the establishment of federal and state laws that mandate certain services for children. The removal of children from their homes is often based on arguments that it is in the best interests of the child or for the child's protection. Laws governing child abuse, foster care, and adoption were all developed to serve the needs of abused, neglected, and dependent children.

Criteria for Child Welfare

Three criteria can be used to examine the impact of child welfare policies on African American children. These criteria are equity, equality, and adequacy.

Equity denotes a conventional sense of fair treatment. It "prescribes that people receive what they deserve based upon their contributions to society, modified only by considerations for those whose inability to contribute is clearly not of their own making" (Gilbert and Specht 1986:41). Flynn defines equity as the extent to which "situations in similar circumstances are dealt with similarly" (1985:54). Thus a program is inequitable when two persons identical in other respects receive different services or resources from it (Jansson 1984). If the child welfare system is equitable, then African American children should receive the same combination of services, exit at similar rates, and achieve permanency at the same rate as white children.

To apply this criterion to African American children, we need to assess whether they are treated similarly to other children in the welfare system. Research findings indicate ethnic differences in decisions regarding foster-care placements. Findings obtained from 4,439 public welfare and social service agencies revealed that children of color tend to stay in care longer than white children and tend to be placed in different types of facilities and in different locations (Jenkins et al. 1983).

Hogan and Sui (1988) argue that the current treatment of children of color in the U.S. welfare system continues to reflect racial bias. In a study tracing the history of the treatment of children of color in the welfare system, they found that African American children were more likely to be in foster homes than white children, had less likelihood of adoptive placement, and tended to be overrepresented in child-abuse-and-neglect reporting.

Jenkins and Diamond (1985), in an analysis of data drawn from the 1980 Census, as well as survey data collected in 1980 by the Office of Civil Rights, found support for the following hypotheses: (1) There is a greater propensity for African American children to be placed in foster care when they constitute a smaller proportion of the population and less propensity when they represent a larger proportion. (2) The differential between African Americans and whites in relation to time spent in care is minimal in the poorest counties and greatest in those counties with the lowest number of poor residents.

Equality is a criterion somewhat open to interpretation. Gilbert and Specht (1986:40) distinguish between numerical equality and proportional equality: "Numerical equality implies the same treatment of everyone—to all an equal share. Proportional equality implies the same treatment of similar persons—to each according to their merit or virtue. [Proportional equality is often discussed as equity.] Social welfare policy is influenced by the value of equality with regard to the outcome of benefit allocations." The value of equality prescribes that the allocation of benefits "equalize the distribution of resources and opportunities available in society" (Gilbert and Specht 1986:40). Accordingly, African American children should be treated equally once they enter the welfare system and they should not be numerically overrepresented within this system. Specifically, regarding our concern here, do African American children in the welfare system benefit equally from the services and other resources provided through foster care, adoption, and supportive activities? To apply the criterion of equality to the care of children of color, it is clear African American children are more likely to be placed in foster care than children of other racial or ethnic groups. Mech (1983) found that compared with a national placement rate of 4 per 1,000 for whites, African American children were placed outside the home at a rate of 9.5 per 1,000, followed by Native American children with a rate of 8.8 per 1,000. African American children constitute only 14 percent of the population under the age of nineteen, but they account for 33 percent of all the children in out-of-home placements. Is this equality?

Adequacy is defined as the degree to which benefits provided meet some predetermined level. African American children are less likely than white children to receive the full range of services in child welfare. Close (1983) found, using a national survey of 1,530 African American, Hispanic, and white children, that service planning was more limited for families of color, that these families received fewer comprehensive services and had less contact with child welfare agencies, and that the agencies responded more slowly to them. Older African American children and younger Hispanic children were particularly at risk of being neglected by the system. Data suggest that the diagnostic and prognostic assessments of families of color are often biased, and that vigilant monitoring of services to this population is needed.

It also appears that African American children do not receive necessary services while in foster care. One study found that African American children in foster care generally received no periodic health or educational assessments but were classified as healthy 75 percent of the time. Eighty percent of the children studied had no record of a psychological or developmental assessment. Older children also face significant disruptions in their education as they move from placement to placement (National Black Child Development Institute 1989:2).

Funding is another factor one needs to consider in examining the adequacy of child welfare policies. The child welfare reform of 1980 offered a new philosophy and framework for child welfare services. Allen and Knitzer (1983:120–121) argue that the Adoption Assistance and Child Welfare Act of 1980 (P.L. 96-272) "uses a carrot-and-stick approach to redirect funds away from inappropriate, often costly, out-of-home care and toward alternatives to placement. It encourages states to implement important protections for children including case plans, periodic reviews, and information systems." The legislation redirects federal fiscal incentives toward the development of preventive and reunification services and adoption subsidies. It has been effective in reducing the numbers of children in institutions, apparently decreasing the numbers of children entering foster care, shortening the period of time children are in placement, and increasing the numbers of children who are returned to their families or adopted (Select Committee on Children, Youth and Families 1989). The law had a positive impact on child welfare philosophy even though it created an enormous amount of paperwork and may have denigrated foster care of all types (Kamerman and Kahn 1990:10–11).

Kamerman and Kahn (1990) argue that "the federal government did not, however, provide the resources on which all else was premised." As a result the 1980 child welfare law has had some undesirable and unanticipated consequences. Among the undesirable consequences has been a shortage and lack of preventive funds to assist troubled families and children who are not necessarily in crisis or at high risk of immediate placement, a decline in the autonomy and flexibility of professional staff to intervene as needed, and a shortage in the supply of foster-care resources (Kamerman and Kahn 1990).

Alternative Policies Based on African American Values

When one examines the impact of child welfare policies and services on African American children by utilizing the criteria of equality, equity, and adequacy, it is apparent that changes are needed. As previously discussed, P.L. 96-272 provided incentives for states to develop mechanisms for permanency planning for children. The law provides financial incentives for states to offer preventive, reunification, and adoption services. Though a nationwide evaluation of the implementation of P.L. 96-272 has not yet been published, certain dominant trends can be observed. Among these are the following: (1) Although fewer children are in care, those who are entering the system need more extensive services. (2) Drug and alcohol addiction, and acquired immune deficiency syndrome are increasingly causes for the number of children entering foster care. (3) African American children enter care at a disproportionately high rate and still remain in care longer than white children. (4) African American children are still considered harder to place for adoption than other children.

Improvements in the implementation of the existing child welfare policies might be made by incorporating African American values. At least three of these values could serve this purpose: the extended family, collective identity, and spirituality.

First, child welfare policies for African Americans need to reflect an increasing reliance on the extended-family system or consanguineal family structure. The current public and private child welfare system cannot replace the family system. Increased efforts need to be made to include maternal and paternal grandparents, aunts, uncles, cousins, and fictive or adopted kin to maintain children in homes. Use of the extended family can allow children to remain with people who know them and their family background, traditions, and culture.

Many public child welfare agencies are utilizing this alternative increasingly. Findings from one study indicate that "agencies considered relatives for placement assistance in nearly 75 percent of total cases and of the relatives considered, nearly 60 percent offered some type of assistance. The most commonly provided resource from relatives was [a] home for the child, while the relative assisting in the majority of the cases was the grandparent" (National Black Child Development Institute 1989:6). When relatives refused to assist, it was often because of lack of financial resources or housing or both. Child welfare services need to continue this trend and consider ways to support concerned relatives who are willing to assist but are unable to do so because of a lack of resources. These relatives may be able to help if provided with financial assistance, respite care, day care, or homemaker services. Placing African American children with relatives may cause far less damage to children than placing them with strangers. Too often, the current system fails to look at natural support networks when removal of the child from the home is deemed necessary. Policies need to be clearly written to require placements with relatives as a first priority.

Second, child welfare services can be improved by focusing on the communalism or collective identity of African Americans. In order to survive racism African Americans have developed a communal perspective: What happens to one of us could potentially affect all of us. Existing groups, organizations, and institutions within African American communities can be tapped to address the needs of children and their families. Sororities, fraternities, community organizations, women's organizations, and churches are available sources of assistance and need to be engaged, recruited, and informed in vigorous and creative ways. The VCIN project described in Chapter 9 is an excellent example of this effort.

Child welfare agencies need to consider expanding existing boundaries and domains in order to make use of existing African American groups and organizations. These groups will respond to requests for help and in many cases will provide leadership in developing networks or programs to assist children. However, they must be made aware of the seriousness of the issue and appealed to for help. Public-awareness efforts must appeal to the sense of community and public service of African Americans. If leaders, groups, and organizations are asked for their input with respect they will respond positively.

Local African American groups and organizations should be encouraged to apply for state funds to develop their own programs to assist parents and children. They have knowledge of and respect for the culture and traditions. Thus, these groups can develop creative approaches to solving these problems. They can also hold their own fund-raising drives to provide supportive services for parents and children.

Training funds need to be provided to increase the pool of African American workers in the social work profession also. Many African Americans would continue their undergraduate and graduate education and commit to working in the public sector if scholarships were made available to them.

Third, spirituality, or religion, remains a major force and source of strength among African Americans. Historically and now, the church is one of the strongest institutions within African American communities. Child welfare agencies must find creative ways to cooperate with these churches to meet the needs of African American children. Religious beliefs are among the major reasons some African Americans become foster parents.

Many churches are organizing various types of supportive services for families already (clothing drives, food drives, soup kitchens, big brothers and big sisters, single-parent support groups, visiting the sick and elderly). Local ministers of various denominations could provide leadership in developing new services to help African American children as well as in recruiting families to help with the existing services in child welfare. If you ask you shall receive. Local church leaders have organized community groups around other pressing issues. They will respond to the plight of scorned children in child welfare if asked.

African American children in the child welfare system are indeed scorned children when one applies the criteria of equity, equality, and adequacy to existing policies and outcomes. Incorporating dominant

African American values of family extendedness, communalism, and spirituality is a way to improve existing policies and services to African American children.

References

Allen, M., and J. Knitzer. 1983. "Child Welfare: Examining the Policy Framework." In *Child Welfare: Current Dilemmas, Future Directions,* edited by B. G. McGowan and W. Meezan, 93–141. Itasca, Ill.: Peacock.

Billingsley, A., and J. M. Giovannoni. 1972. *Children of the Storm: Black Children and American Child Welfare.* New York: Harcourt Brace Jovanovich.

Close, M. M. 1983. "Child Welfare and People of Color: Denial of Equal Access." *Social Work Research and Abstracts* 19(4):13–20.

Costin, L. B., and C. A. Rapp. 1984. *Child Welfare: Policies and Practice.* 3d ed. New York: McGraw-Hill.

Day, P. 1989. *A New History of Social Welfare.* Englewood Cliffs, N.J.: Prentice-Hall.

Dinitto, D., and T. Dye. 1987. *Social Welfare: Politics and Public Policy.* 2d ed., Englewood Cliffs, N.J.: Prentice-Hall.

Flynn, J. P. 1985. *Social Agency Policy: Analysis and Presentation for Community Practice.* Chicago: Nelson-Hall.

Gil, D. G. 1976. *Unravelling Social Policy.* 3d ed. Cambridge, Mass.: Schenckman.

Gilbert, N., and H. Specht. 1986. *Dimensions of Social Welfare Policy.* 2d ed. Englewood Cliffs, N.J.: Prentice-Hall.

Hogan, P. T., and S. F. Sui. 1988. "Minority Children and the Child Welfare System: An Historical Perspective." *Social Work* 33(6):493–498.

Jansson, B. S. 1984. *Theory and Practice of Social Welfare Policy: Analysis, Processes, and Current Issues.* Belmont, Calif.: Wadsworth.

————. 1988. *The Reluctant Welfare State: A History of American Social Welfare.* Belmont, Calif.: Wadsworth.

Jenkins, S., and B. E. Diamond. 1985. "Ethnicity and Foster Care: Census Data as Predictors of Placement Variables." *American Journal of Orthopsychiatry* 55 (2): 267–276.

Jenkins, S., B. E. Diamond, M. Flanzraich, W. W. Gibson, J. Hendricks, and N. Marshood. 1983. "Ethnic Differentials in Foster Care Placements." *Social Work Research Abstracts* 19 (4):41–45.

Johnson, L. C., and C. L. Schwartz. 1988. *Social Welfare: A Response to Human Need.* Boston: Allyn & Bacon.

Kahn, A. J. 1976. *Theory and Practice of Social Planning.* New York: Russell Sage Foundation.

Kamerman, S. B., and A. J. Kahn. 1990. "The Problems Facing Social Services for Children, Youth, and Families in the United States." *Children and Youth Services Review* 1/2:7–20.

McGowan, B. G., and W. Meezan, eds. 1983. *Child Welfare: Current Dilemmas, Future Directions*. Itasca, Ill.: Peacock.

Mech, E. V. 1983. "Out of Home Placement Rates." *Social Service Review* 57(4):659–667.

Miller, G., ed. 1989. *Giving Children a Chance: The Case for More Effective National Policies*. Washington, D.C.: Center for National Policy Press.

Morisey, P. G. 1990. "Black Children in Foster Care." In *Social Work Practice with Black Families: A Culturally Specific Perspective*, edited by S.M.L. Logan, E. M. Freeman, and R. McRoy. 133–147. New York: Longman.

National Black Child Development Institute. 1989. *Who Will Care When Parents Can't?* Washington, D.C.

Prigmore, C. S., and C. R. Atherton. 1979. *Social Welfare Policy: Analysis and Formulation*. Lexington, Mass.: Heath.

Select Committee on Children, Youth and Families. 1989. *U.S. Children and Their Families: Current Conditions and Recent Trends, 1989*. Washington, D.C.: U.S. House of Representatives.

Williams, R. M., Jr. 1967. *American Society: A Sociological Interpretation*. New York: Knopf.

JOYCE E. EVERETT,
SANDRA S. CHIPUNGU,
AND BOGART R. LEASHORE

Conclusion: Within Our Power

This book emerged from a series of conversations about why children of color enter the child welfare system at disproportionate rates. We wondered why so little concern is expressed about their needs in national and state policies, agency practices, and professional publications. The situations families of children of color, especially African American children, endure are hidden—to be revealed when an exceptionally devastating problem such as drug addiction or acquired immune deficiency syndrome threatens the sanctity of family life.

The children we speak about are scorned children who must depend on themselves and hope that someone will care enough to make sure their life chances are equal to those of any child in the United States. They dream that someone will heed their call and ease their pain. These children cannot speak for themselves and often their families are not heard. They are special children, not hard-to-place or high-risk children. Their race and social class elicit a societal response for what Gould in Chapter 3 calls "limiting damage," but today limiting damage is not enough.

In this book we challenge policymakers, practitioners, and educators to struggle with the "race issue" in their deliberations of policy alternatives. Furthermore, we provide an Africentric perspective to shape these deliberations. Clearly, if not lost, race has been relegated to a low position in public debates about how to improve child welfare services and practices. It is seldom raised as a determining factor in the development of policies for families and children. It is, however, frequently identified as a critical indicator of the effectiveness of policy decisions. Rapid changes in the country's demography, due in part to increasing immigration, demand a conscious infusion of the race factor in the policy debate. A delay will only increase the social costs to society and the damage to millions of children.

One might ask, What could be gained by elevating race as a factor in the policy-development phase? We might reply by asking, What could be lost? At the least, a remedial public-education effort would begin in which the historical and cultural tradition of self-help through cooperative family and community efforts for African American children would be acknowledged. The result might be a narrow policy directive similar to that which protects the interests of Native American families and children as well as sectarian interests. Or a policy directive that is responsive, flexible, and humane might emerge. Such a policy might reflect the value of cultural and ethnic diversity and emphasize family function more than family structure. It might encourage the development of community-based preventive services, empowerment models, and training for ethnically sensitive practice.

Resolving the current crisis in child welfare for African American and all children requires changes in both the policies and the practices of child welfare agencies. These changes should be based on a deliberate and conscious recognition of the cultural patterns of various racial and ethnic groups, particularly as these patterns involve cultural traditions and norms about child rearing and family dynamics, so that the approaches used enhance family functioning and the well-being of children. Bold, but effective, initiatives and experiments should be tried when they reflect the cultural patterns of the families and children served. For example, the Indian Child Welfare Act of 1978, among other things, gave important powers to Native Americans in deciding the fate of their children. The chapters in Parts 1 and 2 provide additional insight into African American families and children.

Implicit in the results of Hampton's analysis in Chapter 8 is the question of racial disparities in the American child welfare system. Scorned children are likely to be children who are not white. Corrective measures to ensure that assessment and intervention in cases of alleged child abuse and neglect incorporate an understanding of the experiences of African Americans can reduce the differential involvement of this group in the American child welfare system. Hospital staff in particular must be reeducated about African American families, children, and traditions.

Tatara (Chapter 7) highlights many of the problems that plague child welfare services in the United States. Although the resolution of these problems will not make for a perfect system, improvements can allow children and their families to be served better than they now are. Social policies that address structural changes, such as reducing unemployment, poverty, inadequate health care, and education, are needed. They can be designed so that all Americans benefit. Political actions will be required, including lobbying and the formation of alliances among social workers, lawyers, and advocacy groups and organizations whose missions are to achieve social justice and equality of opportunity for African Americans and others. Scorned children and their families are often isolated from the larger society and sometimes within their own communities. The isolation and vulnerability of these children and families can be reduced through policies and services that are universal in appeal—child care, employment opportunities and training, national health insurance, compensatory education and higher education, and affordable housing.

An Africentric response to child abuse and neglect incorporates kinship ties that extend to assuming social, cultural, and economic responsibilities for children. It involves both sides of the child's family, paternal as well as maternal. Although a child may lose one or both parents, an Africentric response ensures that the extended family is never lost. It treats children as a blessing. Thus, public policies should be established that strengthen the extended family, and child welfare services that meet the needs of the extended family as a resource for children should be available.

In addition, other policies need to be changed. Unwarranted and harmful intervention, disruptive and stigmatizing approaches, wasteful investigations of unfounded reports should be eliminated. Anonymous reports should be rejected, while measures can be taken to ensure confidentiality. Definitions of child abuse and neglect should be narrowed and made specific; litigation for arbitrary applications should be encouraged. Fines should be imposed on states that fail to maintain the child's relationship with the extended family, misuse foster care, or fail to provide adequate services. States should be held accountable for violations of constitutional rights; monetary damages should be encouraged. Legal challenges should be mounted to encourage family preservation and reunification.

Public education about the conditions of scorned children and about the American child welfare system is necessary to prevent the mistreatment of children. A variety of approaches for educating the public, including written or videotaped exposés of the personal circumstances, prevailing conditions, and daily activities of the children who have become wards of the state, would greatly enhance public awareness and concern about the length of placement, access to medical and educational services while in state custody, and efforts toward reunifying families. Each new day brings vulnerability to pain inflicted by a system that is supposed to protect children from harm but instead punishes them for the probable sins of others.

Integration of the Africentric perspective into contemporary child welfare policies and practices can promote the well-being of African American children and their families. Indifference to the cultural patterns of these families will result in continued psychological and social assaults. Indefensible policies and practices must be eliminated; federal mandates should ensure that children and their families have opportunities to maintain healthy attachments. The ultimate measure of successful intervention is when children are no longer scorned.

We need to approach changes and improvements in the child welfare system with a three-step plan. First, we must believe that changes are possible and take the necessary steps to make them. Second, we need to continue those components of the system that are working well, albeit imperfectly. Third, we must fight for large-scale changes that most social workers agree are needed even though, as a society, we continue to refuse to implement them (access to equal education, income, and health care, for example).

Publications on the delivery of services suggest that we already know what to do to serve families and children in need or at risk. Various successful and innovative programs in different areas of the country meet these needs. Key characteristics of these programs are flexibility in service delivery and design, committment and caring on the part of the staff, provision of basic necessities in addition to services, and innovation in service delivery; innovation requires coordination, which can be attained by crossing the professional and programmatic lines of authority or boundaries of service delivery.

Experience should have taught the service community that to serve the needs of African American children, one must involve the community, its leaders, and the institutions that provided services when none existed and continue to provide services when needed. Although there may be a decrease in the number of traditional foster and adoptive parents, there has not been a decrease in the sense of caring for children. Innovative, flexible, and culturally specific recruitment efforts must be made to involve additional members of the African American community. Such outreach would utilize a personalized, respectful, nontraditional approach to potential foster and adoptive parents. Although the law may require a separation of church and state, the African American church is still a powerful and resilient institution. Religious convictions are among the primary reasons African Americans become foster parents. Creative ways of utilizing different family forms as potential placements must also continue to be explored, as must the use of African American groups and organizations as supports for at-risk families.

The emphasis on preventing placement and reunifying foster children with their natural families if possible or the securing of permanent homes for children in care is appropriate. One should not stop an effort that was a culmination of the best studies and opinions of child welfare experts prior to the passage of the Adoption Assistance and Child Welfare Act of 1980 simply because of additional problems discovered during its implementation. Additional paperwork, judicial reviews, case plans, and working with foster children and natural parents are all needed if we are to protect and assist children at risk, as are more well-trained workers with smaller caseloads and a commitment to working with families. Changes in the nature of problems such as drug abuse and drug addiction that require children to be placed in foster care should not be excuses for turning back the clock to increased out-of-home placements or residential facilities. These should be used only as a last rather than first resort. The framework for these changes provided in the Adoption Assistance and Child Welfare Act should be enforced and fully funded in order to meet the needs of children.

There are obviously gaps in our knowledge about what service models exist, which work best, and with whom. Research and policy studies are needed. Starting in the early 1970s, delivery systems shifted under the pressure of massive cuts and reforms in funding sources and patterns, shifts in staff resources, public outcries for accountability, and a change in the demographic character of families and children. To date we know little about how state agencies have responded to these changes. The few studies that are available tend to suggest the feasibility of diverse and innovative models for pooling limited resources by integrating services across departmental and professional lines. The need for further analysis of state efforts to improve services is as important as analyses of federal policies or national data. Because local governments are likely to respond quickly to the particular needs of children in their care, we also need information about any discernible differences in state responses by region. It is also clear that traditional organizational and funding patterns have various aspects that are dysfunctional for children of color and reflect the racism that is endemic to their basic structure (Billingsley and Giovannoni 1972). A central purpose of this book is to provide information about the effects of child welfare services on African American families and children. Further development and application of the Africentric perspective will enhance service delivery to them.

Knowledge about intervention models that work well for particular problems, under certain circumstances, and with particular families and children is vital. These models must be examined through lenses that reveal the color of the faces, the heritage, the strengths, and the weaknesses of those needing child welfare services. Intervention models must be sought from a wide range of sources and disciplines. How do the practices of private child welfare agencies differ from those of public agencies? How do African American agencies deal with the absence of adequate resources, the recruitment of foster and adoptive parents, the reunification of families, and the placement of children? Models provide possible answers: they do not offer guarantees. There are no quick fixes for the problems within the child welfare system: no single policy or practice will remove or minimize the damage imposed on families and children. We must acknowledge the limits of social policy. We must also realize that in 1972 Billingsley and Giovannoni raised the same issues, questioned the same facts, and presented a historical perspective that still shapes public debate about child welfare and African Americans. Today, addressing the needs of African American and all children of color is within our power.

References

Billingsley, A., and J. M. Giovannoni.,1972. *Children of the Storm: Black Children and American Child Welfare.* New York: Harcourt Bradce Jovanovich.

Index

abuse, 3, 171; counseling, 209; decline in, 192; definition of, 9, 215$n1$, 226, 242$n3$; determinations of, 63; effect of employment on, 229; false accusations of, 197; increase in, 193, 227, 286; by nonfamily member, 195; physical, 3, 191–192, 223, 251–252; sexual, 3, 193–195, 224, 252; single parent as factor in, 132; stress as factor in, 229–234; in urban areas, 224. *See also* maltreatment; neglect

access: to adoptive services, 2; to health care, 55

accommodation, 163

acquired immune deficiency syndrome (AIDS), 170, 177, 268, 301, 306

adaptation, as developmental process, 163

adolescence, 43; development in, 169–170; pregnancy in, 19, 87, 107, 131–132

adoption, 266–272, 275; African American services, 2; agency, 71; ethnic differences in, 266–272, 275, 299; formal, 270–272; by foster parents, 269; informal, 9, 48, 70, 81, 101–102, 266–267, 269, 293; modification of procedures in, 2; negative effects of, 260; overreliance on, 250; professional intervention in, 19; rates, 3; reasons for, 101–102; revocation of, 278; subsidies for, 63, 75$n1$

Adoption Assistance and Child Welfare Act (P.L. 96–272), 2–3, 10–11, 75$n1$, 248, 253, 300–301, 310; effects of, 3

advocacy, 17; by guardian, 280; related to maltreatment, 8, 198; services, 9; strategies, 30–31

AFDC, *see* Aid to Families with Dependent Children

African American children: bicultural competence of, 127; developmental processes of, 156–178; and disabilities, 1; exclusion from orphanages, 292; I.Q. testing of, 141–144, 174–175; linguistic models for, 167; mortality, 1–2; removed from home, 1, 248–252. *See also* children

African American community: adoption agencies, 270–271; behaviors, 45; collective identity, 46; disequilibrium in, 147; life expectancy in, 43; material consumption in, 49; as nurturing environment, 70; social institutions, 45; unemployment in, 43; value system, 45

African American families, 85–110; adaptations, 86, 124; adoption exclusion, 270–272; affinal, 86; attitudes toward children, 87, 101; attitudes toward motherhood, 87; behaviors, 11; child abuse in, 220–242; child-rearing practices, 119–148; composition, 92–95; consanguineal, 86, 302; coping strategies in, 11; cultural contexts for, 10; current status, 90–92; deficit view of, 11, 273; development, historical, 88–89; differential experiences of, 127; diversity among, 79; elders in, 50–51, 92–93, 96–99, 105–106; extended, 9, 32, 68–70, 86–96, 267, 302; extranuclear, 89, 92; female-headed, 64, 69, 92–93, 240; function of, 10, 95–102; geographical effects on, 94; grandparents in, 97–99; help-seeking in, 11; implications

313